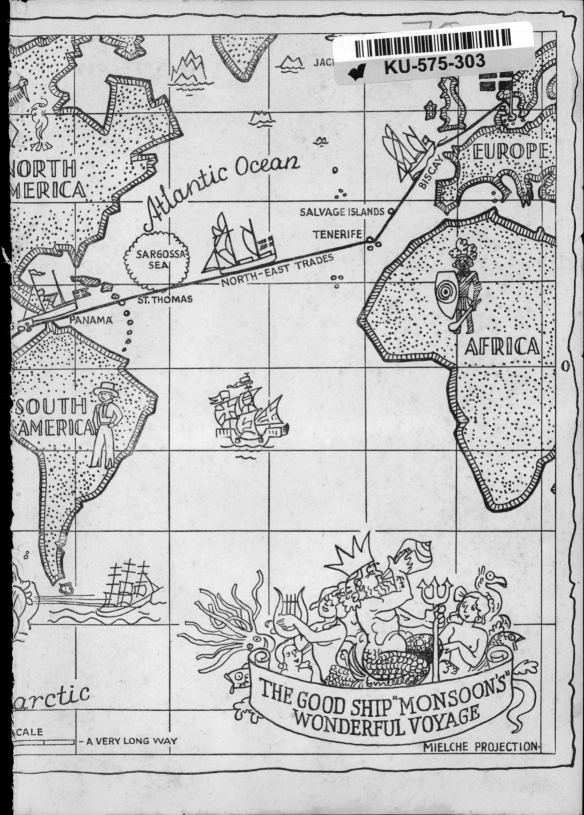

JAC...

EUROPE

BISCAY

Atlantic Ocean

SALVAGE ISLANDS

TENERIFE

NORTH AMERICA

SARGOSSA SEA

NORTH-EAST TRADES

ST. THOMAS

PANAMA

AFRICA

SOUTH AMERICA

arctic

THE GOOD SHIP "MONSOON'S" WONDERFUL VOYAGE

SCALE ▭ — A VERY LONG WAY

MIELCHE PROJECTION

Translated from the Danish by M. A. Michael

First Published - 1938
Reprinted,   -   1944

LET'S SEE IF THE WORLD IS ROUND

BY

HAKON MIELCHE

Author of

JOURNEY TO THE WORLD'S END

LONDON   EDINBURGH   GLASGOW

WILLIAM HODGE AND COMPANY, LIMITED

1944

TO EVA

Printed in Great Britain by Wm. Hodge & Co., Glasgow, Edinburgh, and London.

FOREWORD

THIS account of the *Monsoon's* last voyage, which began so promisingly one sunny day in October and came to such a brutal end ten months later on a coral reef in the Pacific, may disappoint some of those who read it.

It is not in the least scientific as it, perhaps, should have been in view of the whole character and nature of the expedition; nor is it filled with accounts of intrepid sailing or the technical names of ropes and sails, for such are mysteries which the author has not penetrated.

I have tried to write a faithful description of our voyage, neither too solemn, stylish—for we were certainly not that—fantastic, nor exaggerated, for I have to face a jury of five good seamen and two sceptical scientists, with Headmaster Möller as foreman and as I know them, they will not be satisfied with either more or less than the truth.

I am no professional writer. To be quite candid, this is my first attempt to arrange my thoughts and experiences into chapters, so you must not expect a particularly polished style. This is only an ordinary young man's attempt to describe what he experienced on this way round the ball we call the world. Thousands of young men could have done it as well; many better. Still, it was I who drew the prize and the others had to stay at home behind counter and plough, in office and factory, where they have displayed much more resignation, moral courage and endurance than any of us were ever called upon to do throughout the entire voyage; and it is for their pleasure this book has been written.

It will tell of boyish dreams which came crashing down,

of little adventures and unconsidered names on a map which became a reality more beautiful than the fairest dream. It tells of brown, black and white people, of calm sailing in moonshine, of storms and high seas; and, above all, it will show that even when many of your illusions have been shattered, earth and nature are still so diverse that they compensate you richly for what you have lost.

Among its pages you will find serious and light-hearted hours, sentimental minutes and one or two dramatic moments; and I hope, also, a little of the good spirits and wonderful comradeship which stamped the entire voyage and so made it such a great experience for those who took part in it.

The results of the expedition were excellent, even though our shipwreck struck so much from our plans. You may see the things we collected at any time in our museums; and how we found them and where, that you will find in this book. It also takes you through that technical miracle which is the Panama Canal to the curious Galapagos Islands and fabulous Tahiti, and ends somewhere in darkest Melanesia where tom-toms still thunder out their summons to bloody human sacrifices in the primeval forest. It lets you experience a real shipwreck and throws you up on a modern South Sea island, and then lets you go when the solid ground of Europe is once more under your feet.

There is no more to be said. I can only wish you *bon voyage* and cast off fore and aft. May you enjoy the trip is my last wish before I withdraw to my drawing board and leave the real writers to their games on Parnassus.

HAKON MIELCHE.

Vanikoro, Santa Cruz Islands.

CONTENTS

PAGE

CONTENTS

LIST OF ILLUSTRATIONS

CHAPTER I

*Of seeds and sewing, wonderful plans and
strange people*

THE seeds of this adventure were sown one dark winter's evening in the village school of Vejlby, which lies a few miles from Aarhus.

Outside it was raining.

The weather had been filthy and disgusting and the thawing snow lay in puddles alongside the ditches—a proper background for planning long, adventurous journeys to far lands, where the sun, as we supposed, shone the whole year through in a cloudless sky.

Are there any amongst us who have not travelled round the world by way of an atlas and a match? Who doesn't know the wonderful sport of leaving Singapore at 9.15 p.m. and arriving in Batavia at 9.16, shooting a couple of tigers or a crocodile, and getting to Borneo or Tahiti by bedtime? Surely an innocent pleasure—and a cheap one. If one has a little imagination, it makes it more adventurous and exciting than the arrangements of any Thomas Cook or Lunn could ever do—and the company in the Vejlby school house *had* imagination.

At 8.45 they purchased a schooner. At 9 o'clock Director Hans Tholstrup was on his way from the Gold Coast to New York with a mighty cargo of ivory. Quarter of an hour later the owner of the school, Axel Möller, had set course for the eastern hemisphere; while the actor, Eric Hofman, was engaged (quite alone) in

tremendous combat with a wild tribe of savage head-hunters somewhere in the neighbourhood of the equator.

At this point Mrs. Möller raised her head from her sewing and suggested that I should go to Hofman's help. I had, during the summer, earned a certain amount of esteem through my shooting with a target rifle on the moor, and was proud of this appeal to my prowess in the manipulation of heavy armament.

Mrs. Hofman was learning a part and asked us to be a little quieter and leave the savages alone and although the meeting broke up after this, yet the seed was sown.

On the way home each one of us played with the idea, savoured it, and forgot it amidst the prosaic problems of the daily round. The headmaster, Möller, was the only one in whom the idea took deeper root. One fine day he quite unexpectedly sold his school and asked Hans Tholstrup and I if we wanted to come with him. Where we were to go was not quite clear, but we unhesitatingly said yes. Tolstrup dropped out a little later for reasons of a private nature, but I was caught by both feet in the birdlime.

The avalanche gained momentum. The plan took shape.

The ivory was jettisoned owing to a certain ignorance of the dental mysteries of elephants and of the market for this raw material for piano keys and toothpicks, but the idea of the South Seas was planted more and more firmly in Headmaster Möller's head. He wanted to get out into the world and have a look round.

Twelve years of schoolmastering in the country make one long for the sea, and the many curios in his private study were the proof of the interest he took in ethnography and its kindred sciences. There were skin rugs, lampshades made from papyrus with mystic and exciting inscriptions, beer-mugs from Munich, gods from Siam and cushions from Cairo.

How far could we pay for a pleasure cruise round the world by purchasing ethnographic rarities which could be sold to museums and private collectors?

The *Etnografisk Samling* was, as it turned out, interested in the affair, and the inspector gave us several good tips. Later the Zoological Museum came along and its director declared that he would welcome the opportunity of extending the museum's collection with a comprehensive exhibit of the fauna of the South Sea Islands.

That turned the scale. The outlines of the scheme were now to a certain extent sufficiently defined and expert assistance assured, so that Mr. Möller could now look round for a suitable ship. For two months he sped from harbour to harbour in his sorely tried tourer, smoked cigars with shipowners, shook the calloused hands of seamen and looked at ships of every shape and size. For Thurö, Marstal, Svendborg, Halmstad and various other harbour towns he became a veritable Flying Dutchman, and one can still hear the fisherwomen saying to their children: "If you are naughty, Möller will come in his grey car and take you away!"

Shipbrokers sent us long lists and offered miracles of ships from the size of the *Europa* down to dinghies, with or without outboard motor, and it was the plethora of offers that made the choice so difficult.

One day Möller was strolling along the bank of the Frederiksholm Canal in Copenhagen—and he came upon the *Monsoon*. It was a case of love at first sight. She was built forty years ago in Boulogne-sur-Mer from good French oak, and furnished with pitchpine masts made to withstand any storm—which was necessary, too, for she was intended for fishing in the North Atlantic. Although she had led a restless existence since then and been put to many other uses, she was still completely seaworthy. The last few years had tested her severely. Knud Andersen, the Danish author, had sailed the length and breadth of the Atlantic in her and followed the 40° of latitude round the world in the face of roaring westerly gales. She had only recently returned home from her adventuresome travels, and now back in harbour she regarded her surroundings with an expression of melancholy and fretted over the places below the waterline where her paint was peeling off. Knud Andersen had given her to his faithful mate, and she seemed to be condemned to spend the rest of her days in sailing along the coast in seas where storms are rare and the waves ridiculously small.

Then Mr. Möller bought her. If ships had tails to wag, she would have wagged hers. She was just the ship for which he had been looking so long—it was almost as if she had been built for the purpose. Numerous borings and examinations from stem to stern, from the top of the mast to the keel, showed clearly enough that there was no possible doubt as to her seaworthiness. She was towed into Erichsen & Grön's yard, and Mr. Möller, taking up residence with his family in the cabin, personally superintended the process of rejuvenation.

The old lady was dressed up so that she looked like a young girl, and meantime Mr. Möller wore out the steps in Copenhagen and the provinces, and made all the lifts in the public buildings cry out for oil long before the regulation time. The results piled up on the *Monsoon's* deck.

4

Guns, revolvers, nautical instruments, fuel oil, charts, tarpaulins and a thousand other things were willingly lent us by the parsimonious Naval Stores in such generous quantities that we began to be seriously afraid of what would happen should war break out during our absence. A chemical factory sent us vitamins in bottles and pills, both A and B plus the whole alphabet, sufficient to last for many years; while the gifts of friends and equipment we had borrowed flowed in over the rail and filled the hold up to the brim.

The vitamins were stowed at the bottom, and some bottles of "aquavit," Maltese Cross brand, at the top, but that must just have been a coincidence. Unfortunately, they disappeared in the reverse order. It is said that schnapps can only be drunk in the colder regions. That is not true. When he had recovered from his first choking fit, the Governor of the Galapagos pronounced the beverage wonderful—and that was plumb on the equator!

The question of a crew began to occupy us. Who should come with us? That was not so easy to decide. An advertisement in the papers brought hundreds of replies. To look them through was in itself a colossal task. They were built up in two piles on Mr. Möller's desk—on the left the possibles, and on the right the impossibles. The latter pile was decidedly the higher.

There were young ladies who wanted jobs as stewardesses; barbers trying to persuade themselves and Mr. Möller that they were indispensable; and clerks who could do double-entry bookkeeping, conduct business correspondence in English and, in addition, were enthusiastic rowers in their spare time. There were stewards who could play the mouth organ, stuff birds and play bridge; carters who were quite certain that their right place was on the sea—to say nothing of a tragic pile of unemployed of every profession seeking a way out of their idleness. There was also quite a number of qualified applicants, old South Sea fishermen, young mates and whalers, men who knew the tropics, and men with the best of references to show. All were ready to come for a small wage and all of them were out for the adventure. Mr. Möller had only to weed them out and choose. After careful sifting there were still too many.

The *Monsoon* only needed a crew of five—a skipper, a mate, two deck-hands and a cook. This latter situation was filled in advance by the ship's former master of the pots, the youthful prodigy "Sonny Boy," who was the only fixture taken over with the ship when she was bought. During the summer he had functioned as cook to the Möller household on board, blown the noses of Mr. Möller's two young daughters and told so many tall stories of the legendary "last voyage" that the air in the cabin and galley became quite thick while all the iron fittings blushed and had to be repainted. His good humour was quite unshakable and he had to give his own most disrespectful annotations to every conceivable subject, even those which had absolutely nothing to do with him. When he came on board, he was so spoiled as to be quite ruined; nor did he get over it till we had left Panama behind us.

After the "last voyage" with Knud Andersen countless nice old ladies had patted his cheek and given him sweets and knitted scarves; his picture had been in the papers and he had been interviewed. In other words, everything had been done to turn the boy's head. He imagined himself as a cross between Columbus and Maurice

6

Chevalier, but all the same we eventually succeeded in bringing him down to earth (or rather the deck), so that in the end he was able to cook sausages without posturing in front of the stove as though he were about to be photographed. But—he had an excuse. He was twenty-three, but looked as if he were still of the age when every woman feels an irresistible desire to take you upon her knee, say "Keek-keek," and carefully feel if your nappy is still dry. In other words: enviable.

Thus the galley and its pots were in the best of hands. It was only the bunks fore and aft which required to be filled, and, finally, that also was successfully done after much lengthy consideration.

Peter Bundaberg Thomsen became skipper. He was engaged on the warmest of recommendations from Knud Andersen and because he was one of those real good old windjammer men whom it hurts when they see as much as the smoking chimney of one of those modern coal-buckets described in the dictionary as "steamers." He had sailed the seven seas, chewed salt horse on his way round the Horn and shortened many a sail in many a squall on the Tasman Sea. During the War he had been interned for five long years with a thousand other sailors in a camp on the north coast of Australia where he had learned his curious English. He sang chanteys, but would have done better not to. His memory was such that he was excellent at forgetting what time it was twenty-four hours ago, or where he had put his foul but beloved pipe; but ask him the name of the ship that passed Cape Hatteras at four o'clock in the afternoon of 4th April, 1898, and, without blinking, he would tell you that it was the Danish barque *Margaret,* that she had sprung a leak on the starboard waterline three feet below the

7

Plimsoll line, that she was carrying that-and-that sail, that the chronometer lost two seconds a week, and the wind was three points aft, strength seven, and that the master was called Olsen and drank like a fish.

When the skipper came on board he was wearing a beret and was clean shaven; when he was paid off he wore a soft hat and full beard; but in spite of this mighty disguise he was the same pleasant, comic, good-humoured skipper he had always been and always will be. You will meet him all through the book as "the skipper"—we delete the mister as well as the P. Bundaberg Thomsen, which we only used at governors' receptions and on other rare occasions when we wore socks and ties and were polite to each other.

As mate we chose forty-year-old Sören Nielsen. He, too, was an "old timer," and knew everything about the profession and five times as much again. In his younger days he had been whaling off South Georgia, and later he had sailed on big liners. He was an excellent sailor, quiet and reliable in any situation, and a bit of a genius when it came to mechanics. He had a quiet sense of humour, and his little remarks were as dry as the sand in the Sahara and very much to the point. He it was who "borrowed" a majestic black policeman's baton on Christmas eve and brought it home as a souvenir of San Cristobal. We soon saw that the man with the nut-cracker face and monosyllabic moroseness whom we came up against during the first days on board the *Monsoon* possessed quite a lot of surprisingly good characteristics which we gradually learned to value. He knew what he wanted to do, and he did it as it ought to be done. He became the skipper's indispensable assistant and our good companion. He was one of those who maintain discipline without you noticing it.

The deck-hands were soon engaged. Nor for a second do I hesitate to say that they were the best of the hundreds who applied. They were quite different in character and temperament. There was nothing to choose between them, and they formed an ideal couple.

Jack Mortensen had sailed in everything, from tankers which exploded in the middle of the Atlantic to pleasure yachts nearly bursting with the sense of their own importance. He was an optimistic pessimist, usually with a face beaming like the sun, but now and then dark and gloomy like a wood at night when there are no reassuring patches of light to be seen above. If we hadn't had Jack at the harpoon, we wouldn't have had any dolphin steak, and would have contracted beri-beri, scurvy and spots, or one or other of all the things which, according to the predictions of science, you are sure to catch if you go three days or more without fresh food. When he hurled his big crochet-needle from the jib-boom, there it was stuck in red flesh—if he happened to hit. Jack was the best shot in the expedition. He could kill any animal if he had cartridges and time enough—and, of course, provided the animal kept reasonably still and was not too far away!

Carl Pedersen was his exact opposite, blonde, sunburned to the colour of beetroot and as unshakable as the Alps. He regarded the voyage as a kind of extended pleasure jaunt, and only went ashore when this was quite unavoidable—as, for instance, on 10th August on Vanikoro. He possessed the courage of his convictions, in which respect it must be mentioned that he was something of a peaceful, friendly quarreller. He couldn't

9

understand how scientists could assert that the world was round, that apples fall to the ground, and that as far as pimples are concerned chiropractic is not better than surgery. "Kalle" was the ship's element of eternal unrest, its never-resting opposition and the source of many a heated discussion. He was capable of asserting with the greatest calmness that the whale is a tree lizard, lays eggs and is related to the giraffe, if he could only cause sufficient commotion at the table to enable him to shovel three or four rissoles on to his plate without being noticed. He was the only one on board who didn't collect something or other. He had difficulty enough in collecting his own thoughts when every now and again he tried to write down his experiences and adventures in the finest diary on board.

That was the crew.

Those were the five men to whom were entrusted our welfare and that of the ship. They were our companions and our comrades through thick and thin, and I can with good conscience say that they were well chosen. They never came to blows, never really quarrelled, which perhaps will disappoint those of my readers who have a taste for mutiny and finely sketched character studies of hard-bidden sea-dogs. Instead of whistling uppercuts, they must content themselves with friendly smiles, and as a substitute for hefty oaths and romantic quarters they will find polite talk round the table of a living-room, with flowers and pictures on the wall. From a Marryat point of view that is boring, but you can bet your bottom dollar that it was wonderful for us.

The crew came aboard. Their kit was emptied out on to the cabin table and photographs of their girls fixed up on the bulkhead with four rusty drawing pins.

The *Monsoon* came to life. There were sounds of whistling, hammering, cleaning and carpentering, and then came the awful day when the 35 h.p. motor had to be shipped. That was a bit awkward. It was something of a sacrilege—like putting steel furniture in a rococo drawing-room. However, we had no choice. If we didn't want to row the *Monsoon* half the way, the 35 h.p. would have to come to our help, for our voyage took us suspiciously near the region of calms round the equator where the wind is one day as incalculable as a woman— according to the classics—and the next week disappears altogether and goes to sleep on the horizon under the clouds drifting with the trades, and laughs at the poor hulk with its fluttering sails and cursing crew.

Meantime there had been a number of conferences. The charts were already torn to bits. Mr. Möller had decided on the advice of professionals to go left instead of right when he reached Gibraltar, and thus make better use of the trades. Science had formulated its desires and given good advice as to how they were best to be fulfilled.

There were missing only the two scientists who were to represent the museums and form the expert portion of the *Monsoon's* crew. It was actually quite exciting. We were absolutely dependent on the museum's choice. No sorting of material was possible here. Would we be given a couple of good fellows, or would we have to depart with two such monsters as we all know from the comic papers, with horn-rimmed spectacles, long beards and forgotten umbrellas? The job was unpaid and they had to provide their own pocket money, so that competition was not particularly keen.

One couple had had enough by the time they had

reached the ship's rail—as a race ethnographists seem to be rather unadventurous—and it was only a week or two before we left that the complement of two was complete. Neither of them had horn-rimmed spectacles and both were clean shaven at least once a week, and if there was anything they forgot it was to forget their umbrellas. In explanation of this phenomenon it must be explained that they were both young.

The zoologist, Knud-Erich Stubbe-Teglbjerg, we discovered, as soon as we had got over his complicated names, to be an extraordinarily good sort. In this book he will be called "Stubbe" pure and simple. For this he has to thank not me but the compositors, who demanded an increased wage if they were to have to keep on setting his name in full! At this time he was twenty-seven, well-dressed—according to provincial standards—and the possessor of an engaging eloquence. He was the ship's memory expert. He knew the entire *Encyclopædia Britannica* off by heart, with the exception of the supplementary volumes, and every one of the songs in the *Students' Song Book,* to say nothing of all the jazz hits of the last three years with their tunes and lyrics. When his mouth was not filled with his whistling or the scientific names of snouted beetles and setaceous worms, he unfortunately sang. As he had a brother who was a doctor, he was elected supreme chief of the medicine chest and conducted minor and major operations with "The Seafarers' Medical Guide" in one hand and a pocket knife in the other. Curiously enough nobody died of misprints. The man who was to look after the ethnographical collection was called Jan Degenkolw. He was twenty-five and still in the midst of his studies. He was taller than the stories the barber tells and thinner than the weakest of tea, but at anyrate his name was at least pronounceable. "Jan"—you will find him thus labelled later—Degenkolw is a charming name, but we will leave it here in this first chapter parked with the other titles.

Like Stubbe and me, he was an old Boy Scout, and was to find a use for all the attributes which Baden-Powell developed in the Matabele War, which, as everyone knows, was arranged purely and simply to provide material for *Scouting for Boys*. Actually Jan was not an ethnographist by profession, but he had taken an exhaustive course under Professor Thomsen of the National Museum, and that this bore fruit is amply shown by the things that were saved when the *Monsoon* was wrecked. For this reason his bridge is forgiven him. He educated us to a high degree of self-control by offering to make up a four to oblige and then falling asleep in the middle of the first exciting rubber.

"Bobby" arrived two days after Jan. He was a six-months-old bull-mastiff who became our acknowledged darling throughout the whole voyage, cheered us up during the long weeks at sea, and was our greatest source of amusement on sea and land. Coming straight from the kennels he had no idea of the earnestness of life. His baroque face lay in deep folds and his brown eyes betrayed the deepest melancholy and disappointment as he was emptied out of his box on to the deck and surveyed the crowd of extraordinary beings around him. He resigned himself to the situation with a heavy sigh, graciously wagged his two-inch stump of a tail, and took a turn round the place to give licks of greeting to sea-boots, gym and patent-leather shoes.

At last the crew of the *Monsoon* was complete.

Erichsen & Grön went over the boat with rag and

brush, and then handed her over all ship-shape to Mr. Möller in the first week of October. The tool was ready and the work could begin. A few final conferences were held with the museum officials and various other authorities, to say nothing of nautical experts. Our route was decided on in its smallest detail and letters of introduction obtained from the Foreign Office to foreign governments and Danish consuls.

It was a perfect ship, a rejuvenated edition of the old *Monsoon* which strained at her moorings at eleven o'clock of that fourteenth day of October. The deck swarmed with relations, friends, press photographers and people who had no business to be there. Jan presided over a circle of Boy Scouts who regarded "the old eagle" with awe and worship, and in the cabin Dr. Mortensen, an old East Indiaman, made a short farewell speech and gave us a word or two of good advice for the road. It was the first time that the idea of malaria or head hunters occurred to us properly, and the first time that the pleasant shiver of anticipation ran down our spines. Then came good wishes, port wine, biscuits, emotional returns of thanks by Mr. Möller, curious lumps in one's throat, rapid steps up the companionway and over the bridge. The deck was cleared, the hawsers drawn in—a bevy of white handkerchiefs—faces which became more and more indistinct. The first waves in the bay began to splash against the bows: the sails came to life and filled; the voyage had begun.

But not in real earnest yet. Our last port of call was to be Aarhus, for we wished to say good-bye to our own town, and, besides, the last of our equipment was to be taken on board there. A little customs cruiser came up alongside us to wish us *bon voyage*. There was quite a nice breeze. It was a slow business sailing against the wind over the grey waves of the Kattegatt. Bobby was seasick, but curiously enough he was the only one. Mr. Möller read "The Wicked Eyes of London" far into the night, and we others slept the sleep of the just in spite of the curious movements of bed and bedroom.

Next morning we saw the slender spire of Aarhus Cathedral, and at twelve o'clock ran alongside the quay with the neat precision of a taxi driving into the small space between two others on the rank. All our boring preparations lay behind us; before us the whole world.

CHAPTER II

Concerning bad advice and favourable wind,
haughty steamers and a wild rabbit

"SHUT your face!" said the mate—and quite right too.

For three whole days the *Monsoon* had been an exhibition piece in Aarhus Harbour. Friendly people had told us that the ship was too small; that we would sink before we got as far as Skagen; that even if we passed through the Bay of Biscay we would be eaten later in New Guinea; that we were all quite mad, and would do better to stay at home with our wives and families; and that we could consider ourselves lucky if we escaped with nothing worse than malaria! Anxious ladies asked us about woollen drawers and vests, and optimists confided to us that they intended to make the same voyage in a cutter when they could find the time. Now some drowsy messenger boy had hit the nail on the head by saying that our spanker boom was too thin.

We were waiting for a valve for the engine. It had been sent ashore early in the morning to be repaired, and now the hands of the cathedral clock were drawing critically near to eleven, our zero hour which had been ceremoniously announced in the papers. A quarter-past eleven and we looked everywhere except at the quay. We were embarrassed. Where the devil was the skipper and the valve?

The flowers piled up in the cabin. Deputations appeared. Friends and acquaintances drank port to pass the time and a couple of extra speeches were made. At eleven-sixteen the skipper arrived with the valve. The last of the flowers were handed over the rail. Everybody shouted hurrah and sang the national anthem. Some were busily engaged in blowing their noses, Mr. Möller made nervous gestures with his hands, and the rest of us tried to look unconcerned and to talk of something else.

The small strip of dark-green water that separated us from the quay and the faces we knew, grew broader, became all too broad, became the sea. The star-spangled burgee of the yacht club sank slowly down and up again; the motor puffed quite unaffected by the seriousness of the situation. We passed yet another small group of people gathered on the end of the mole, shouted a couple of bad and out-of-place jokes at a group of fishermen at the last of the light-buoys—and were on the high seas.

No longer did we feel like monkeys in a cake. We stopped attempting to smile and look intelligent for the clicking cameras of the press photographers. We were at sea, bound for Teneriffe, palms, sunshine and adventure.

The long voyage had begun in earnest. Ties were torn off, collars flew about the cabin, and our natty suitings were gathered more or less tidily together and hung on the pegs. A prep-school boy couldn't have behaved more ridiculously on the first day of the summer holidays.

Helgenäs slipped astern and Hjelm appeared before us. A passing fishing boat took a couple of postcards back to land, and then began the nautical eduction of the novices. Jan, Stubbe and I took turns at the wheel, while the crew set sail. Contrary to the expectations of common sense, we escaped all the sandbanks, although it did for a moment look as though Jan wanted to go

straight over Hjelm. There was a good breeze from the south-east and the mate prophesied that we would be off Skagan by the following midday—and with this information the non-maritime portion of the crew retired below deck, closed the hatch over their heads and left the watch to Kalle and the mate.

They looked quite pleased and relieved as we disappeared, but were not to find our absence such a great relief, as there were still a large number of cases and other things over which to stumble. I sketched for a little, to accustom myself to the movement of the ship and my new workroom. The others read, and the evening finished with a short but daring rubber, the first of a long series.

The *Monsoon* slipped surely and quietly through the waves. Now and again she shipped a little water. Next morning, despite the not very optimistic prophecy of the mate, found us, with Lange Maren to port, running into the North Sea with all sails set and the water foaming at our bows. The old girl longed for the open seas. She was as frolicsome as a colt and went straight for the post like a racehorse. She wanted to amuse herself, and brought us to Teneriffe in the record time of seventeen days. She had a bit of the devil in her.

We were on deck most of the day. We grinned triumphantly at the heavily laden tramps ploughing their way north through the heavy seas, whilst even the skipper, who usually suffered from an inferiority complex as regards speed, imagined himself a rosy little angel wearing a sou-wester and large white wings on top of his sweater.

Some joinering was being done in the cabin. Shelves were put up in the most impossible places and there was a brisk demand for planks and canvas. Hell was made inhabitable, and with books, cards and tobacco we went into winter quarters. It was cold. The North Sea showed its roughest winter side. The wind howled in the rigging and long lines of grey-blue waves swept continuously past; but they were going our way and gave us many a friendly slap on the tail to speed us up, so that we made eight knots. Migrating birds rested in the rigging, and we showed them every hospitality—for were we not of the same blood and had not our desires the same goal? Away from the rain and the cold, on to sun, south and warmth!

A jackdaw stayed with us for a long time. It came on my birthday and received a fair share of the cake. A fleet of Dutch trawlers appeared and vanished astern, and then we were in the Channel. The tremendous speed had left us quite breathless. The skipper paced the deck shaking his head with perplexity. East wind—in the second half of October—in the North Sea—that was a breach of every known etiquette of the seas. But there could be no doubt. There were the white cliffs of Dover glistening to starboard in the sun, and there was one of the cross-channel express boats tearing through the water at twenty-two knots. Then the wind disappeared; the sea grew calm, and we didn't move forward an inch.

It was Sunday. Jan had oiled and brushed his hair and there were not a few clean finger-nails to be seen round the breakfast table. Mr. Möller was wearing a tie. Dolphins played at the bow and large steamers throbbed past us on their way in or out of the Channel.

We were not off Dover till the next day, when field-glasses made their appearance and Dover Castle, our first piece of foreign land, was inspected. Then we

lowered "Moses," our flat-bottomed Norwegian dinghy, on to the water, rowed to the harbour, where we made fast at the pier beside the swimming pool, and took our first letters to the post. Newspapers were bought and we told each other how awful it was to have been nearly five days without contact with the world. Later we were to be thankful for a three-months-old *Times* in which some purchases had been wrapped.

Our departure was delayed on the quay by three uniformed men who were most inquisitive and wanted to know the reasons for our rather unceremonious landing. They were gentlemen, however, and were satisfied when their attention was drawn to the Danes' thousand-year-old tendency to raid the English coast, so that we arrived back on board safe and sound with our boxes of sweets, cigarettes, nuts and four-inch nails, the product of a lightning tour round this amusing little town with its narrow streets, its many pubs and pithy faces set between handkerchief and hooker.

On we sailed. The sun was shining, and it was nearly warm. A gentle breeze began to play with the flag on the mizzen. Off Dungeness we set all sail, at Beachy Head we stopped the engine, and at our eight knots sailed on towards the Lizard.

The skipper remained silent and uncommunicative. He growled like an angry Bobby if we spoke of the favourable wind, and nearly exploded when we dared to say that we would be in the roads of Santa Cruz on such and such a day; but in spite of his scepticism and ever-growing amazement the wind continued to blow steadily from the north-east. Under all canvas the *Monsoon* ran over the moody Bay, danced the polka with the waves and created the record run of the whole voyage, 197 miles in twenty-four hours, and the record speed of eleven knots. The fates were ever gracious, and the *Monsoon* their darling.

As we were running down the coast of Portugal, just off Finisterre a storm blew up from the north-west, the dangerous direction for small ships, for it drives them farther and farther into the mouse-trap of the Bay of Biscay and finally slings them against the steel jaws of the cliffs. A mizzen-mast drifted past us telling its sorrowful tale to the seagulls and the fishes, but we were already out of the Bay's clutches, and the north-wester meant only increased speed, a faster voyage.

The wind was responsible for Lisbon being struck off our itinerary, where it had figured as a possible intermediate stop on the way to Teneriffe. The *Monsoon* laid herself again on the port bow and let port wine be port wine. The wind sang in the rigging and the breakers piled up aft, splashing against the sides and sending cascades of water over the deck. The sun went in and came out again, cheering us up and strewing dazzling spangles on olive-green velvet, giving us an opportunity of snapping His Majesty the Sea in his shirt sleeves. It was our first storm, and in the seven months to come was to remain our only one. We enjoyed it like a refreshing douche, a farewell from the north and the cold.

The novices were making progress. Jan no longer talked of "Going across to the right and pulling the ropes," Stubbe had learned the difference between "sailing wide" and "close-hauled," one only had to give him a little time to think, and I myself began to understand that the wind couldn't "veer" and "remain steady" at the same time. Stubbe with his dachshund legs easily

kept his balance on the rolling deck, but Jan in his efforts to make his stilts react at the same time and with the necessary harmony to the incalculable whims of the deck, moved like a louse on a flypaper.

It became milder. A couple of large steamers crossed our course on their way to Gibraltar. The north wind took us swiftly and surely southwards.

We fell victim to a bout of tropic frenzy and ran amok. Stubbe and Mr. Möller took a bathe on deck and the rest of us cast sweaters and scarves aside and put on shorts. The sky was blue with light white clouds and the temperature of the water 66° Fahrenheit. We sampled our armoury. A bottle was put on the rail, where it stood like Nelson at the battle of Trafalgar, while the bullets splintered the woodwork for yards on either side. However, it was smashed in the end, because Sonny pulled the trigger by mistake before he had had time to spoil his chances by taking aim.

And then our sweaters made their appearance again, and our shorts were laid aside. From that day we became more impatient to get on for hadn't we at long last said good-bye to the cold and everyday life. We didn't rightly understand why adventure had not arrived.

That evening a huge tourist steamer ran right across the *Monsoon's* bows completely dwarfing her, without even giving us a glance, while a thousand lights shone from her sides; no scuttles these, but common or garden windows with plate glass. From her ballroom sounded music, men and women in evening clothes strolled the deck and white-clad stewards brought cocktails to delicate editions of *Vogue* lying puffing at Abdulla cigarettes in striped deck-chairs.

We gathered for-ard and stared—then spat disdainfully

to leeward, lit our pipes and went to have a talk about wind and sea with the skipper. We had become sailors.

The floating sanatorium for tired business men and pampered Americans caused not a spark of envy under our sweaters. We were almost sorry for them and at the same time glanced up to see how the top-sail was. We ate tinned cow and maggoty rice which we swilled down with tepid water. Yes, we had become sailors.

Science proposed to try out our apparatus for surface fishing. We caught, it is true, nothing worth mentioning—a few crabs and spawn—but it provided an amusing hour or two round the microscope for layman and learned and showed that the apparatus was in perfect order for future and more important use.

Our beards grew and it became warmer. The breeze became a breath and ended in a calm. A school of blue whales appeared, blowing for our benefit before being lost to sight. Then came the wind again, by a miracle from the right quarter. The skipper looked like a teetotaller who had just discovered that beer is a healthy and nourishing beverage. He no longer dared to believe in his own superstitions! We sat on improvised deck-chairs and waited for the mountains of Teneriffe to appear. Not a bad waiting-room! We dipped into our store of books and magazines, and it so happened that Stubbe picked up the book of sailing directions where he stumbled across a description of the Salvage Islands, a pair of cliffs half-way between Madeira and the Canaries. That name had a magical effect on Sonny. While the sauce burned and the water in the kettles boiled away in the galley, he began again to weave the yarn which Knud Andersen had begun in his young mind. It unfolded and broadened out, and before he was finished,

the Salvage Islands had become a country where there were rabbits and buried treasure in such quantities that one could scarcely find room to put down one's sea-boots.

Knud Andersen had never been on the islands and Sonny had only seen them as grey spots on the horizon, but our curiosity was aroused, and despite the skipper's feeble protests at moving even an inch from our course, an overwhelming majority decided to land there. We were longing for variety. The thought of treasure tempted us, for who will not willingly secure his old age, his Rolls-Royce and two hot meals a day, if it costs no more trouble than to place oneself between the great oaks and take two hundred steps in the direction of the north star in order to find the ironbound chest full of Spanish doubloons under the big stone with the cross? Besides, there were rabbits there.

Our longing for fresh meat was nearly as great as our gold fever and desire for precious stones in costly settings, and should we not find the one then we could always console ourselves with the other. The wheel was spun three points to starboard and the murmurings of the indignant skipper were completely drowned in Sonny's triumphant cries.

On the way we met a Hamburg-America liner steaming north and dipped our flag in friendly greeting, so that she should not feel that we looked down on her because she was only a steamer. She didn't even look at us, but went straight past like a S.A. man who has to pass a Jew on a narrow pavement. That constituted our final break with these proletariat of the sea. Still, we behaved like gentlemen and contented ourselves with sticking out our tongues at her as she waddled fatly northwards. If only her engines would break down!

At noon we saw our first flying-fish, which aroused wild glee. It was a symbol, a foretaste of what was to come. Later those sparrows of the South Atlantic were to become a daily occurrence which could no longer cause us to raise so much as an eyelid, so quickly does man accustom himself to different conditions; an ability which the encyclopædia and other philosophers call intelligence, but should rather be called a kind of slackness.

We sighted the Salvage Islands at five o'clock on the morning of 3rd November. By "we" is meant the two poor devils who were forced to be on deck at that barbarous hour. Salvage—islands of rescue: christened thus by some grateful sailor the day after he had been shipwrecked as he sat in safety on a rock out of reach of the grasping breakers, and emptied the water from his seaboots. The dull, tattered piece of rock towards which we were steering seemed, besides, just about the most melancholy and comfortless place one could imagine. There was not the slightest mitigating glimpse of green, only sheer cliffs towering up to a height of more than three hundred feet. At the top was a flat plateau, running slightly up to a pinnacle at the south-east point—the Devil's Head is its attractive name on the map.

The greatest excitement reigned on board. It was our first landing on uncivilized ground, our first encounter with untouched nature beyond the bounds of law and order. "Moses" was launched; guns and rucksacks filled with provisions were handed down into him and we left our parent ship to swing restlessly on the long Atlantic rollers. The skipper stood in the bows and regarded our endeavours with the expression of a mother duck watching her ducklings waddling down to the water for the first time.

25

The breakers were worse than we had thought. They spurted high up the damp, smooth face of the cliff and now and again burst with the roar of a cannon, sending a column of spray shooting skywards. We succeeded, however, in finding a stretch of shore studded with large boulders where a landing seemed possible, and while we were still arguing as to the possibility of getting it over safely, a fussy little wave came along, seized "Moses" by the collar and, lifting him up a yard or two, tossed him roughly on to the shore, where our argument abruptly came to an end. We declared, not the landing possible, but the return journey doubtful.

We filled "Moses" with boulders, threw rucksacks and guns over our shoulders, and looked upwards. There must be a direct opposite of vertigo. This occurs when one sees a wall the height of a good-sized church tower rising vertically before one, and at the same time knows that all the treasures of earth and the entire world of rabbit await one at the top. In the course of the next hour we discovered that it is possible for a heavy rifle to adopt one hundred and eighteen different positions during the ascent of a mountain, and that none of these are calculated to increase the climbers' speed.

The Salvage Islands owe their origin to a volcanic outbreak, and volcanoes have a stupid hereditary tendency to consist of lava which always breaks off just at the moment when you think that a secure foothold has been found. Jack, below me, had a bad volcanic and vituperative outbreak, and Sonny vainly sought to take my life by staging avalanches of stones ranging in size from soup plate to large cannon ball. In spite of everything we reached the top.

There lay the plateau—eighty acres of earth covered

26

with parched grass and stunted bushes. Every step was a trap, for the ground was undermined by rabbits, though the holes were unoccupied. The plateau had been the scene of tragedy. Shortly before our arrival the Black Death had ravaged the rabbit population. Rotting flesh and white bones were everywhere, but there wasn't a live rabbit to be seen. Birds of prey hovered over the carrion and the seagulls came sweeping in on their white wings and shrieked hoarsely above our heads. No wonder they were alarmed by our visit. The Salvage Islands are uninhabited. An attempt at colonization was abandoned many years ago, but once a year boats come out from Teneriffe and massacre the breeding grounds. The birds are killed without regard for age or sex to make dried seagull meat, which is a choice delicacy on the shores of the Mediterranean. Deep down below us lay the *Monsoon* like a little toy ship on a sea of blue, more splendid than we had ever dared to dream.

We split into two groups. One consisted of the scientists armed with a butterfly-net and collecting-boxes, the other was formed by the rest of us with our various murderous weapons. The scientists had the greater success. When the whistle blew for time, they triumphantly showed a couple of rare geckos, a glass jar with some oil-beetles and one or two butterflies and lizards; while all we had to show was the island's guaranteed last rabbit, a lonely bachelor, and a half-grown seagull. This last was for stuffing, the rabbit for the skipper, who had shown so much mistrust and scepticism regarding the island and ourselves, and had sworn that anything we could shoot he would eat raw, skin, hair and all.

We ate our lunch and started to climb down. The sun beat down on the cliff wall, the heat radiated out from

the baking stones, and deep below lay the breakers foaming at the mouth with desire for the little dots dangling above them between heaven and earth. However, we disappointed them of their meal, which made them so angry that at the first attempt to get "Moses" into the water they swamped him, and then, when we tried again, nearly choked Jack and me. Wet and tired, we reached the ship before the sun set, but forgot all our trials when we saw the skipper's face as he caught sight of the rabbit.

We had had a grand day, and Bobby as much as any of us, for he had taken the opportunity of demonstrating the same crying ignorance of the noble sport of hunting as had all of us.

Sail was set, and turning our backs on the island, we steered south away from the rabbits to the Canaries. Astern the contours of the Salvage Islands merged more and more into the gathering darkness. Wild, rough and unapproachable was the impression they left on our minds; and so will we always remember these first islands of ours. Majestic in their wildness, proud in their inaccessibility, they will go on standing there for thousands of years yet, sterile and poor, and untrodden by man, in their sun-singed wigs, away from all public ways and stages.

"They are of volcanic origin," said our sages, and looked unutterably wise as they spread rancid butter from a tin on to their bread.

"They are all that is left of Atlantis," said Sonny as he put the pot with an argumentative bump on the torn oil-cloth on the table. We were inclined to agree with him.

The Salvage Islands look as though they were brooding

over an enigma greater than shipwreck or freebooters' buried treasure. They are like a man with a past.

The night wrapped us up in a black cloth, and the next morning Teneriffe lay in front of us in the early sunshine.

CHAPTER III

*In which we attend a disrobing, inspect a volcano and
meet an angel who talks Spanish*

THE island slowly peeled off its kimono of morning mist.
A soft, round contour made itself visible; a stately
shoulder and an entrancing dimple appeared; like a
beautiful coquette Teneriffe hesitated to reveal all her
glories at once. Entranced, we glided nearer and saw her
powder herself with green woods and place a necklace
of snow-white swansdown round the violet blue of her
neck. We saw the sun play in her hair and the waves
kiss her feet.

Eight young men stood in the bows and gaped in
amazement, while the ninth let the rudder go at will
and only came to himself when the ship had wandered
eight points off her course and the sails had begun to
flap. That is the effect Teneriffe, in the radiance of the
sun, had on a prosaic northerner, and that is the reason
why our first encounter with this outpost of palms and
bananas in the Atlantic was made the occasion of
celebration.

Teneriffe's volcano, Pico del Teide, had a headache
after his last attack of hysteria, and had plastered his
temples with white, wet cotton-wool which looked like
cloud; but we didn't miss him in the panorama—there
was enough to see. Strewn about the valleys lay terraces
of vines, plantations of bananas and fields of sugar cane,
while toy towns gave us a friendly smile from every slope
where nature had fashioned an inlet between the cliffs.

And then the palms! They were real big palms, not the sickly little greenhouse affairs which we had formerly associated with this botanical label.

Before we had time to shut our gaping mouths the pilot came on board, we heard our first Spanish, and gaped in amazement again like country bumpkins, and this was the expression which the boys on the training ship *Danmark* saw as we glided into the harbour and dipped our flag in greeting to them. The *Danmark* was on her maiden voyage and had gone as far as Santa Cruz. She was now carrying out exercises in these waters while waiting for Santa Claus. After the presents had been doled out, she was to cross the Atlantic and visit Saint Thomas, but meanwhile the boys had a glorious time on this island of lotus eaters, for such is Teneriffe for those who smell the tropics for the first time. For him who comes from northern climes, it is an earthly paradise. Just warm enough, just strange enough, and yet civilized with its manicure salons and picture-post-card shops. Not too much of the latter, for Teneriffe has not yet been able to compete with Madeira for the tourists, which is a pity for the island and the town but a good thing for us others.

Santa Cruz is the capital of this island province of Spain. It has sixty thousand inhabitants, more than half of whom appear to be industriously engaged in polishing shoes, whilst the only work of the others seems to consist  in having their shoes polished. This, of course, is one of those remarks which call forth protests from indignantly quivering consuls-general and chambers of commerce. Hence I hasten to explain that it is only a jocular first impression of this hard-working and enterprising town, into which one makes one's way over sleeping lazzaronis who occupy no small portion of the harbour square and the town's finest market place.

The noise in Santa Cruz is wonderful. No modern composer could write a jazz symphony which could even attempt to reproduce its discord. The leading instruments are newspaper boys, taxicab horns and tram drivers who amuse themselves wonderfully the whole day long and bet amongst themselves as to who can wear out the most bells in a week. The cars tearing through the narrow streets are instruments of murder, for the streets are no broader than will allow a man in the fourth storey to amuse himself by spitting across into the open-air shop on the pavement where the barber regales his customers with the latest political scandal. The wild scurry of trams and taxis only stops when a donkey lies down in the middle of the street and refuses to be driven on with kicks. Buxom Spanish peasant women with miniature straw hats and fluttering ribbons quietly steer their way through the crowds with a pyramid of milk cans on their heads and knitting in their hands; majestic policemen with coalscuttle helmets of varnished tin and white glacé gloves direct and confound the traffic in a way that would make black-clothed undertakers laugh joyfully in anticipation of increased earnings—and then there are the shoe-blacks. They are to be found of all ages, from the nimble dark-eyed five-year-old to the quivering grandfather of eighty. No one can escape them, and you begin to wonder whether you will not find them at the dentist, in the theatre or in the cathedral. If you have a speck of dust on your shoes, the next shoeblack you meet will give you a look that will make you blush like a schoolgirl, and if you let him remove the speck with three different creams and elixirs you will receive into the

bargain the *chronique scandaleuse* of the whole town, including a talented criticism of the town council's latest bye-law. Give him a tip and say no to the next, else all your money will go in cleaning your shoes, and when the sun goes down behind the roofs of the plaza there will be only the soles left.

Santa Cruz is wonderfully free from the atmosphere of a capital city. You may easily see a heavily laden camel plodding down the main thoroughfare, and you are certain to notice the numbers of cages with real live canaries hanging over the street on the walls. Remember that the Spaniard pays much more attention to his court-yard than he does to the façade of his house, and you will get a rough idea of how many canaries are twittering in this city! They sing in the woods all over the island; not the yellow, degenerate, artificial toy birds that we get in the north, but the real, original canary, an incon-spicuous little brown song-bird rather like a nightingale.

Santa Cruz breathes in a wonderful mixture of petrol fumes and the scent of flowers. On the *ramblas,* the big wide boulevards which are the pride of every Spanish town, the flowers triumph over the petrol. A thousand and one miracles, large and small and of bright colour, grow between eucalyptus and laurel trees. They hit you in the face, and the scents penetrate right into your heart, so that you forget that at home people are leaving their goloshes in the porch.

Rambla a XI Febrero—evening.

At one end of the promenade is the bull ring, two large cinemas at the other and in between a mass of blazing arc lamps. The grasshoppers are singing and their song sounds like the string accompaniment to the Pilgrims' Chorus. The black-eyed señoritas of Santa

Cruz stroll arm in arm up and down under the trees, and the dons lounge there likewise in groups of four and five, while fiery glances stab the air like Toledo blades. This is Love's hotbed, where he slaves evening after evening when the weather allows—and the climate of Teneriffe doesn't permit him many days of rest in the year. But Love is a little boy with clipped wings subservient to Spanish domestic discipline, and can only flirt from a distance. El padre and la madre sit at home behind their green shutters and keep an eye on the clock. Inviting a girl to coffee and cakes or to the cinema is a thing unknown in Santa Cruz, and the most dashing of señoritas turns into a pillar of lava which has been petrified under ice, should some daring youth dare to speak to her during the evening promenade on the *rambla*. When a girl eventually finds a Don Juan or Don Carlos, then they must give expression to their feelings through the little grille in the door, while father and mother hang about in the dim background like watchful dragons who cannot be shaken off. Then the guitar begins to sob out in the dusk, and perhaps Dolores' heart may melt, but not that of her inexorable parents nor the solid iron bars of her cage. That is the reason why each evening the streets and alleys of Santa Cruz sob and whine like a nursery for strings, and that is also the reason why the Canary Islander who marries can be sure of getting a pure, innocent wife whom he can deceive.

In Santa Cruz we met Mrs. Knud Andersen and her children, Lis, Jan and Thure. On entering their old Atlantic home, they looked amazed at the different arrangements and the alterations we had made. It was through Mrs. Andersen that we got to know Talavera. This miracle of a Spaniard was a pilot, a charming bachelor and a sworn supporter of Denmark and every-thing Danish. He completely shattered our former opinion that Danish hospitality stood in a class by itself and overwhelmed us again and again with his Spanish grandezza. He loved his island and spread all it had to show before our eyes in a series of motor trips throughout its length and breadth. He was our guardian angel during our stay in Santa Cruz, and we shall remember his hospitality when every other memory of our trip has faded. Imagine a man with the appearance of one of the few film stars whom men can look at without feeling sick, give him the most winning personality that you can think of, and finally add a modesty like that of Francis of Assissi, and even then you will have a poor reflection of what nature had made Francisco Garcia Talavera.

One morning he rolled up on to the quay in a spacious Hispano-Suiza which he had hired for a sum that must have been equivalent to the pilot fees for two large steamers and a liner. We got in, and the motor purred like a sleepy kitten over the wonderful motor roads of Teneriffe. We passed through La Laguna, stopped in Masala, a little village set amongst blooming fig-cactus, and drank wine in a little inn that clung to the edge of the cliff like an eagle's aerie. The kitchen door opened right over the cliff and the slops went down for three hundred feet where they were collected with great punctuality by the rising tide. The wine was good and we praised it before a numerous crowd of friendly peasants and black-eyed children who devoutly stood around us while we tested the local product. From Masala we went down into the Orotava valley and stopped for a moment to recover our breath after meeting this, the most beautiful valley in the island, with its emerald banana fields,

ruby roofs and sapphire sea. Orotava is the jewel coffer of Teneriffe, where real stones look like coloured glass.

The road wound along like a white snake, hidden in the shadows of forking cork trees and majestic eucalyptus, and framed in a galaxy of red and white roses, pinks and jasmine. Yoked to their wooden ploughs, oxen walked thoughtfully up and down in the fields, and a pair of ruminating camels looked sadly up as we drove past. Mighty cisterns, Teneriffe's weapon against drought and a necessity for the cultivation of bananas, lay to left and right of us on the heights, with water channels running down the slopes on every side like a spider's web. We came to a sharp bend in the road, the brakes screeched nervously as we went round, and then began the climb up to the Pico, that high, old volcano that is the island's landmark and the pride of the population.

At three thousand feet we drove into the clouds, seeing nothing but damp trees and a strip of road in front of us. A quarter of an hour later we emerged into the purest air and the most dazzling sunshine imaginable, into a peacefulness that for our city nerves had something almost uncanny about it, and into a feeling of cold that we thought we had left behind somewhere in the latitude of Gibraltar. It made one think of a countryside bathed in moonlight on some far-off, extinct star. Round about lay huge boulders that some mighty eruption had strewn over the plateau, while the gravel on the road was of pumice stone. The volcano itself rose from the salver-like plateau in graceful majesty, forked by streams of lava and grey with ash. We felt as though we had been transplanted to some spiritual sphere, and Talavera had difficulty in getting us back into the car.

The next afternoon I bumped into Stallknecht from

the *Danmark* on the quay. He was striding up and down the pavement in elegant, Spanish-cleaned shoes, smoking cigarettes and looking at his watch every five seconds. It was twenty past four. He was waiting for the representatives of the local press whom the consul, who was sitting in the longboat wiping the sweat from his forehead with a blue-edged handkerchief, had invited to visit the ship at four o'clock punctually. It was half-past four. Stallknecht had now not many cigarettes left and his arm was quite sore with looking at his watch. The consul sighed. He knew his Spaniard from forty years' experience and this was nothing unexpected. The gentlemen of the press had no doubt gone to sleep over their desks with a dead cigarette and a mañana on their lips. As Stallknecht threw his last cigarette stump into the water, Mr. Möller came unsuspectingly along the quay with a hand-embroidered Japanese kimono in one hand and half-eaten ice in the other. We were both bundled into the motor boat.

We were received on board by Ankersö, captain of the *Danmark*. He was in his finest gala uniform and not a quiver on his quiet seaman's face betrayed his surprise at seeing the correspondent of the *Jyllandsposten* as sole representative of the entire Spanish press. The boys were all paraded on deck, washed clean and standing to attention, and then the consul, Mr. Möller and I walked down their ranks with the captain. Not one of the boys laughed. Discipline is a wonderful thing.

We were shown the ship from keelson to refrigerators, and only properly thawed when we had collected in the officers' mess round a tray of sandwiches, which had been arranged to give the Spaniards a never-to-be-forgotten impression of Danish cooking which, together with the

37

"Norwegian" Holberg and the "German" Andersen, has laid the foundations of Denmark's reputation in the world at large.

Mr. Möller and I felt homesick and our eyes had a race with the beer glasses as to which should grow dim first. We honoured the Spanish knights of the pen with a glass of aquavit and that closed the official part of the visit. The rest of the time passed in swapping lies and homely conversation. We listen to Captain Ankersö's tales of his days in the South Seas, and grew to like more and more this old sea-dog with his quiet, smiling eyes and clergyman's face, who had been put in charge of the education of a hundred bright young boys.

The days flew along as though on wings. We enjoyed being tourists and men of the world, were invited to  lunches, dinners and suppers, and ourselves made a shy attempt to return all this hospitality with a party on board. I made a painted table-cloth with Indian ink, water-colours and writing paper, and the others all vied with each other in attempting to hide my marvellous designs under an extravagance of table decorations. The result was that when the guests arrived the table looked like an old-clothes shop with flower counters. I think they enjoyed themselves. It was late when they left and on awakening next morning we discovered to our dismay that it was time to leave Teneriffe.

We went ashore to take a last look at the town, drank cocktails at an hour which made every orthodox patron of the café lift his eyebrows and had our shoes cleaned three times in succession. A couple of handshakes, a well-meant hurrah from nine men in the *Monsoon* and a ringing one from a hundred young throats in the

Danmark, and we were out of the harbour, *en route* for America.

We felt a little sad. Even Bobby tried to put his cropped stump between his legs and look melancholy, even though some stupid quarantine paragraph in some dusty law book had prevented him from having shore-leave. Then Stubbe related two of his experiences in Santa Cruz. He had visited the best school in the island, the local Eton. During the break he had been surrounded by well-dressed boys who looked round to see if the master was watching and then stretched out their hands and asked for sixpence. On leaving the school he met a funeral. A poor man was going to be buried. Being the good fellow that he is at heart, Stubbe stood aside to let it pass and took off his hat. As the coffin was being carried past him, a small boy in the procession stretched out his hand and asked him for a penny. When the procession had practically passed, several grown-ups stretched both hands out and asked for the same amount, and when he put his hat on again all the man's mourning survivors roared and shouted the same request in his ear and the procession became hopelessly disorganized. That is Teneriffe as it is and as it lives, the reverse side of the medal the face of which is ornamented by Talvera and men of his type.

These tales enlivened us a little and Bobby began to wag his stump once more. We felt at home on the Atlantic, which behaved very well on seeing us again and sent us a nice little north wind which filled the sails and took us southwards right into the arms of the north-east trades which were to be our companion over the Atlantic. Flocks of flying-fish played about our bows and in the evening the light of the sea shimmered most gloriously in our wake for as far as the eye could see.

In front of us Venus shone so brightly that she formed her own little moonbeam over the sea. This was the beam along which we were to try to go, this was the star we were to try to catch; and it was the consciousness of this romantic chase after distant stars that made us forget our sorrow at having to leave Teneriffe with its sun, its friendly smiles and its blissful laziness.

When we turned out next morning Pico del Teide had sunk below the horizon, and we were alone with the trades and the Atlantic. I stood in the bows with my arm round the bow-sprit and whispered to a dolphin playing at the bow the age-old motto of Spain: "Mañana"! It seemed to understand and tore on before us.

CHAPTER IV

*In which we learn third-form history, wave to a turtle,
and finally arrive at Saint Thomas*

THE days that now followed were long. The white
clouds drifted along with the trades over our heads and
the *Monsoon* tried to keep pace with them as best she
could. A little painting was done on board, and science
investigated the sea every now and again, bringing up
all kinds of small animals and curious bits of slime in
its finely meshed net.

One watch relieved the other and one game after
another made rubber. Birthdays were celebrated and
songs sung for the occasion and each imagined himself a
little Columbus. But all the same we were sailing along
Columbus' route. The *Monsoon* was a *Santa Maria* that
was a good four hundred years late. Can you wonder
then that now and again we let our thoughts go back to
the World War, Napoleon's fall, and the centuries before,
and relived this epoch-making event?

Columbus had to stay at Teneriffe for four weeks in
order to repair the rudder of the caravel *Pinto*. He must
have felt a little afraid when he saw the snow-clad peak
of Pico del Teide, the last of the Old World, the boundary of reality, disappear below the horizon. Before him
lay the unknown with which unreined imagination
could wrestle without restraint. The three caravels drew
close together. *Santa Maria*, *Pinto* and *Nina* formed a
living part of Europe that had broken off from the mouth
of the Rio Tinto at Palos in South Andalusia, and was

41

now drifting westwards, cradled on the broad Atlantic rollers, bound for the land of adventures—for India. The trades blew consistently, the high, white clouds hurried on above their heads like birds pointing out the way, and the sun shone down day after day on the hundred and twenty adventurous sailors.

This voyage has given birth to legends such as have been woven likewise about the son of the Genoese weaver who stood in the narrow captain's cabin of the *Santa Maria* bent over a primitive chart—but history has made an end of most of them. Columbus was not a nobleman who had studied at the geographical faculty of Pavia. This myth must be ascribed to his son Fernando trying to give his family tree golden leaves. He himself relates that, like so many boys of his age, he went to sea at fourteen; that he lived at home with his father and helped him at the loom when times were bad and his search for work fruitless. Perhaps he served in the small boats which carried wine from Chios and other ports of the Mediterranean.

It must have been during the long days and clear starry nights on deck that he first began to dream of a sea route to India, urged on by the stories of the sailors and strange tales of far, unknown lands away under the setting sun. The great idea never left his head, but took deeper and deeper root, found support with various rich families, and became the alpha and omega of Christopher Columbus' life. He fought for it with the energy of a lion and the obstinacy of a donkey, while he drew charts to make a living.

Finally, in the spring of 1492, on 17th April to be precise, he signed the contract with the Spanish crown, and Queen Isabella gave him money and material to

carry out the voyage. The road now lay open, the road
to titles and riches, to fame and power. He reaped his
reward to excess and became a great man, but spoiled it
all for himself on account of the fact that he was unable
to govern the golden lands he found. The seaman, the
man of action who does not understand the ins and outs
of diplomacy—there has always been this type of man
and his fate has for ever been that of Columbus. But
enough! Leave the tragic tales of history and follow us
along the broad road of the trades in the wake of
Columbus!

We glided along over the great heaving carpet, the
water desert which had to be conquered before the
Monsoon could let go her anchor chain in the harbour
of Saint Thomas. In earlier times this route used to be
thronged with traffic, it was the thoroughfare between
the Old World and the New, but now the twentieth
degree northerly latitude lies as deserted as it was at
the time of Columbus. Round about in the harbours lie
the few ships that are left of the great full-rigged fleets,
waiting in vain for a freight to Rio or Melbourne. The
steamers run in and out of the harbours groaning and
grunting, sweating stokers appear out of hatchways and
dry their black, glistening faces with a handful of waste
before they have to return to their glowing hells to feed
the greedy jaws of the furnace with shovels of coal.
Steam has left the wind behind, and prose has strangled
the poetry which flourished between jib and mizzen.
That is why the trades are deserted.

The rusty iron ships plough the seas like trams, laugh
at wind and weather, and draw their course from harbour
to harbour as though with a ruler. That is why the
trades blow in vain, and nobody would miss them if they

suddenly became annoyed and stopped work. Yet they still have a task to do for the old, honoured equator, which is surely as hot as any stoker and needs a little air now and again.

The water was blue here, bluer than the Mediterranean whose praises are so often sung. It had the colouring of the great depths. It was four miles to the bottom below us, so for the moment there was no danger of running aground.

It was along this track that the three adventurers, Columbus and the two brothers Pinzon, who commanded the *Pinto* and the *Nina,* waddled in the heavy caravels. Caravels were no racing boats, they were too log-like for that. What is this track like, that is old and yet eternally young? What did Columbus and the old full-riggers see? What did we see? They sailed under the same sun, in the same heavy rollers as we; but did not get on quite so fast.

Above all, a sparkling blue sky with white cumulus clouds driving across the heavens. The atmosphere is thin and unusually dry for sea-air, and so sunset is an event of overwhelming and ever-changing beauty. It has all the brightest colours of the spectrum, now flaming in a fire of red that bathes sea and sky as in blood, now painted with the most delicate of pastel shades, unearthly clear and pure, in finest contrast to the violet clouds standing out in relief in front of this glorious background. We pointed our jib-boom towards it all and steered straight into the flaming sun. No fortune-hunter ever had a more promising omen! There in front below the horizon lay adventure, to which Columbus had given us the key and we followed in his tracks.

Since those days much has changed, though the sea

itself remains as of old and there is the same urge to chase on after the sun which one can discern even in children when they stretch out their hands to the glowing ball, and which, hidden under a layer of dust, habit and veneer, survives to some extent in everyone.

The darkness comes as soon as the sun has dipped down into the waves. It rolls up from the east with a speed quite unknown in the northern lands of twilight. In the space of a quarter of an hour it gets so dark that Venus stands out in sharp relief just above the last soft colourings of the dying sunset. The stars come out in their myriads above our heads, but only accentuate the black darkness they are unable to dissipate, just as the distant sounds of bells or the baying of a dog makes a silence deeper still.

At night the flying-fish come aboard. During the day a natural shyness keeps them from doing so, but they follow us and cross our course in thousands. Now and again a devil enters into them and they shoot out of the water in hundreds and glide for several ship's lengths with fantastic speed and elegance on quivering "wings." They look like little green birds in hurried flight from the neighbour's cat—and they are in flight too. They are hunted in the waters below by large, greedy bonitos, the natural cousins of the tunny fish and the mackerel, and the flying-fish's worst enemy. In order to get peace, they take a run, spread their large, pointed side-fins and fly like a seaplane over the foam. Every now and again they forced land, but start off again the same instant in another direction, like a stone with which one plays ducks and drakes. The bonitos follow them from time to time with a clumsy jump above the surface, but plump back again at once.

The little airmen land on our deck with a wet smack when it gets dark and the reflection from the skylight lights up the mainsail. The light attracts them and they whistle through the air like little shells. They hurt when they hit you.

Kalle was standing there one night dreaming of his girl at home when he suddenly cried out. A flying-fish had kissed his cheek with a little more aplomb than his girl did. The same night our lifeboat developed a swelling where another projectile had hit it, and after that we had a little more respect for Kalle's cheek bones which had shown themselves to have more power of resistance than solid oak planks. Our flying-fish were subjected to Stubbe's zoological dictatorship, and in sorrow we watched several specimens find their way straight into the formalin bottle. This brought mutiny into Sonny's eyes, for he would gladly have seen these shining, herring-like fish in a pot in his galley, and we others shared his egotistical and unscientific desires. Flying-fish are tasy morsels and in the long run beef which tastes of tin becomes a little monotonous!

Bobby was the only one to defy science. He personally investigated the specimens which came his way during his nightly prowl of the deck, and what was left when he had finished was no longer worthy of being included in even a beginner's zoological collection.

We lived in the hope of catching a dolphin that was too big to get into the formalin bottle. Dolphin's flesh is very tasty and its liver is food for the gods. Day and night the harpoon lay ready in the bows, but these speedy little whales only honoured us with a French or nocturnal visit, and it is more difficult than you think to harpoon

46

patches of phosphorescence and snorts when the night is as black as pitch!

There was a minimum of bird life. A large bird of the genus Puffinus accompanied us part of the way from Teneriffe; a little stormy-petrel zigzagged about the main mast, and a long-tailed tropical bird bade us welcome at fifty degrees west. The surface of the sea itself changed as we went farther and farther west. In the middle of the ocean drifting bits of seaweed came to warn us of the existence of the Sargasso Sea, that curious island of sea-weed in the Atlantic which gave Columbus' men such a shock. In a western part of the ocean the currents have driven huge masses of seaweed together, the circulation of the current keeps them in the same spot and the sea-weed fosters an exotic animal life. Polyzoon, toad-fish, and limacidæ live here in the warm, salt water far from land. Shipping avoids the place, for it is not amusing to sail through a thick layer of seaweed which fastens itself around rudder and screw and hinders a sailing ship's progress. The seaweed itself belongs to the sargassum family whose respectable members lead a permanent and orderly bourgeois existence on the coast of America. The rolling-stone branch of the family has gradually so accustomed itself to its Bohemian life that it is able to obtain sustenance from the sea with its entire surface, quite independent of roots or other formalities.

Legend has put a ships' graveyard in the middle of the Sargasso Sea where the wrecks are said to drift around caught in the devil's dance of the current and bound together with hawsers of seaweed. Imaginative authors and film directors have occupied themselves with the idea, but, like the seaweed, it lacks proper roots.

We were standing on deck one glorious morning and

talking of turtles. There was a tremendous argument as to the size to which turtles grow. We always revised our lessons early, and on that day the Galapagos were on the time-table and it was their rich and curious fauna that had given rise to the discussion. Somebody maintained that turtles grew to a length of from twenty-six to thirty-two inches at the most and we all expressed our sorrow that we would have to wait till we got to the other side of the isthmus of Panama before the argument could be settled. Then a golden brown spot appeared in front of us and passed the side of the ship at a distance of thirty feet. It was a giant turtle quite twenty-seven inches long.

Dozing quietly on the surface (water 81°, air 86°) it cheekily waved to us with its starboard fin as it glided astern gently bobbing in our wake. Someone pulled a long face and all of us were a little surprised. We had met the first representative of the New World more than a thousand miles from land, calmly swimming against wind and tide—a sea-turtle on an Atlantic voyage!

The next day we saw a whale blow, a fin-back the mate said, and he ought to know, for in his callow youth he had hunted fin-backs off Spitzbergen. It shot through the water with the speed of a torpedo-boat, making the flying-fish dive out of the way to either side. Its white belly showed up a shiny green as it ploughed along three feet under the surface, and when it came up to breathe the spurt from its blow-hole shot up like a fountain. It circled in front of our bows for a while, investigated our keel and inspected us with seeming benevolence from stem to stern, then taking a couple of turns round the ship it disappeared southwards in search of greater deeds.

The skipper played with our little harpoon, but then

reconsidered the matter. The *Monsoon* was not built as a submarine and our harpoon tackle could not even hold a tunny if it sneezed.

The birds became more numerous. Large flocks of them came to meet us from the land which was quite close below the horizon, and circled with loud cries round our masts. It was the flocks of birds which made Pinzon persuade Columbus to alter his original course, so that he steered southwards in the direction whence the birds came. They are responsible for the little island of San Salvador and the adjacent Antilles being discovered first. If Columbus had followed out his original reckoning he would have set foot on the coast of Florida and thus on the mainland of America. That would have concentrated the field of his activities; the islands broke it up, and into the bargain he let the *Santa Maria* pile up on the rocky coast of Haiti on Christmas Eve. There she stayed and from the salvage of the wreck he built a fort, which was later razed to the ground by rebellious natives.

We also altered our course and followed the birds, but did not let ourselves be seduced into any indiscretions for all that. The chart of Saint Thomas lay spread out on the cabin table. In a small bay the name "Charlotte Amalie" was printed and it was there that we intended to drop anchor.

The next few days saw us hard at work washing and ironing trousers, for, though most of us had almost forgotten how to tie a tie, we rather wanted to make a presentable appearance in this old Danish colony where there might still happen to be a few Danes.

Bobby put his forepaws on the rail and smelt land, and on the 29th November, after a nine days' voyage in the wake of Columbus, the skipper juggled us through rocks and reefs into the harbour of Saint Thomas.

We had arrived in good condition in a new part of the world. The first person to jump over the rail after the quarantine doctor's visit was, wonderful to relate, a Dane smiling all over his face. He was the bank manager, Consul-General Axel O. Thage, come to bid us welcome.

CHAPTER V

*We are tourists in the seventh heaven, visit a rich
American who was not at home and learn a
little of an old Danish Colony*

THE consul brought us a large bundle of letters and gave
us time to read them and note all their kisses and kind
remembrances before showering upon us the hospitality
and friendliness which continued to flow ceaselessly all
the days that we were to stay in Saint Thomas, and
which still seemed to be inexhausible when we came to
leave the island.

The fifty or so Danes who were still on Saint Thomas
indulged in fierce competition to see who could make our
stay the most unforgettable. It was a dead heat, for there
was no definite winner. Even to-day this December week
seems like a dream. It was on this island that my
personal idea of paradise first took definite shape. No
longer is it a vague conception: I can describe it with
minute exactitude. Here is my idea of El Dorado: In
the middle of a large, blue sea a small green island where
are palms, hibiscus and bougainvillæas. The sun is just as
warm as it ought to be and the sky so blue that it seems
improbable it can belong to this world. You are called
in the morning with a specially prepared cocktail, cool
and lively, and tasting like a sleigh-ride through a wine-
cellar, if you understand what I mean. The day passes
in a kind of idleness that lets you believe that you have
done quite a lot, and in your ample spare time you sit on
a veranda drinking rum fit for the gods and accepting

invitations to teas, dinners and picnics where you gorge yourself with pigs roasted whole, swill down tremendous beakers of ice-cold drinks, and fill in the corners with the culinary refinements of the entire world.

We left Aarhus in torn, old sweaters and thought ourselves Vikings: when we left Saint Thomas we were more than anything else like Romans from the time of the decline. We had been fearfully spoiled—and it was glorious. But I see the reader beetling his brow and looking angry. He bought a travel book and can dispense with the gastronomic fantasies of an epicurean cocktail drinker, and would much prefer to learn something about this former Danish colony now under American dominion, so I hasten to lay the rudder hard over and set all sail in order to make up for lost time.

The best view of Saint Thomas is obtained from the Luise Heights which rise up to the north-east of Charlotte Amalie. In the old days there was a Danish plantation here and, after the island was sold, this was bought by Mr. Fairchild, an eccentric American bachelor. Mr. Fairchild made his money speculating in real estate in New York and now spends his time in visiting Saint Thomas and travelling all over the world. On the Luise Heights he has created a veritable Garden of Eden, a show place with tropical plants growing in a luxuriance that beggars description.

Here the "Queen of the Night" winds its stem up rare trees, for it grows wild on Saint Thomas, and during the months it flowers it fills the island with a stupefying exotic scent. Green overgrown stone steps alternate with loggias where the blood-red of the bougainvillæa stands out like a Chinese lantern from the dark green of the palms, and suddenly one is confronted by a Sleeping

Beauty's castle—Mr. Fairchild's home, his pride and his passion. He has spent a great deal of money on building and extending it, and this money has been a boon to the poor native workmen of the island. He added wing to wing and stone to stone until the house with its tower and balconies assumed the shape it had already had in his imagination when he danced with the others round the golden calf in the gilded hell of Wall Street.

It may be that the house is very American, a little too distinctively Hollywood. Its architecture is certainly theatrical, but it is good theatre and many sins may be forgiven it—even the fact that a large number of stones its owner had ferreted out and brought back from his travels have been built into the walls. There is marble from Rome, rock crystal from the Tirol and sandstone ornaments from Tunis.

Inside, the house is gloomy and quiet. Heavy old furniture stands in the rooms whose shutters are closed waiting for the Lord of the Castle to return. His dining-room is an impressive poem in dark Renaissance. It is a huge room with a mighty table and at the table is a single chair dominating the entire room. It broods gloomily over its melancholy and tells a vivid story of the lonely meals of a lonely man far from the sound of happy voices and the bright laughter of children. It is the gloomy cave of a hermit set right in the heart of paradise.

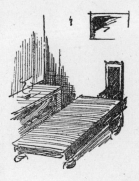

Mr. Fairchild likes beautiful views. Wherever he turns, to windows, balcony or door, his eyes encounter wonderful panoramas: to the north he sees the islands of Saint John, Hans Lollik and Jost van Dyck, at the foot of the cliff lies laughing Magens Bay, and to the south he has the town, the harbour and the sun—more beautiful views than these are scarcely to be found in this world. Down below, Bluebeard's Castle greets his eyes in all its venerable majesty. In the olden days the much-feared, young French pirate, Edouard à la Barbe Bleue, sat behind its strong turret walls keeping watch for his prey. He sat in his aerie, as haughty as a sea-eagle, till one day the hot passion of a lady of Spain drew him far away to where the sun sets.

His colleague, Captain Teach, lived a musket shot away in Blackbeard Castle, but he, too, had to flee the island to which he had retired to enjoy his *otium cum dig* as an honourable shipowner, for a Danish captain brought him into the limelight and unmasked him as the notorious freebooter. Teach fled headlong from the island, but he took his young ward with him—and she loved the Danish captain with all her loyal and faithful heart. It has always been red blood that coursed in the veins of the people of Saint Thomas.

The Caribbeans put up a bitter struggle against Columbus and his men, until finally superior forces drove them to the mainland, since when possession of the islands continually changed hands. The Dutch, Spanish, French and English have each hoisted their flag on Signal Hill, until in 1667 the Danes set foot ashore and only left when one day in 1917 twenty-five million chinking American dollars slipped in Denmark's depleted treasury and vanished again without the taxpayers noticing any relief.

The first fort which the Danes built to protect the harbour still stands. With its crenellated walls, unpretentious square tower and reddish hue, it looks like one of those little wooden fortresses which inflamed our young hearts to mighty deeds when we were ten and our toy soldiers executed strong attacks from the base of grand-mother's footstool. The fort is now a police station. Giant negroes in yellow khaki grin at the visitor, and from the depths of the dungeons come the penitent cries of some native boy who has been caught stealing a motor car lamp.

Christian the Ninth is enthroned in lonely majesty on a granite block opposite the fort. Agaves and palms give a comical effect to the homely Danish characters on the base, an effect which is further heightened when one sees that the next street is called "Nörregade" and that all the other streets have retained their old Danish name-plates. The Americans do know what piety is. Or is it rather indifference?

Even though ex-President Hoover may have exag-gerated a little when once, in anger, he called the former Danish West Indies "America's Poorhouse," yet Saint Thomas is really a place of poverty. These islands cannot support themselves, but neither could they under Danish rule, and since then times have grown considerably worse. The life-blood of Saint Thomas is its harbour, and this has been hit by the Panama Canal and the great advance of the motor ship, which now throbs past Saint Thomas with many oil barrels on deck and small use for bunker berths after its long voyage across the Atlantic.

Agriculture is not of much importance for Saint Thomas. Any systematic cultivation is of itself prohibited by the nature of the ground and the long, incalculable periods of drought. But cattle breeding does pay to a certain extent.

The cattle of Saint Thomas are in great demand throughout the whole Caribbean. They are a hardy breed, which is always kept supplied with new blood by

importing Friesian bulls. The cattle graze at liberty in the knee-high, scrubby grass on the slopes of the hills. They clamber like chamois in and out of the mango and calabash trees and in the evenings are driven down to the farm to be milked.

In material respects it is no lotus eaters' land over which the governor in the big house on the heights rules. Here flows neither milk nor honey.

The governor is a good man for the islands. Dr. Paul M. Pearson is a small, white-haired man who lives behind a large desk in the airy government buildings, smiling benevolently through the glasses of his spectacles. He understands the noble art of getting things done. Himself a teacher, he has created a school organization that is fit to rank with those of most of the great countries. The negroes have admittance to the secondary schools and can take the examinations as well as any white, and one really cannot grudge them that. But is that farseeing? Does this sudden cultural elevation bring the negroes of Saint Thomas happiness?

We must call a halt here and have a bit of a breather after all this running about, and survey the situation as we did the town from the Luise Heights.

Saint Thomas is a small island. Blacks and whites live side by side, but their elements and colours may in no wise be mixed. The whites live on the heights, the blacks in the valley. Should a "coloured man" work his way up, make money and achieve a position, he still remains a "coloured man," even though the shade is so slight that only the practised eye can discern it. That is the inexorable law of America, and it is so difficult for us Northerners to understand it properly because we have no such problem. Still it is the law wherever the whites

are in the minority, whether they be Dutch, English or American. Why then educate the "coloured man" for the professions of the white? Does that not mean the temptation of a new-born ambition, and will it not run its head against the wall until it loses its reason? A negro cannot think of emigrating. U.S.A. has quite enough to do to look after its own unemployed children, and everywhere the doors are closed with seven seals which no negro at any rate dare break.

What will be the result of this good school education? Will it mean that the small, smiling negro children from the tin huts will be turned into big, unsatisfied young people who look down on their kin, feel themselves too good for manual work and cast envious glances at the whites who live on the heights behind those invisible walls which are stronger than any others in the world and older than the great wall of China? No one will dispute what is best from the purely ideal point of view, but how are the negroes best served in the long run and under present conditions? No one who has seen happy and primitive negroes, who have passed no examinations, sitting gathered round a banjo on a doorstep with a piece of sugar cane in their mouths, will seriously take up cudgels in defence of the culture given by the schools, whose fair portals lead direct into a morass where there are neither roads nor paths.

A few cents a day, a little salt fish and much sunshine have for centuries created natives who are unreflecting and therefore happy. Logarithms, philosophy and Beethoven sonatas have made out of this material a race of black unemployed with high ambitions. Of what use are a pound of ham, a little milk and some sugar to a man who can quote Goethe in the original?

It is very beautiful in Mosquito Bay when the full moon shines on the gently breathing sea. It is a quiet and unforgettable experience to see the moulded cupolas of the hills, where the wind gently stirs the leaves of the palms while the fireflies sparkle in the bushes and the cicadas sing their evening song.

We three Danes sat on a bench on the shore and, absorbing all this beauty, grew very quiet and still. Why couldn't these smiling islands remain Danish? Couldn't we afford this little luxury, this feather in our grey everyday cap? Is everything in this world then only money, money and again money?

The whispering palms gave no reply. A bird called hoarsely from the bushes. We went home.

CHAPTER VI

We eat liquid dynamite, sail thirty yards over the sea and vainly court Miss Diana

IN spite of countless invitations to stop and celebrate Christmas in this friendly and hospitable Danish colony, Mr. Möller adhered to his decision to be in the Pacific before the New Year. One makes an itinerary to follow it, and even if we now and again allowed ourselves to be a day or two late, following the Danish State Railway's example, yet there were limits beyond which we could not go. So we had to carry on.

We left on 4th December, at lunch-time exactly, and all our friends stood on the quay and waved good-bye while their black cooks at home rolled their eyes in despair because the soup was getting cold and the ice hot.

We felt no particular pleasure at the thought that now new and unknown cities awaited us. Feelings on board were almost a little depressed and, as this is simply not the thing on a voyage such as ours, the *Monsoon* decided to do something quite special. She gave a little shake to the mainmast, so that the throat of the gaff broke and in consequence the whole boom fell with a thundering crack on deck, and by the time the damage was repaired and the sail hoisted again, we were in good spirits once more. We stuffed Saint Thomas right at the bottom of our kitbags and began to look about us.

The Caribbean was ruffled blue and we made good speed through it. Flying-fishes jumped and bonitos tried to spoil their fun; it was the trades over again but a

59

shade warmer and milder. Mr. Möller hammered and whistled lullabies in the cabin where he was taking down boards to make room to put them up again, the skipper sewed at a torn sail, and Jack caught a couple of dolphins with the harpoon.

It was thundering over Venezuela and there was a rainbow over Columbia, and before we realized it we were tossing in the wake of huge steamers and waiting for pilots and quarantine boats in the roads of Colon at the entrance to the most famous short cut in the world, the Panama Canal.

Colon is a thing by itself. It is like nothing else in the world, with the exception of its big twin brother at the other end of the canal, Panama City, and is extremely amusing on the first day, quite funny on the second and absolutely unbearable before a week has passed. It had a Spanish mother with quite a lot of Indian blood in her veins, and its father seems to have been a kind of League of Nations whose nationality is not easily determinable. The town has now come under the guardianship of Uncle Sam, and though that may not have made the colour of the children's skin less dusky, it has helped to soothe its nervous system.

Colon has twenty thousand inhabitants, most of whom are coloured black, gold, brown or some shade in between. There are groups of Indian shops near the harbour and in the tourist quarter where they offer with ununderstandable pride the worst trash produced by the old and new worlds, to which, to give local colour to the business, they add panama hats, which actually are made in Ecuador, and dried Indian heads made from papier-mâché and horse-hair. The prices on the other hand are real enough and the shopkeepers' energy and

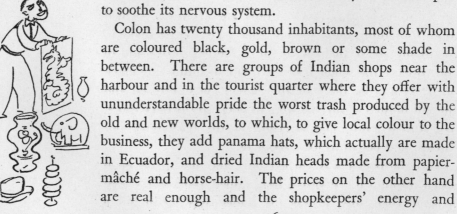

impertinence equally so. They will take off your coat as you pass in order to convince you that you need a new shirt of hard, disgusting artificial silk, and they weep or swear if you buy nothing.

The Chinese and Japanese have taken possession of all the barber's, greengrocer's and butcher's shops, and naturally Colon also has a number of Chop Suey restaurants above whose buffets yellow faces shine like full moons. Colon is the extreme advance post of the yellow races in the commercial war which rages openly from Suez to Panama and secretly in all the rest of the world. I shall return to this problem later and so leave it for the time being.

The original inhabitants of Panama, the small, thick-set Indians with flat noses and raven-black hair, feel that they are completely superfluous. Their gay eagle's feathers have given way to stupid straw hats, they wear a dirty shirt over a pair of dungarees and tread with curious clumsiness the pavement which lies exactly on the spot where only twenty years ago alligators waddled in the swamp between the stake foundations of the huts of one or two pioneers.  Colon has shot up out of the swamp like a mushroom. Huge cemeteries outside the town tell their own terse tale of the lives that were sacrificed here to yellow fever before the American Gorgas seized it by the throat and thrust it back, while the engineers drew the Panama Canal from ocean to ocean as though with a pencil. Colon bears the unmistakable stamp of a rapid birth. Nearly all the houses are of planks put together anyhow, and the shores of the artificial island on which the town is built are still being filled up.

Broad balconies jut out over all the pavements. You

only appreciate their real worth when you are surprised in front of a house with no balcony by one of the sharp tropical downpours. A hundred and twenty-eight inches of rain fall every year in Panama, more than six times as much as in Denmark, and it comes in the form of violent squalls at lunch time.

America governs in San Cristobal and the Republic of Panama in Colon. The two towns are built close together and the boundary runs down the middle of the twin towns' main street, the Avenida Simon Bolivar. This occasioned many curious incidents during the years that America was dry. There were, then, many American marines stationed on the Coco-solo peninsula, and on the American side of the street they could only get ice-cream and malted milk, while well-stocked bars and gay posters beckoned temptingly to them from the other side. When the donkey only has one bundle of hay, his choice is not difficult, and the result was a never-ending stream of Panama "heads" across the invisible frontier!

On the other hand, if you wanted to beat, shoot or only lynch a negro, you had to take him across into the U.S.A., for Uncle Sam looks at such things quite differently to the Panama police, of whom one in three is black and the others chocolate-coloured.

The Avenida Simon Bolivar looks like a huge exhibition of bars and bar-furnishings, and in the evening when the lights burn in "Moulin Rouge," "Atlantide" and "Sailor's Rest," the electric pianos and cinema organs make such a deafening din that you dive in horror into a side street, only to discover too late that a swarm of Scyllas and Charybdis are feeling lonely and long for the company of an understanding soul. Colon in the evening is as decorative and amusing in its colours as a summer

fair, but as a field of study for town councillors can only be recommended to those of Marseilles and Port Said.

God's own Americans have, of course, brought their racial distinctions with them to Panama. Above the entrances to all the many public buildings, post offices and banks are decorative and discreet plates on which are written "Gold" and "Silver." This does not mean that gold coins are received at one end of the building and silver at the other. It is only the American's tactful way of asking the whites to regard themselves as the golden doubloons and the blacks as inferior small change. We felt very golden in those days, although the banks did their best to convince us to the contrary when we changed our devalued Danish crowns into heavy dollars. They were only enough for a modest cinema ticket next to the silver seats, a glass of beer and a native meal in one of the least fashionable restaurants of Colon.

In this restaurant there was a jar of pickles on the table. On the label was printed "Pickled Onions" and we did think that the onions looked a bit queer, but every country has its own customs and shapes for vegetables. Actually it was pickled cayenne pepper which, if anything, most nearly resembles liquid dynamite beaten up in sulphuric acid and spiced with drawing pins. Throughout the whole voyage we were never nearer to death than in that moment. There was an explosion somewhere in our throats which carefully removed the skin from their entire inner surface and then shot like blue acetylene gas flames over our swollen tongues. Meanwhile Spaniards and Indians sat on either side of us and ate it as though it were marzipan. That was our last impression of Colon.

We still had the taste in our mouths when the pilot

came on board, and we still had tears in our eyes as we were raised by the three mighty locks and let out into Lake Gatun ninety feet above sea-level.

The Atlantic lay deep below us in peaceful majesty. It looked at us thoughtfully, rolled its eyes a little and spat after us over the mole into the harbour basin, and then went on with its work of carrying heavy steamers on its back from one part of the world to the other. The Atlantic had waved its last farewell to its old friend the *Monsoon*.

We were now in fresh water on the huge artificial lake which was formed when the Americans took over from the bankrupt de Lesseps and built the Panama Canal with granite. Mountains were cut through with dynamite and extensive swamps filled up with human bodies and millions of shining dollars. Nowadays the canal is like a high road which you take for granted, running across the northern outriders of the Andes, and the hospital at Ancon rises up a worthy monument to the real victor, Dr. William Gorgas, who fought and exterminated malaria and yellow fever, thus making the fulfilment of the great plan possible.

Leafless trunks stick their black branches out of the water, for where primeval forest formerly was is now deep water covering decaying swamps, and the steamers of all nations traverse the old hunting grounds of the jaguar.

The primeval forest comes right down to the shore of the lake and howling-monkeys compete with the shrieking sirens as the steamers come round the dangerous corners in the canal. The contrast between untouched nature and modern technique is so curious that we asked the American Government's permission to park for a

The Crew of the *Monsoon*
From left to right: Skipper Thomsen; the mate Nielsen; "Sonny Boy"; Degenkolw;
Stubbe-Teglbjerg; Mr. Moller; Mortensen; Pedersen; and the author

An Old House on St. Thomas

day or two in this main thoroughfare. This we received and made ready to study the canal's private life.

An animal reserve has been made on an island in the middle of Lake Gatun. Next time you are going through the canal and you see a small green island with little white buildings you will know that this is Barro Colorado, the kingdom of Professor Zetek, where he holds sway over a veritable Noah's Ark. There are not only ants, bird-spiders and howling-monkeys there; but snakes and monkeys, pumas, jaguars, wild pig and tapirs as well, together with an eternal twittering chorus of gaily coloured birds and humming-birds with buzzing wings and long pointed beaks. When the engineers closed the Gatun dams and opened those where the Chagres flows into the valley of Culebra, the water rose inch by inch in the primeval forest and the animals took refuge in the heights. The largest and highest became a big island and thither came Noah and set up his tent.

That is the reason why Barro Colorado to-day has a rich animal life that is unique, and it was this the scientists we had brought with us were now to inspect with their large wondering child's eyes. They set out with their butterfly-nets and specimen cases and found large numbers of Gadus morrhua, Trichechus rosmarus, typlonectes, Mistichthys luzonensis, and whatever else the little dears may be called that crawl about in the tree-tops and amongst the leaves on the ground. My readers who are interested in zoology must excuse me, but I am only in a position to name the worms and insects most frequently to be found.

We others employed our time in taking a look round and being amazed at what we saw.

The virgin forest stretches its green fingers straight into

the water. Curious birds and brightly coloured flowers look out from between the branches and bid you welcome, and if you take only ten steps into the forest you will be right in the Sleeping Beauty's garden. Large gay butterflies swarm about your head, many of them are cobalt blue and have a wing span of half a yard. That's really true. Ask Stubbe!

Orchids flower in such confused profusion as to make the hearts of a collector and of every woman beat in ecstasy. From the ground there rises a narcotic mixture of flower scent and putrefaction, which makes you think of a greenhouse and a cemetery at the same time—the stifling hot perfume of the tropical forest.

The machete, that long Spanish knife, must come out of its sheath and carve you a path through the spider's web of the creepers, and long loops make intricate traps for your feet. The humming-birds look like gay flowers and the flowers look like humming-birds on waving stems. It is like paradise, but a paradise for sinful connoisseurs of beauty, if one can imagine such a thing without coming into too severe conflict with the dogmas of this world and the next.

Some Indians appeared and lent us long, narrow canoes which we not only learned to balance but at the same time to paddle. The days passed like tepid dreams, and then we suddenly decided to go hunting. Away, to shoot pumas, crocodiles and jaguar.

We manned "Moses" and landed on a small island clad in sou-westers, mackintoshes, sea-boots, gym shoes, straw hats, or whatever we had been able to find in our hurry. We looked awful, but we were well armed. Six rifles, a saloon pistol, four revolvers and two shot-guns were divided amongst six men, four of whom had never fired a thing more murderous than an airgun.

No one was shot, for the gods were with us. But they were with the animals too, for, if there were any on the island at all, they didn't let themselves be seen. We warned them in plenty of time.

We went through the bush like a herd of young elephants and for most of the time the cracking of branches and twigs drowned the sounds of our loud voices and the beating of our hearts. The jaguars did not come to have a look.

We had both hands full in making a way for ourselves and it is not certain what we would have said to a savage beast if we had had the bad luck to meet one. Later we discovered that the island was a peninsula and that our trek had taken place over a piece of ground lying between a banana field and some native huts. So, as one couldn't expect to find many pumas close to a frequented main road, the riddle was solved— but that did not happen till afterwards.

We waded in a stream up to our middles in water, and slid on our behinds down smooth, steep slopes between thorny tree-trunks. We were so wet that we never felt the rain that poured down on us from above. Sonny was bitten by an ant that had the jaws of a tiger, and then Mr. Möller photographed us in a clearing surrounded by breast-high reeds. We were modest and retiring, without the usual heaped up trophies which normally disfigure photographs of swaggering big game hunters in clearings surrounded by breast-high reeds.

It had been a glorious day. We were tired and fell asleep while the fireflies flew above the deck giving expression to their views on driving game in light-signals whose code we luckily could not decipher. The jaguars and pumas on Barro Colorado roared all night triumphant and challenging, so that in our shame we pulled the sheets over our heads. Nobody mentioned going hunting at night!

Next morning José and Gonzales brought us whole cargoes of ripe bananas and juicy paw-paws from the science station, and Sonny and I went on a little expedition and found some native huts where we bought eggs and lemons for a couple of old Kodak spools. Two stark naked, ebony children accompanied us right down to the water's edge and waved to us like small living statues. We took a photograph of them in all their glory and in parting presented them with an empty spool, which delighted them so much that they disappeared like lightning into the bush; presumably being terrified lest we regret our extravagance and demand that they give our present back. That was our last impression of Lake Gatun.

When we got back on board, the pilot had come out from Colon in a motor-boat and we continued our interrupted journey from one mighty ocean to the other.

The dead trees disappeared, the American flag on the station on Barro Colorado dipped in greeting, and we glided out of the lake and into the narrow, costly part of the canal, through the Culebra Cut where a bronze plaque in the rock tells of defeated forces of nature, and on into the locks at Pedro Miguel and Miraflores, where electric locomotives creep up and down the ramps on the dock side like ants, pulling the heavy cruising liners from one lock into another.

The *Monsoon* managed without a locomotive. We made fast with four hawsers and lay in the middle of the mighty dock like a spider in a bath and tried to look as though we filled the space quite nicely and were considering whether it mightn't be necessary to hang out fenders.

Our efforts to blow ourselves out were, however, not crowned with success. The tops of our masts scarcely peeped above the quay, and we made an amusing show for the passengers of a luxury twenty-thousand-ton tourist liner coming from the other direction, which settled down in the neighbouring dock like a turkey cock. We were filmed—with Baby Pathé—and the ladies waved to us and blew us kisses. Altogether we were the centre of attraction in a nice situation and were regarded like a toy in a shop window.

Toy! At home in Denmark they would be looking at the Christmas displays in the shops, and garlands of pine would be hung across the streets; and perhaps it would be snowing nice and thickly. In a week it would be Christmas Eve, and we sat on a coil of rope and sweated.

Then a tropical squall came and washed the sweat away, and when the rain had stopped, the steamer and the giggling girls had disappeared and the *Monsoon* was sailing in the waters of the Pacific. We had cheated Cape Horn and taken instead a promenade on an island sea. Dredging machines are an excellent invention when their work is so well camouflaged as has been done by nature along the shores of the Panama Canal!

The Pacific lay most temptingly there waiting for us, but we put the rudder hard over to port and went alongside the quay at Balboa, the American appendage to Panama City. The town looks like Colon, only it is larger and has trams and a cathedral with a hideous roof made of oyster shells. The *Monsoon* chafed at the posts of the quay. Sometimes her flag was quite near the bollard, and sometimes we could jump from the rail on to the quay, there being a difference of eighteen feet between ebb and high tide, so that it really did look as though we had arrived in the great and Pacific Ocean, which was what we wished to conquer, once we had eaten our Christmas turkey and unpacked our presents!

CHAPTER VII

*We celebrate Christmas in our shirt-sleeves, meet a nurse
and a loathsome crocodile, dance the rumba by
moonlight—and end among pearl-fishers*

THERE were a number of Danes in Panama City and district. To us they were kindness itself and vied with each
other to give us a good time. None of us will forget that
Christmas in Panama. While the others were feasting
ashore, I lay on my back in the cabin holding Bobby's
paw, who was suffering from an attack of fever and all
the attendant pains which, according to "Everyman his
own Doctor," one can contract in head, stomach and
other parts of the body. In a warehouse close to the
ship some negroes were singing carols, and it was so
beautiful that for a time I believed that I was dead and
had arrived at a place where, strictly speaking, I had no
right to be. Thus I got a little foretaste of Christmas
before I opened my stocking and ceremoniously shook
Bobby's paw and wished him "A Merry Christmas."

We were invited to a moonlight picnic on the shores
of the Miraflores Lake and it was there that we were
introduced to Elvira Filandino.

Normally she is a nurse in the Gorgas hospital, but
every year in her summer holidays she makes trips into
the forest in search of the still savage Indian tribes. She
is afraid of ants and snakes, but good friends with all the
blood-thirsty chieftains and fanatic medicine men between
Columbia and Nicaragua.

She packs her rucksack, laces up her riding boots and

then either on horseback or by canoe penetrates as deep into the jungle as she can. She once had a lovely picnic with the primitive tribes on the San Blas Islands and is very friendly with the Darien Indians. She looks after the sick and gives the women good advice on house-keeping, and then returns to her small room in the hospital with whole chests full of presents which would make the museums of the world lick their lips.

Every day she came aboard and chatted with us on deck, and before we left Panama City we were able to send a couple of cases of valuable ethnographic specimens to the National Museum in Copenhagen as a present from the little Elvira. We came to think very highly of this delicate, feminine explorer and through her we learned to love the country which she has chosen for her home and field of study, the country which under the bloody conquistadors of the sixteenth century wrote its name in history and then fell into a Sleeping Beauty sleep which was only broken by the puffing of the dredging machines and the hammering of the pile-drivers.

It was from the mountains of Panama that the first white man, Vasco Nuñez de Balboa, saw the mighty surface of the Pacific glittering in the sun and it was over this isthmus that native slaves carried heavy loads of pearls, silver and gold to the Spanish ships in the Gulf of Mexico. There are still traces of the old paths through the wilderness, and the alligators continue to roll about in the slimy rivers through which the porters had to go. Panama is a country with a bloody history.

Ghosts still walk the ruins of Old Panama at midnight. Old Panama lies a few miles south of the new canal town. In the old days it was the capital of the New World, once the country's original inhabitants had been killed or driven out. That cost streams of blood, but from this blood arose a city, rich and powerful, with a cathedral whose square tower points to heaven, with beautiful bridges swung over its rivers and richly clad men and women on the side-walks of the streets. Now, set amid the ruins of the past, there is a modern dance restaurant. Every evening the orchestra echoes shrilly through the silent squares, yet the music is in strange accord with the past. It is the rumba, the national dance of Mid-America—wild, exciting rhythms, staccato of drums and rattling gourds, that are akin to the ground we tread and all that has been.

The rumba is both enervating and stimulating at the same time. It is the harmony of the virgin forest, the expression of the national soul of Panama, what jazz in its original form was for Africa and what the tango is for the gaucho of the wide Argentine pampas.

The moon shines down cold and white on the ruined city. The long Pacific rollers break against the foundations of the houses and their muffled roar has a hypnotic power on your mood. The hectic, monotonous melodies of the orchestra seem to recede more and more into the distance, until finally they are only a muted accompaniment in your subconsciousness.

Then the walls of Old Panama rise again. The old bridges stand out sharply against the background of the primeval forest and lie mirrored once more in the water. White doves flutter out from the arrow slits in the cathedral and the whole city rings with the muffled clink of pieces of eight as they are counted and piled up. Indian slaves wander over the bridges with their heavy loads. They have a strap round their foreheads and fastened to this strap is a basket filled with silver and jewels plun-

dered from the treasure stores and graves of the ancient Incas. They walk bowed deep under their loads—a caravan on its way to the caravels anchored in the Gulf of Mexico. There is a rustle of silk in the streets and at the hour a heavy bronze bell sends its ringing note out over the proud, vain city. There comes Henry Morgan, the daring English pirate who is the terror of the Spanish conquerors. He comes like a fox from one of his many hiding-places on the coast, and where the fox bites, blood flows.

One day, in the year of our grace 1671 Morgan came sailing over the seas with his ships, which seem to have been an inexhaustible treasure store for pearls and mother-of-pearl; his bearded pirates went ravaging through the streets; flames shot up from the cathedral; a column of smoke stood over the city and the Spanish nobles fled mad with terror into the jungle, the treasure that they had gathered together in their haste fastened in a bundle on their backs. The walls of the slave market fell in; the warehouses were a sea of flame; and Henry Morgan plundered the city till only its bare walls were left.

Then the jungle took possession of the land that had been reft from it. Creepers twined across the dilapidated bridges, orchids bloomed between the stones and a giant snake crawled across the grass of the street.

Mother Nature has laid her hand gently on the blackened walls and time has planted wild flowers in the arrow slits of the cathedral, so that they no longer stare like the empty eye-sockets of death. It is only at night, when the full moon shines clear enough and the music of the native orchestra mingles in harmony with the roar of the tide, that the casual observer is permitted for a

few short seconds to see the walls rise up again, and then
Old Panama shines in all its glory, resplendent once more
with colour, love and life.

The past, present and future go side by side even in
Panama's everyday life. The Indian peasant still grinds
his maize between two stones and lives in a clay hut with
a roof of palm leaves, while his wife wears a nose-ring of
metal as was the custom when the conquerors first came.
His brother in the city rides in trams and speaks into the
telephone, but even he is mentally fast embedded in the
sixteenth century.

Some people will perhaps feel sorry for the Red Indians
who a few centuries ago rode naked and savage on the
track of the bison as they hunted over the plains, when
they see them stoning raisins in some shop or waiting
for a chance hire in the market. They seem more to be
pitied than any tiger that has to sit in a cage and beg
for sugar.

But the world progresses and disregards such problems.

American influence in Panama is growing from day
to day, and in its wake follows the corrugated-iron hut.
In a few decades it is sure to rule the land alone, which
will then be standardized. Every man will have his
Ford and no home will be without its vacuum cleaner, to
the greater glory of Wall Street but to the sorrow of
those few of us who still find joy in the fact that all
houses are not the same.

However, you can still find people in Panama who
have no idea that Joan Crawford paints her nails green
and who live in complete ignorance of the fact that
Wrigley is one of mankind's most unselfish benefactors,
and you can find things every day which cannot be calculated in terms of sheer dollars and cents but which make

life worth living and lend colour to the greyness of the days.

The *Monsoon* gave a Christmas party with an awning over the deck and ice-cold drinks. Rosita danced a rumba and Dolores a tango, while the whole company swayed across the laboriously scoured deck to the strains of a Danish "hit" to which our American guests listened in amazement. Our new ice-box made a brilliant debut and Mr. Möller wound the gramophone with sullen energy.  Bobby sat on the skylight and watched with awe, while twenty-five coal-black dockers stood on the quay, caught by the bright light of our lanterns. We dripped and spoke of winter in Denmark.

We took a look round the town and were a little surprised that it was so difficult to find a sober American at Christmas time, and that his first thought when he finally became sober was concentrated on what he was going to drink next.

Then Elvira Filandino came and fetched us one evening at twelve o'clock to go alligator hunting in the swamps of the River Chagres. Her car was so old that in spirit it still lived in the age of the shimmy (or was it a rumba that it tried to show us?), but all the same we  reached our hunting ground safe and sound, hard on the heels of our leader, a red-haired mechanic, who drove as though he were Sir Malcolm Campbell fleeing from the traffic police. We stepped out, cocked our rifles and switched on two large pocket torches. The light danced over the low river bank, bringing tree trunks to life, and suddenly caught two glowing red points, two cat's eyes in the darkness—an alligator!

"Red's" explosive bullet flung up a fountain of water and mud three inches from the monster's head and a mighty splash told us that the beast had retired in dudgeon. All became still as death again. The light continued its search. Another pair of eyes! Only two fireflies. Another pair! A huge alligator! A shot, a splash: we had it!

Jack waded in up to his thighs in mud and water, but it would have cost him his life to have got the body, and so we gave it up. A good sailor on deck is better than ten alligators in the mud. Then suddenly another two red lights gleamed ten yards away from us. "Red" fired and we got that one too. This time I was the retriever. Carefully I waded out between the rotting trunks, carefully I seized the monster and, after a short but heroic struggle, hauled it with a tight grip round its tail on land. It measured a little less than ten inches from the tip of its snout to the tip of its tail. Unfortunately it was too dark to take a photograph.

Should anyone doubt my courage or the size of the monster, they may go to the Zoological Museum in Copenhagen where the dragon lies in a glass case on its *lit de parade,* while St. George is quite prepared, should his way lead to Aarhus, to tell him the story over again. Perhaps in the meantime the alligator may have grown a couple of yards or so, but that will be the only falsehood in the story.

Jan roasted an excellent steak over our camp fire and we ate it under a roof of straw in the forest. Sonny swore that in future he would always roast his cutlets over a fire on deck, and then we went home, while the car danced an abandoned can-can to show its pleasure at the result.

New Year's Day was drawing to a close and we were beginning to get a little tired of Panama. We had stayed there long enough, and there was quite a lot of work waiting for us in the big puddle in the west.

Kalle contracted a really disturbing attack of fever which delayed us for a day; then the engine developed piston slap which made us later still. But after that the hour of departure really came. We waved good-bye, cast off from the quay, passed a huge motor ship, the *Tacoma,* and ran past Port Amador which guards the entrance to the canal, its batteries concealed by green plants and red flowers, like a savage watch dog on a chain. One or two officers were swimming in a pool cut off by a solid wire net, in front of which some sharks wagged their tails but they were not allowed to play.

Evening came, then night and the morning. Seven o'clock found us standing on deck and looking down. The *Monsoon's* stern was resting securely on a mighty coral rock, while her bows lay on the nice, white sand. It looked as though the ship had seen something interesting in the water and was now trying to dig it out with the jib-boom.

The night before the skipper had brought us wreathed in smiles into the harbour which is considered safe at high tide; the lead had recorded any amount of water under the keel; but he had forgotten that we were in the Gulf of Panama where there is a difference of eighteen feet between high and low tide, which is more than one usually reckons with; and now the *Monsoon* was well and truly stuck. There was no sea and at noon we had another bathe and dropped the anchor a little farther out.

A mile or two away from the ship lay a green island. Four miles to the north-west lay another, and to port a smooth broad bay which became a swamp when the tide was out, while on the shore of the bay were a hundred or two straw-roofed huts with a church tower in their middle. Some ragged negroes paddled out to the ship in their hollowed-out tree trunks. They were pearl fishers on their way to work and the islands were the pearl islands, Islas de las Perlas, the old treasure store of the Spaniards, the refuge of the bucaneers and the ancient burial ground of the mainland Indians. At the present time there is a slump in pearls, because some wily Jap had the idea of feeding pearl oysters with sand so that they laid well-shaped pearls, and that is why the Pearl Islands are so indescribably poor. They still dive there and every day naked black bodies fetch gleaming pearls out of a sea that is infested with sharks, but the divers wait in vain for the white schooners of the buyers, who in the old days used to fight for who was to get there first and bid the most. Nowadays the fishers live from the sale of the oyster shells from which prosaic shirt-buttons are made, and keep their pearls for the occasional tourists whom some chance or another brings to the islands at intervals of years.

The mate bought five unopened shells to try his luck and found a pearl worth anything between fourpence and fivepence. In size it was between that of a pinhead and a match head. Then the mate ran amok, and long before evening he was practically covered with oyster shells, and his one and only pearl had cost him a pair of trousers, a shirt that was practically new, five packets of Camel and two and a half dollars in cash. Luck had turned her back on him and he had two hundred and fourteen blanks in his hat, whereupon he turned his back on Luck and whistled the "Marseillaise" to a brand new tune.

All this time Science was at work. Jan dug out an ancient Indian dwelling and Stubbe caught insects and was himself caught by sandflies—nice little animals about the size of a grain of sand which bite without barking first and whose bite leaves a prickling irritation which takes days to disappear. We did not see much of our sages those days. They left in the morning with sandwiches and a thermos flask. Jan took his toy pail and Stubbe his botanical specimen case and they were put on shore where they could play in the sand all day long. They were fetched at sunset, just early enough to wash their little faces before they tumbled, tired out, into their bunks.

The rest of us took a look at the town. The inhabitants' ideas of cosiness were somewhat different from ours. According to the negro point of view, a black-spotted pig and a few clucking hens make a hut habitable, and if the interior can be finished off with a rocking-chair and a table covered with glasses of every conceivable shape and colour, it only needs one or two whisky posters and some coloured illustrations from magazines on the walls to make a harmonious whole.

The streets were the sewers and the sewers the dustbins, while in the middle of the market place were dance hall, inn and church, the first two well patronized. The church had not been used for a century or more, since white marauders had pulled up the floor in their search for gold coins in the old graves.

The centre of the town's spiritual life was the cock-fight arena, a round straw hut bigger than the others, where all the male inhabitants of the town sat on perches and enjoyed the bloody spectacle being played out on the white sand. Being New Year's Eve there was a

grand gala performance. Two ruffled cocks were peck-
ing each other's eyes out with their pointed beaks; blood
spurted from the arena up into the glistening black faces
of the spectators, but the negroes paid no attention to it,
only grunting like hungry hyenas while their eyes became
bloodshot with ecstasy. Each betted on his own cock
and hoarse howls sought to spur the bleeding animals
on. Silver coins were thrown into the arena and an old
negro, the owner of the losing cock, groaned as though
he were dying.

It was not the bleeding cocks which were the most
revolting. No north-European can understand the mentality necessary to enjoy such a disgusting spectacle. A
bull fight is something a little different, for there the
toreador stakes his life against that of the bull, and there
is still a vestige of fair play hidden in the torture of the
animal, but cock fighting lacks even these saving
moments. It is a perversion of the lowest kind.

The black remembrance of the cock fight weighed on
us the whole day and we did not recover our spirits until
the evening when, glass in hand, we wished each other
a happy New Year.

The first days of the new year saw us still in our
sheltered bay of Pedro Miguel. Jan found a number of
interesting pieces of pottery in his sandpit and said that
they were most important proofs of the ancient Incas'
high state of culture, and we others were rather surprised
to find that even in those days servants were so careless
in washing up and when handling the household china.

Jack brought down a wild boar, or, what is much
more likely, a tame pig gone wild, one whose forefathers
had grunted in the pigstys of the ancient Spaniards. It
is at any rate possible that our pig really had belonged

to one of the old conquistadors in the sixteenth century; it was quite tough enough for that. Mr. Möller sought to kill a pelican, but the butt of his gun flew backwards and nearly killed him. Luckily he only received a large cut over one eye which Stubbe treated, but in spite of that the wound healed very quickly.

The entire crew slept at night in hammocks slung on deck. During the day it was so hot that we began to wonder whether there was not an article of clothing more suited to this climate than the warm fig-leaves we were wearing.

Early on the morning of 6th January we set sail for Galera, the most westerly of the Pearl Islands. Huge shoals of fish made the calm sea boil, and when a wave lifted "Moses" on to the chalky white shore of Galera thousands of inquisitive seabirds swarmed crying round our heads. We shot several specimens for stuffing, frigate-birds, petrels and puffins, and the only difficulty we experienced in our shoot was in getting the birds to keep a sufficient distance from the muzzle of the gun. We waded in a sea of gulls' nests and said "How do you do?" to most attractive young gulls in white silk dresses, who spat at us from their nests between the palms and banana trees.

When we got back to the ship the entire jib-boom was occupied by a Sunday school of young gannets, two sharks were circling round the screw, a whale was blowing on the horizon while a fine black-sea-snake with a yellow belly hunted small fish under the keel. It was obvious that it was the birthday of our zoologist, Stubbe, and that the animal world had sent deputations from far and near to congratulate him.

We caught a shark, sixteen feet long and our biggest

yet, and induced a sea-snake to enter the butterfly-net, when it was hauled on deck and taken for a ride straight into the formalin bottle where it met a swift death.

These snakes were one of our greatest zoological surprises. We knew from "Brehm" and all the other zoology books that the ship possessed, that the sea-serpent is the cobra of the sea; that to be bitten by one means instant death and that the greatest care has to be exercised when catching one. To begin with, we took hold of them with an ingenious pair of tongs and the fear of death, and felt very brave whenever we had overpowered one of these monsters. Then we came to Fiji  and saw whites playing with the serpents as they bathed. They let them twine round their arms, lick their ears and form the tenderest of folds round their necks. The native children dragged them along to us and tried to sell them for cigarettes. They held them by the tail, in the middle or by the head, and did not seem to have the slightest fear of these "cobras of the sea." We investigated the matter and sought information all over the island. Always we were given the same answer. Nobody had ever been killed by a sea-serpent and they were everywhere regarded as toys and considered quite harmless to humans. After Fiji we were not quite so proud of our exploits as serpent tamers!

The gannets had covered the jib-boom with sufficient guano to turn the desert into a waving field of corn and we had to kick the birds to get them to move a couple of inches. Towards evening a flock of horn-fish shot like  glistening projectiles out of the water and the largest of them wedged its snout fast under a piece of metal plate on the hull, where it remained hanging, so Stubbe had it for his birthday supper. That night he was sick. The

general supposition was that it was the result of over-
eating and too rich chocolate, yet we decided to stay
where we were till the morning and see if he felt better,
for we were now bound for places where hospitals and
doctors do not hang on every tree. But anyway where
do they?

We could have spared ourselves the trouble. In the
morning Stubbe was heaving on the capstan for dear
life, and he and Jan spent the whole day stuffing birds
while the *Monsoon* drove southwards under full sail. A
pencil line marked our course on the chart, nine hundred
sea miles across the ocean to where it ended among some
curiously shaped spots—the Galapagos, some of the most
desolate and least known islands in the world.

CHAPTER VIII

Tells of long days with short squalls, sharks and dolphins.
We are visited by Mr. and Mrs. Neptune and
reach the Galapagos like giants refreshed

NINE HUNDRED miles of sea is no mean distance. Even
in the most favourable of circumstances one cannot do the
voyage in under a week, and on board a sailing ship in
the regions where calms are more frequent than wind, the
way can become fairly long. Although the engine was
running most of the time, the *Monsoon* took twenty-three
days for the voyage.

Jack harpooned dolphins, the skipper sewed sails and
murmured something about youth in days long past,
which had had more respect for grey hairs, &c.—but in
doing so he avoided looking at anybody and so there was
no resultant scrimmage.

Now and again we were wakened up at night by
hammering and trampling on deck and sat up prepared
for the worst, till we realized that it was the mate and
Kalle still engaged in their everlasting game of blind
man's buff with the light, capricious breezes. The sails
hung lifeless and powerless and only occasionally were
they filled by a breath of air, to fall back again into their
state of somnolence five minutes later. Our hair was
getting long and Jack's was cut by Stubbe, Jan, Sonny
and one or two others. When it was finished his head
looked like a relief map of the Bernese Oberland with
soaring peaks and deep valleys into which never a ray
of sunshine penetrated.

85

One dark night the mate saw a bird circling about the mast. When he looked up again a little later, he saw a dark shadow that had settled down to rest up there in the darkness. Silently as a cat with rubber boots he crept up the rigging and threw his coat over his prey— one of the halyard blocks. Once down on deck again he whistled an air and took a furtive glance at Kalle, whose expression was luckily hidden by the darkness.

Then they were given something else to think about. A squall came up and whipped the rain down on the deck, whilst our little violinist, a cricket that had stowed away on board in Panama, packed up his instrument and sought refuge under the water tank.

Those were long days and long evenings, and we had many a grateful thought for Mrs. Wanger of Aarhus who had brought us an armful of detective thrillers which we now read from title-page to end-paper. When we were tired of reading, we sat on the bow-sprit and looked down into Neptune's huge aquarium, and it was like looking into a sapphire of unthought-of dimensions, not one of the cold, dead ones that gleam in Maharajahs' turbans— no, this sapphire had warmth and life.

The water under our stem swarmed with fish of every colour, striped, golden, red and black, silver-shimmering fish of every colour in the spectrum swimming in a bowl of sapphire—an Arabian Nights of the sea, told by the Sea Virgin on longitude two degrees north, while the *Monsoon* lay on the seas with fluttering sails like a seagull that had been shot.

The oaken planks of the deck burned under our bare feet and Bobby took panting shelter under the lifeboat. The man at the helm rolled himself a cigarette without even deigning to look at the compass. The ship had no way on her, and the sea was as calm as a pond. Now and again an inquisitive frigate-bird would circle round our masts, take a couple of wing-beats out to sea and then back again, and finally disappear towards where the horizon quivered in the heat, where it became a tiny, black speck finally swallowed up in space.

From time to time there was a commotion under our bows, when a flotilla of dorados on the war-path shot through the swarms of little fish. The dorado is one of the most beautiful things in the sea. It is about five feet long with beautiful lines, a swimming symphony in colours, whose notes continually change while it hunts. It changes from verdigris to the brightest blue, turns on its side and becomes striped with black and yellow like a mackerel, and the whole fish shines like bronze. Its huge belly turns from green to yellow with a speed as though the colours were electrically controlled, and finally lights up a brilliant violet.

Now you must not try to catch this living neon light with a hook and line. Firstly, they are difficult to catch and, secondly, they become silver-grey and boring as soon as they come out of the water. The beautiful bubble bursts leaving behind a little colourless soapy water in the palm of your hand. As they flashed hither and thither under the jib-boom, the small fish darted confusedly in every direction, but the dorados knew how to make the most of their panic, for a monster raged with gaping jaws beneath each mask of beauty. Suddenly deep below the wild chase appeared a grey-black shadow, another, and then a third. They glided along questing and sinister in their slowness, turned under the keel and came back again. Three voices rang out from the stern,

eager and excited, and the call shattered the sleepy quietness of noon like a bomb: Shark!

That instant the dead ship woke to life. Bare feet smacked across the deck, someone shot out of the forehatch and the mate who was spending his watch below in the arms of Morpheus in his bunk jumped up and rubbed his eyes in confusion. The man at the wheel tore himself from his meditations with a jerk that could not be reconciled with the state of the thermometer, spilling half his tobacco, and Sonny threw a clattering casserole lid on the floor as he rushed out of the galley swinging the carving knife above his head.

The ice-chest was plundered of its content of salt pork and not two minutes after the shout had echoed across the deck, the shark hook slid tempting and treacherous over the rail.

In the clear water the white bait was visible for a long way; embedded in the pork was a hook that could lift a couple of tons and joining it to the rope that we used as a line were two feet of our best steel wire, a precautionary measure that the loss of two shark-hooks had taught us.

Once more the shadows became visible in the water. This time they came right up to the surface. One could see them and their wicked yellow eyes quite clearly. A mighty fin whipped the water as one of them inquisitively circled round and round the hook; yet again the shark swam round the tempting morsel in a wide circle, then shot straight at it, turning a little on its side so that the white of its belly glistened in the water—and bit. An instant of nerve-racking tension was broken by the triumphant shout of the man at the line: "We have it!" and the struggle began.

The tiger of the sea didn't give in easily. It whipped the water with its tail, the giant strength of which can break a man's bones like matches. But we had taken a turn of the rope round a belaying pin and the shark was slowly hauled nearer and nearer to the surface and the side of the ship. It was a well-grown fellow of about 13 feet. It prepared itself for a mighty wrestling bout with the side of the ship as a spring board, but then a revolver sang two short verses in its honour and these were the shark's funeral psalm. A mighty jerk and it hung there motionless. Blood flowed out of its mouth and dyed the foam red. The man-eater was dead.

Sailors have no mercy where sharks are concerned, and anyone who has seen the head of a man-eating shark appear above the side with its gaping jaws and evil eyes, will understand why that is. The shark is the personification of ruthlessness and cruelty its only finery. It is one of the most efficiently equipped machines that nature has designed for murder.

We dropped a running bowline over its tail and pulled it up to the rigging. Nervous convulsions still shook the blue-black body and the tail fins even beat long after the head had been severed.

If the proud albatross harbours the souls of fine, old sailors, then the shark is the reincarnation of all that is vile from the filthy fo'c'sles of days long past when knives flew from their sheaths, and the stink from the harbour inns of Shanghai and the whale factories of the South Seas hung in the air. The shark is the reverse side of all that is straightforward and noble in the sea's character—an assassin with an evil heart, and sailors hate them.

Life is not always a Sunday School and the Pacific by no means so peaceful as its name, but now it returned to its dreams in the sun. The sharks disappeared into the depths and cyclones were only a name that was to be found in handbooks. A school of dolphins came up close to us and played like naughty children.

First, they marched in rank and file with military exactitude, rising to the surface to breathe in files of more than twenty black-shirted fascists, then the next moment pairs of lovers separated from the main body and took an extra turn round the ship, then round again until some rejected suitor had the idea of shooting out of the water like an arrow, turning an elegant cartwheel over the head of his rival—and so it went on for several minutes. One after another the slender bodies spun through the air in competition for the honour and title of the best jumper, till the water foamed white on their playground. Five minutes and this game too, became boring and off they went, away from the ship to new playgrounds across the sea.

We watched them go with a smile, but Jack licked his hungry lips and his hand loosened its grip on the shaft of the harpoon. Not this time! We understood him only to well, but for the time being we had forgotten our culinary desires in our enjoyment of the dolphins' merry, carefree games. Dolphin steak is very tasty, and their liver something to be experienced. What a pity they've escaped! and yet—

Neptune's inexhaustible acquarium offers you much amusement. When His Majesty is playing a hand of poker with the gods of the winds behind the great ice wall of the South Pole, where they can find a little coolness, then it is that his dumb subjects play tig on the surface for the entertainment of those who, like us, wait for wind to fill their flapping sails.

Flying-fish darted like arrows over the waves and the bonitos chased them with clumsy jumps—but whoever has seen a tramp overtake a streamlined seaplane? In the mighty smack with which the bonito land on the water after their awkward flight one can hear their anger and disappointment.

Turtles paddled sleepily along and gaily coloured sea-snakes turned and twisted in the quiet depths below. An inquisitive swordfish stuck up its horny snout a few yards from the ship and the water at our bows was split by the mighty back fins of a sailor-fish just where five minutes before a giant ray had been.

By now all the wind gods had left the gaming table and a slight breeze from the south announced their arrival. A squall was coming, with the wind now from the east, now from the west, swinging round the entire compass in an instant.

We were in the region of calms, close to the equator, in the world's most unstable weather zone where, theoretically, the wind should blow horizontally upwards from the surface of the sea to the zenith, but where in practice it exhibits the characteristics of the most fickle of women and blows from every direction in one and the same minute, so that the skipper's beard got tangled round his neck making him quite confused and he whispered a mighty oath, while the main-boom swung about madly.

For one day we made progress till the wind thought that the joke had gone on long enough and quietly stole away, whereupon the sea quickly quietened down and a dead calm reigned once again.

It was midday and the sun had reached its zenith, exactly in the north. An observation was on the point of being made when suddenly there arose a commotion

by the stern capstan. Strange voices sounded in the usual chorus and unknown faces appeared behind the mainmast. Strange visitors! What the devil had happened?

We were at the equator, the middle of the earth, and the almighty Lord of all the Seas wished to see our passports. Since time immemorial he has exercised his right of search on all ships that wish to cross the line and eat up knots on the other side of the world. None may cross without a passport and the passport is a certificate of baptism, a legal document from the mighty hand of Neptune himself recording that you have been baptized on the equator after being thoroughly examined and your guts being pronounced worthy of bringing the Lord of the Seas the necessary sacrifice when he whips the waves into foam with his trident.

Neptune himself was a small, thick-set man with a golden crown and bearded chin and spoke with an east-Jutland accent. It is amazing how often one meets one's countrymen in other parts of the world! In fact we were so used to it, that we scarcely felt any surprise when we found that the Regent of the Seas also came of Jutland stock. His wife was small and dumpy and the hair falling down over her shoulders was like straw. Her clothes were most simple and practical, and she smoked Chesterfields like a chimney—a true product of the twentieth century.

The procession was brought up by Neptune's executioner, barber and surgeon, all three being incorporated, in view of the general depression, in one and the same person. In view of his trinity this Jack-of-all-trades was clothed with the most luxurious tattooing all over his body. In his hat he wore a cockade of a skull and crossbones, which, by the way, had been made from a number of the *Jyllands-Posten* of 18th October, a really charming tribute to us, for that was the date on which we left Aarhus harbour.

Neptune negotiated with the skipper. The mate, Sonny and Jack had disappeared from the deck. They had been christened before, and so left the field free for the unchristened and the Lord of the Seas. The skipper handed His Majesty the ship's papers together with a list of those who had not been christened, and then the ceremony began.

Each shaking, trembling lamb is led away by the executioner and subjected to a careful examination in which the principal parts are played by a wooden club, a file and an oilcan. Not till the doctor has declared the patient healthy and made him swallow a mystic medicine of foul ingredients can the baptism take place. The novice receives a drop of water from a cup without a handle on his head and breathes again—it hasn't been nearly so bad as he had thought.

Smiling and proud he rises from his uncomfortable seat and in that moment gets drenched from behind with water from a pail, yelps with surprise and jumps as though shot in the backside. Then and then only is the baptism complete and he can take his place among the great ones of the sea—Nelson, Drake and all the rest—and enjoy the spectacle of his successor in the torture chamber.

All earthly suffering comes to an end in time. Soon the last candidate rose from his baptism and shook the water from him like a dog and Neptune bade us all welcome to his domain. We each received nice typewritten certificates of baptism and to my great surprise I saw that Neptune's typewriter had the same blurred A's,

O's and E's as my own small "Olivetti." But who worries about such bagatelles on a day like that!

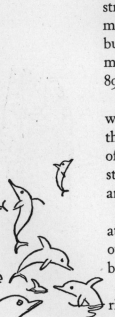

Jan received the name of "Needle-fish," Stubbe became "Nile-fish" and Kalle had to put "Flounder" before his Petersen, while I was christened "Octopus." Even Bobby had to submit to the showerbath and wagged his stump of a tail at the honour of being given the title of "Water Hound."

Our way was now clear and we could roam as we liked through the whole extent of Neptune's wide domains. The old boy himself stood in the bows and worked out the reckoning with the skipper. His nautical instruments were very old fashioned. His sextant consisted of three rulers, a cigar box and a film spool, tied together with string. His dividers were a tripod and his glasses were made of two long-necked soda-water bottles tied together, but they worked as they ought and our position was marked with the greatest exactitude on an aged chart—89.25° west and 0.00° latitude.

The solemn moment had come and we crossed the line while Neptune signed a mighty, ceremonial passport for the ship, which had been composed in a suitable mixture of English, French, German, Spanish and Danish. Bobby stood with his forepaws on the rail and stared cheekily and challengingly at the equator.

With a firm handshake Neptune took his leave, and at the same instant a school of giant dolphins raced across our bows, turning somersaults in the air and generally behaving like a festive display of fireworks.

The last that we saw of Neptune and his staff was a richly tattooed executioner sitting, paper hat on the back of his head, on the end of the bow-sprit and swinging a harpoon at the fiery steeds of the sea. His voice had a slight Danish accent as he swore when his throw missed, but perhaps that was only our imagination.

Neptune and his wife disappeared in the general confusion. Perhaps they dived down to their seaweed castle with its shell roof in the sea, or a ready-saddled dolphin and sidecar took them off to visit another ship.

We did not know. We only saw a school of dolphins that disappeared in the distance in a cloud of foam. Then Sonny sounded the bell and we went below to the day's feast of ham, cabbage and ice-cold beer. We sang songs which had been specially composed for the day and told the mate, Jack and Sonny of our experiences. They seemed to be sorry not to have been there.

When we went up on deck again the compass was pointing to the south where a chain of mountains lay like the edge of a saw on the horizon. They were the Galapagos, those curious islands right on the equator whose animal world seems to descend from that of another planet. Neptune had kept them in the background as a small christening present for his new subjects.

When he left he had sent us a light, fresh breeze from the north-east, so that we anchored in Wreck Bay before evening in a good ten fathoms of water.

We had reached the Galapagos!

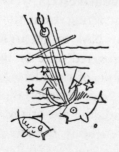

95

CHAPTER IX

*In which you read of Danish schnapps, an Ecuadorian
major, two foundered horses, a 'cello—and
a postman on the road to Paradise*

THESE lonely islands lying nine hundred miles from the
nearest land have no real history. Their origin is a matter
of dispute among scientists, one camp declaring that they
were thrown up by some volcanic outburst, while the
other maintains that they are the western spurs of the
Andes and that the connecting link with South America
disappeared under the waves, similarly in some volcanic
disturbance. At any rate volcanoes have played a prepon-
derating rôle in the Galapagos' past, and although they
are only still to be found in the main island, Isabella, all
the other islands give abundant indication of the commotion of their birth. They are black and rough, with
scant vegetation on their hard lava and basalt.

People have never been attracted either by their appearance or by the poverty of their dry and sterile soil. The
islands are seldom visited except when chance sailors and
whalers have sought refuge from storms there or landed
in one of the many bays to get fresh stores and water.
They had been discovered once or twice—and forgotten
again, till the Republic of Ecuador occupied the cliffs and
turned them into a place of deportation for her murderers
and criminals. With the aid of these prisoners peaceful
colonists tried to run haciendas and plantations, but the
last and greatest of them, the tyrant Manuel Cobos, was

murdered by his own workmen some twenty years ago, and after that colonization stopped of its own accord.

It was at these islands that Darwin stopped for some time during his voyage round the world in the frigate *Beagle* and scientists from all over the world have come from time to time to study the curious fauna of the Galapagos, which includes many rare species and among them giant turtles and iguanas that look like denizens of prehistoric swamps in miniature.

We, too, wished to see these rarities, but first there were formalities to be gone through and the local authorities had to be welcomed. They rowed out in a boat and consisted of the governor, the noble Major Aguilera, and his adjutant. A large section of this book must be devoted to the Ecuador garrison on Chatham Island, the capital of its civilization. I shall devote the greatest possible seriousness to this section and describe conditions exactly as they were, for I do not wish to be considered one of those authors of the baser sort who make South American Republics ridiculous and bring them down to the level of low-class musical comedy. You cannot do that sort of thing to a defenceless country.

Major Aguilera was quite small and slight, but so was Napoleon, before he grew fat. His uniform was impressive, even though the gold had turned black in places and the verdant green cloth was not quite free from grease spots. He had several weeks growth of beard and his nails were too long for every bit of them to be clean. His army consisted of thirteen men, half of whom guarded the town in the centre of the island, while the other half kept watch on the shore. Presumably the unlucky thirteenth ran with messages between town and shore in order to preserve the balance.

The military possessed thirteen rifles and twenty cartridges which were cleaned once a quarter till they shone as though twice that number. As regards uniforms, the equipment of the army left something to be desired. Some of the warriors had uniform trousers and woollen shirts, others wore tunics over a pair of bathing drawers. They all grinned benevolently.

In his spare time the governor sold dried cod and dried sea-lions' skins. They were stored in the hall of his shaky wooden palace and you had to get used to the odour before you could stand it. We stayed too short a time on Chatham to learn how.

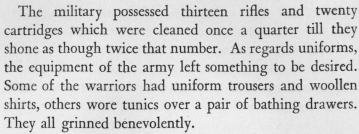

Apart from preventing enemy warships from effecting a landing, the most important duty assigned to the shore detachment was that of tending the light—a storm-lantern on top of a green-painted pole. A former governor had discovered that the good paraffin brought in much more money when he sold it to the town's inhabitants. Every sailing guide in the world describes this light as being unreliable in the extreme, but as no ships ever come to Chatham, there has never been an accident. But all that belongs to the past and the dark days of the harbour's history. The light was not burning the evening we arrived either, but the Governor had it kept alight all the next night, just to show us that he was an honourable man and confined his activities to dried fish.

He apologized for the flag not being hoisted, excusing himself on the grounds that it was so tattered and torn that it could only be hoisted on perfectly calm days. When some days later we paid him a visit, he regaled us with home-made lemonade. It tasted good and so we overlooked the fact that the glass was filled in the hall and brought in on a tea tray to be taken out again and refilled and presented once more bearing the mark of the first guest's lips—a nice, clean half-moon on its dirty opaque rim.

However, to return to our story. When we received the Governor on the *Monsoon's* deck things got somewhat mixed.

We had on board two people who were of the opinion that they could speak and understand Spanish. One of them was the skipper. He had first turn and after a long talk with the Major on deck he told us that the man was a customs official, very hungry and wished to spend the night on board.

Then Stubbe had a try. According to him Aguilera was a general and a bachelor and only wished to say good-bye before he rowed off again. And besides—thank you very much—but he had just had lunch.

Spanish as a language is easy to learn, but evidently it has too many different dialects.

The Major was given a glass of schnapps. We thought he was going to choke in the resulting paroxysm of coughing. However, when he finally got his breath back, he said: "Muy delicioso," smacked his lips, and was immediately drunk. Such is the stuff heroes are made of!

Other guests came aboard. Manuel Cobos' son came with his dark-haired, shy but still Norwegian wife, Karin, and they brought another Norwegian, Trygve Nuggeröd, with them.

Some years ago three expeditions left what was then Christiania to found a colony in this part of the world. All three were colossal fiascos. They lacked cohesion, understanding and capital, and Karin, her father and brother Nuggeröd, and his friend Stampa, together with Engineer Worm-Müller and his wife, were the only ones remaining in that abandoned Norwegian stronghold, where they wrought out an existence for themselves by fishing and farming in a small way.

Karin lived with her husband and her two charming children, the golden-haired Dagfinn and the raven-black Manuel, on Chatham, while the other three families had set up their tents on Santa Cruz, one of the other small islands.

Karin played on Jan's harmonica so that the planks of the deck sang and both the Major and his hard-bitten adjutant stared with enchanted black eyes at the one and only white woman of the place—both hopelessly in love and bewitched by "The Milk-Maid's Sunday" which the noise-box wheezed out immediately after the Norwegian national anthem. It would not have taken much for us to have joined their company, for Karin Guldberg Cobos was really a beauty of the first water, and was all the more enchanting because even in this far corner of the earth she was as fresh and lively as a Venus risen from the waves.

Those of us who could sit astride a horse were invited to visit the Cobos' hacienda. It was only six miles away, we were told, the horses as gentle as lambs, the road good and the food even better.

Three men volunteered. Mr. Möller said that he was an old hand, the mate had once led a horse by the bridle, and I had ridden races on Iceland ponies when I was nine and they twenty. We were a wonderful sight in our self-manufactured riding kit and the effect was that of a jig-saw puzzle wrongly put together.

We rowed ashore and waited for the lambs that had been promised us. They were rather late, but that was a relief, for they couldn't then be absolute racehorses.

Before they came the Major tugged at Mr. Möller's sleeve and whispered that he would be only too glad to do anything he could for us during our stay among the islands—only we must not say anything about it to the Adjutant. He could not quite be relied on. The same was promised me by the Adjutant, if I didn't say anything to the Major.

Then the horses came. A cloud of dust appeared in the distance and shot towards us like a falling star. When the dust had settled, we discovered five wild mustangs standing there stamping impatiently with their fore-feet while foam flecked their—isn't it "flank"?—and the sand. A cowboy grinned satanically from the back of the least nervous of the horses and held his lasso ready.

I don't know how I got on my horse. I chose the one that was nearest the ground, shut my eyes and jumped. I shall never be able to tell how the others fared, for before I had my feet in the stirrups I, or more properly the horse, took the lead and assured itself of the inside position.

I never needed to touch the self-starter. The brute set off with better acceleration than the composer of any car advertisement has ever dreamed of. My kidneys thumped against my shoulder blades and my camera jumped up and hammered the nape of my neck. My left hand was frenziedly clamped round a knob that was luckily in the right place, and I never discovered what the other hand did. I think I should be right in saying that the horse ran away with me.

At first the road was good, then it grew bad and finally became only a narrow path where rocks, cliffs and narrow bridges took care of one's entertainment. We took jumps of several yards and threw ourselves sideways over the ditches which now and again were ten feet deep, and my camera made such desperate efforts to beat me to death that the strap broke and it fell helpless on to a rock.

People are always so curious to know what other people think when they are drowning, burning or starving to death or dying of rage. I thought of the six miles, and how many miles an hour the brute could do. Then I tried to calculate how long the ride would last if I kept hold of my knob, but I never worked it out, for the figures sprang here and there and would not stay still. I lost one stirrup and got my foot back in again, but even to this day I do not know how.

Then I heard a curiously breathless voice behind me ceaselessly crying "Stop! Stop!" It was the mate. He, too, had been run away with. I had the idea that he was advising me to stop with such urgency purely because he wanted most frightfully to know how one brought off such a trick. We said: "Prrr" and "Stop" and all sorts of words that weren't evidence of a good upbringing. We spoke English, French and something that we considered to be Spanish to the horses, but they just laid their ears back and pretended not to understand.

Their wind gave out as we were going up a steep rise. They fell into a trot and ended in a quiet walk. We tried to look as though we had been enjoying ourselves. We began to experiment with the reins, and the mate, to show his superior technical knowledge, started telling me that the brutes had curbs. When, later, the other members of the expedition, Mr. Möller, the Governor and the cowboy, caught us up at a fast gallop, we had happily got so far with the brutes that we could move them forwards, sideways and backwards, and we impressed the others by asking them in amazement where on earth they had been.

They thought that we had been run away with and had lost control of our horses! We made the nags do a pass to the left and convinced them that they were mistaken. The mate whistled the "Finnish Cavalry March," and there was deep admiration in the eyes of the Governor and even the cowboy looked stupid. We told him that we rode in the Danish style, which was slightly different from the English, but thought that our style made better use of the horse's inborn energy. Mr. Möller silently handed me my camera, which the cowboy had picked up.

We discovered later that "Prrr" in Spanish equestrian terminology meant the same as "Gee up" and that loose reins had a similar significance. It also appeared that the bagatelle of touching the horse's starboard or port side with one's spur also had a meaning. Mr. Möller made one or two low, disloyal remarks, luckily in Danish, but when some minutes later his horse plunged to larboard when he had signalled hard to port, even he grew dumb and hit his nose against a mango so that it bled.

Once in the town our ways parted. I was in front and went down one street while the Major and the others turned without my knowledge into another, and shortly afterwards despite all my calls and manipulation of the reins, my horse steered its way to a stable where everything pointed to it being at home. The inhabitants of the village gathered expectantly round me to await further developments. Something had to happen.

I took the reins in one hand and, placing the other on my hip, as I have often seen Tom Mix do, asked if someone could not ride in front and show me the way

to El Senor Cobos' hacienda. The owner of the horse and stable thereupon obliged. He clambered on top of a colleague of my mustang's, and the dear brute followed at his friend's heels till we reached the gate of the hacienda. I kept one hand on my hip the whole way, while the reins lay in the other.

During our really excellent meal none of us felt the urge to expatiate on our ride on the gentle lambs, and we enjoyed a couple of delightful hours with our charming hostess before it was time to go. Curiously enough an invitation to view the estate's extensive coffee plantations on horseback, did not arouse much enthusiasm. Even Mr. Möller, who is most interested in farming, produced a most illuminating excuse.

The ride back went off quite peacefully, although we made feeble attempts to ride in the English style, not because it looks better, but because by doing so you are not always coming into contact with the hard saddle.

All next day we preferred to stand, and the mate talked incessantly of Beefsteak à la Tartare.

Then we sailed away. The weather was calm, so that the Governor was able to hoist and dip the flag for us. Nuggeröd came with us as pilot, and his wife became seasick. The small cigar box in which he usually earned his daily bread was towed astern, steered by his entire crew, an Ecuadorian fisherman by name Trevino, who sat in the trailer and bared his teeth in a huge grin of pleasure at the speed which the old *Dynamit* was going.

In the cabin we had some sea-lions' skins, a gift from the Governor, and some of the famous giant turtles trotted about on deck and got between the sailors' legs just when they were in a particular hurry.

Shortly before midnight we reached our next port of call, the island of Floreana, and anchored in Post Office Bay, which takes its name from the world's most primitive pillar box, a barrel in which in olden days the whalers used to put their letters to be forwarded by any ship that called at the island. The barrel still stood there and was used by passing steamers, schooners, and the three families on the island. Near us on the other side of the bay we saw a silhouette that looked something like that of a destroyer. In the light of the morning sun it turned out to be an elegant, white pleasure yacht, *Velero III,* that belonged to the American multimillionaire and Railway King, G. Allan Hancock. He it was that financed Kingsford-Smith's famous long-distance flight across the Pacific to Australia. Like several other rich Americans he was interested in science, and every year he placed the *Velero* at the disposal of a dozen or so scientists and himself went with them on a two or three months' cruise in the part of the world they were investigating.

The ship was a perfect miracle with its soft-carpeted salons, Steinway piano and luxurious single cabins with real beds and bathrooms. Modern laboratories, huge aquariums and every conceivable up-to-date accessory were at the disposal of those investigating nature, and in the evenings after the day's work they gathered for a quiet hour in the music salon where famous American virtuosi plied fiddle, flute and piano, while Hancock himself played on a 'cello that had cost a fortune with a bow worth twelve hundred dollars. Hancock was passionately fond of music and the clink of his many dollars was lost in the music he conjured forth.

Our own scientists went alternately green and yellow when they saw the working conditions which reigned on the *Velero*. The rest of us congratulated ourselves that we did not need to change for dinner and did not in the least feel like poor sparrows in comparison to this rich bird with its thirty-two knots.

When you ship before the mast, you do not want that sort of thing, and as far as music was concerned, Mr. Möller was not at all bad on his mouth-organ, which cost ninepence, and Stubbe and I were pretty close rivals on a banjo.

Next day found a newcomer anchored between *Monsoon* and *Velero*. She was the *Stella Polaris,* the big Norwegian pleasure yacht, which under the name *Hohenzollern* used to belong to Kaiser Wilhelm, and we began to feel that we were keeping too fine company. However, the *Stella Polaris* sailed away again the same day.

Her boats were lowered even before she had dropped anchor. Some American tourists were set ashore, where they said "Cute" seventeen times, and "O.K." nine times, photographed each other, put into the barrel a couple of hundred post cards with: "If only you were here, Kind regards," and had themselves put back on board again firmly convinced that they had seen the Galapagos. Two hours after her arrival the *Stella Polaris* put out to sea again, tearing breathlessly to her next port of call, the Marquesas. It was with a feeling of relief that I waved good-bye to her.

All the same, these luxury hotels have their advantages. The *Velero* had a dark-room and a ship's photographer, a decent young Norwegian, who developed a good part of my films, which otherwise would have been ruined by the heat and the long time that would pass before we reached the next Kodak depot. He left them at the Post Office in Hiva-Oa, and it is his fault that this book contains photographs taken between Panama and the Galapagos. Shortly after the *Stella Polaris* had disappeared behind the point, the *Velero* also weighed anchor and set course for South America. Our scientists took envious leave of their colleagues, who in their turn envied them their unrestricted life aboard the *Monsoon*.  We were invited to a small farewell party, at which the "Hancock Syncopators" played Carl Nielson and Grieg, while Hancock's first mate, first photographer and best friend, the red-haired Real-Estate King Charley Smith, showed us films taken by the *Velero's* film expert, the Swedish-American Emery Johnson. Twice during the concert the wireless operator brought in radiograms from his Los Angeles Office and Hancock wrote the answers during a piano solo—buying, perhaps, a railway during a Beethoven sonata and deciding under the influence of a Chopin prelude to sell an oil territory.

Then the *Velero,* too, disappeared from our view, with its mahogany doors and its two humming diesel engines. When its wake had settled, the *Monsoon* was left cock of the dunghill, a feeling that made it at once a little broader and a little longer.

Mr. Möller and Nuggeröd went up the cliffs and caught crabs and starfish, while Jan and Stubbe plundered the bushes in their search for unknown insects, and one or two trawls of the sea's bottom brought fantastic sea animals to light.

We paid a visit to a shallow saltwater lagoon where flocks of flamingoes stood on one leg enjoying their exotic reflexions in the calm water, till one of them fell  to Jack's gun and ended its existence under Stubbe's skilful hands with arsenic under its skin, cotton-wool in its eyes and the Easter edition of the *Berlingske Tidende* for a coffin.

One day I suddenly came across a bundle of letters which the Governor on Chatham had handed over to me for delivery on Floreana. They were all for three different addresses: Baroness Wagner-Bousquet, Dr. Ritter and pure and simple Mr. Wittmer. I asked Nuggeröd where these people were to be found, turned Jan's haversack into a postman's satchel, put on a sun-helmet and set off.

I trotted quietly along the dry, dusty, narrow path never dreaming that my new profession of country postman in the Galapagos would lead me into Paradise and a situation that was to prove the most grotesque and fantastic of the whole voyage.

On the shore stood a board on which was fastened a pencilled notice which in itself was full of significance, but the events of the day completely out-trumped it. This was the notice—

WHOEVER YOU ARE—FRIENDS!

Two hours from here is the hacienda "Paradise." It is a spot where the tired traveller has the happiness to find peace, refreshment and quiet on his way through life.

Life—this small portion of eternity which is bound to a clock, is so short—so let us then be happy—let us be good!

In Paradise you have only one name—Friend!

With you we will share the salt of the sea, the vegetables of our garden and the fruit of our trees, the cold water which runs down our cliffs and the good things friends brought us when they passed this way.

We will spend one or two moments of life with you and give you the happiness and peace that God planted in our hearts and souls when we left the restless metropolis and journeyed away to the quiet of the ages, which has spread its cloak over the Galapagos!

(Signed) BARONESS WAGNER-BOUSQUET.

CHAPTER X

In which you will convict the author of mendacity

I KNEW that the road to Paradise was long and difficult, yet my teachers had omitted to inform me that it was paved with red-hot stones and wound between thorn bushes, prickly lemon-trees and infernal cactus.

My desire for Paradise lent wings to my feet and they bore me through the prickly thorns up the hot path to the waiting vegetables, the salt of the sea, and the ancient but still protective cloak. One of the sons of the metropolis was on his way to a better place.

It turned out that in the two hours mentioned in the notice one was supposed to cover exactly ten miles and the maquis gave no shadow. It was on a large plateau scorched by the sun that I found the first signs of the presence of man. The skeletons of a couple of wild cows lay there. At first glance I thought that it was the work of roving wild dogs, but a closer investigation revealed that both thighs and ribs were missing from the assembly of bones, and that in the middle of the forehead there was a hole—the result of a dum-dum bullet.

The path from the plateau was marked all along its length by perforated skulls, from which one might conclude that the Baroness and her archangel lived on something other than mere cold water and the fruits of the trees. The road wound on across plateaux, through passes and over rocks, and seemed as if it would never come to an end. From the position of the sun the business had lasted too long for me already, but, finally, I did reach my journey's end, with my tongue hanging out and a sucked-out lemon between my lips—if the reader can imagine such a combination.

At the end of the path stood an unhappy and curiously out-of-place Japanese gate with "Welcome" painted on it in vulgarly large red letters which bored into my eyes that were already smarting from the sun. A donkey hee-hawed somewhere behind the gate; and there came a spirit lightly tripping over the stones—the Baroness von and zu Wagner-Bousquet and Floreana.

I fought heroically with my sense of humour and sent it flying into the bushes with a well-aimed upper-cut before I dared look at her again. She stood beside me, apparently not at all surprised at my coming. She tendered me a white little hand, and we glided into Paradise, past the local St. Peter who hee-hawed his blessing behind us.

The Baroness was small, but one could not say that she was beautiful. In front of her swollen lids she wore strong spectacles and her mouth, though too large, was yet unable to cover her long, yellow, rabbit teeth. She reminded one of a very vicious caricature of Mistinguette. Her hanks of hair were kept in place by means of a pink shoulder strap round her head, and she wore a kind of baby's rompers, like the trunks the ladies of the chorus wear when rehearsing. She moved in that hopping manner which jockeys call a "canter."

I cantered beside her as well as I could, till, by way of a change and to show a little personal character and independence, I tried one or two chassé steps, but unfortunately stumbled over a large lump of lava.

Such was our entry into the hacienda "Paradise," a

wooden hut set in the middle of a vegetable garden, where a powerfully built, blond youth gave me a paw and was introduced by the Baroness as "My Baby."

Baby looked as though he had been a gigolo in a very cheap restaurant somewhere in Berlin, W. His eyes were a watery blue, his hair was curly and his smile much too sweet. In private life he was Herr Rudolf Philipson of Berlin, aged 28. A German cook, tubercular and with one foot in the grave, smiled sicklily from the background and brought tea.

The interior of the hacienda "Paradise" hardly lived up to the promise of the notice on the shore. The furniture consisted of two broad double divans with revoltingly bright cross-stitch work on large cushions lying on covers which lost nothing by being hidden. The walls were decorated with photos of the Baroness as a South Sea Princess, "little Gardener" and society lady. In the last, taken by a Parisian photographer who had greatly flattered her, she seemed to represent a canary which had been treated with peroxide, given empty eyes and a Coty mouth.

Nestling with dreamy, half-closed eyes in a corner of one of the divans the Baroness—quite unasked—related her romantic story, the gospel of her life, as she called it, while Baby stroked her hands and arranged the cushion behind her. Here is the pith of her story, just as she herself told it.

She was born in Austria—I suppose at least forty years ago—the daughter of a high official, who was sent to the East to superintend the construction of the Bagdad railway and took his child with him. In Syria she met a daring young Frenchman, naturally in the Air Force, who married her and introduced her as Baroness Bousquet into the highest society in Paris.

Her beauty, she said, placed her immediately in the front rank, and the dresses she wore at Longchamps and Auteuil were described in greater detail than the last debate on the budget in the senate. She was over-whelmed with invitations and people competed to secure her wonderful voice for charity bazaars—so she said.

Then this fêted queen of the boulevards and salons happened to meet Rudolf Philipson. She ran into his arms at the Colonial Exhibition in the Bois de Vincennes, and they went arm in arm from one stand to another, looking at pictures of far and beautiful islands.

Shortly afterwards the sky went up in flames, as the aviator was not modern enough to tolerate a lover in his household, and a divorce was put through. The two lovers went for walks in the Bois de Boulogne and amongst the birds, flowers and stinking motor-cars found their way to the beating heart of Father Jean-Jacques Rousseau. They were tired of city life, its alcohol, its evil people and its noise. They were finished with the metropolis. They decided to find their way back to the bosom of mother nature. They spun a globe on its pedestal, stopped it with a finger and lo! a little, red varnished nail pointed exactly to the island of Floreana in the Galapagos group.

Shortly afterwards a steamer left Le Havre. On its deck stood the Baroness and Baby with their arms about each other, and close behind them Lorenz, the cook, sucking his bleached moustache. Their luggage con-sisted of a cheque book, a pile of gardening books, two or three dozen dresses and a swarm of bees. These later gave rise to an amusing little episode on board the

steamer from Guayaquil to the Galapagos. The dear little animals escaped from their skep and so roused several of the passengers that they gave vent to unconsidered words in several languages. This hurt the Baroness, and when with Baby's help she had finally recaptured the swarm from an elderly gentleman's beard, she retired like a whipped dog to her cabin, disappointed and embittered against mankind in general.

Such was her farewell to the ugly, ugly world and she did not revive till she started to tell Baby and Lorenz how she would build the house on Floreana.

On the voyage the Baroness became religious. Her religion included most of the doctrines already known, plus one or two Wagner-Bousquetian dogma, which were largely concerned with love and more or less with strong drink.

The Galapagos suffer severely from lack of rain even during the wettest period of the year, and this lack of water makes itself felt in many parts. Yet the Baroness's faith was such that she believed she could even perform miracles. She remembered having read somewhere about striking a rock so that water flowed. For days on end Lorenz and Baby searched for a spot where the grass was green in the midst of the parched brown, for a cliff where the earth was muddy and damp. Finally they found such a place and called their mistress who at that moment happened to be unpacking silk stockings and rouge from a cabin trunk.

She came, saw and struck with her little hand against the hard wall of rock, and so great was her spiritual power and so strong her belief that water actually dripped out of a fault in the rock—after Lorenz and Baby had plied it with hammer and chisel for a time.

The Baroness fell silent a moment and looked at me with enchanting, earnest eyes. Then she said that a French journalist visited her once, and the whole time that she was speaking he never shifted his gaze from her lips. He was completely carried away.

I felt a prick of conscience, for during half of the conversation my glance had rested on a well-assorted collection of tinned foods lying on a shelf and the rest of the time on a number of empty bottles with really fine labels that were piled up in a corner of the yard. Then for the first time I looked at her lips; but lacking the Frenchman's ability to say in the most charming way possible the exact opposite of what he is thinking, I preferred to say nothing and that chilled the communion of our souls.

Baby was sharply ordered to clear the table, and I was given to understand that if I wanted to take some photographs of her, now was the time. I must indeed have stared a little too long at the good things which good friends had brought when they passed that way. With the sureness and the tired smile of the much-photographed film-star, who is pestered by her publicity agent, the Baroness took up her pose and my modest little camera blushed at having to take this marzipan figure, but there was no way out—the object was given and even the background settled beforehand. The audience was at an end.

The Baroness is a fat titbit for the press. A few years ago fantastic stories circulated in the newspapers of the world. A woman was supposed to have made herself ruler of the Galapagos, to have proclaimed herself Empress of the Pacific, waged war with Ecuador and with her hordes of indomitable freebooters made the waters of that sea unsafe. Even the old *Times* fell into the trap and a Copenhagen newspaper turned it into a front page item. Some young Greek idealists (a hundred lovers of beauty and freedom), formed a league, and offered to help her in her struggle. There wasn't a grain of truth in it all, but whoever the Baroness's publicity agent was, he at any rate knew his business.

The Americans were quite mad about her. She was the correspondent of several papers in the States, and when the millionaires' yachts brought the curious to see the lonely Queen of Floreana she received many nice presents. She was by no means so lonely either.

The next letters in my satchel were addressed to Dr. Ritter. He lived a couple of miles away from the Baroness and a notice at his gate said that one should call loudly once or twice before entering. I roared like a foghorn and there was a rustling in the bushes. Dr. and Mrs. Ritter were exponents of the nudist cult, but not exhibitionists. They received you in more suitable clothing and once you had seen them you were glad. Their paradise was called "Eden." It was a log-house like the Baroness's, but the garden was larger and the trees higher.

The Ritters were the first to come to the island. They constituted the island's ancient aristocracy and were furious with the Baroness, the parvenu, for taking away half their fame as hermits and the greater proportion of the Americans.

Feminine charm will always triumph over the realities of science, however genial and vague, and for a democratic American a baroness is pure heaven—"How shocking! what a thrill."

When the Baroness arrived on the island the Ritters refused to give her water, but instead gave her donkey a whole bucketful of the precious fluid, and what it left was poured on the grass at the feet of the Baroness—for the Ritters love animals and plants.

Ritter was a philosopher. He was fairly small, his legs had been screwed on wrong, so that his toes pointed inwards. His nose was long and pointed, he had watery, protruding eyes and the hair of a prophet. His disciple, Miss Dora, smiled a toothless welcome. The couple had at their disposal only one pair of false teeth and this was Ritter's day.

Miss Dora wore beach pyjamas and had large, naked, black feet. Her neck had not been washed for at least a month, and had been given a marbled effect by the passage of drops of sweat.

Nudism is above all a healthy movement, but the Galapagos are so short of water!

Before his exile Dr. Ritter had been a dentist in Berlin. He had married an opera singer who had had no appreciation of subtle philosophies, and then little Miss Dora came across his path. She understood him. They moved together to the Galapagos, although Brunhilde would not consent to a divorce. So now he was expecting that she would arrive one fine day on Lohengrin's swan and demand him back. Her longing for him would drive her to it—or so he said.

In the meantime Ritter sat in a wooden chair and philosophized with Dora kneeling at his turned-in feet. Like the Baroness's faith, his philosophy was a comprehensive cocktail of the strangest ingredients, a curious mixture of foreign words, faded theories and well-chewed phrases. His ambition was one day to map the human brain but so far he had not finished measuring it. His web was involved enough to impose on coal kings and oil magnates, and a brand new typewriter and a private edition of his own works bound in oasis morocco told of admiration for his work in that, as yet, uncharted wilderness.

When I asked to be allowed to photograph him, he agreed readily and got up on to his bed. He worked at a board which hung suspended over the bed, and above his head swung a storm lantern "made in Thuringia." This he lit—it was midday and blazing sunshine—then he ran his hands through his hair, put finger to his forehead and asked me straight out if I didn't think he looked like Faust.

On leaving the Ritter Elysium, I was rather afraid of carrying out my last mission. There was still Mr. Wittmer left. In my satchel lay a *Vossische Zeitung* and two or three letters for him—but was I capable of absorbing further impressions of this kind to-day, without taking harm and becoming mad myself? I slung the satchel over my shoulder and resumed my pilgrimage into the unknown.

My fears were unfounded. Wittmer was quite an ordinary person living in an uncommonly beautiful stone house set in a large, well-cultivated garden. He had a charming, natural wife, and two children quieter and better behaved than children usually are.

I was so tired that I sank into a chair and asked for a glass of water. I was given tea and home-made paw-paw marmalade, and after amusing ourselves a little with my account of the day's events I gradually wormed Wittmer's story out of him. It was tragically ordinary and gloriously unromantic.

He was a German. When war broke out, he was a lieutenant in the reserve and worked in an office. He was thrust into the trenches, where for four years he lived through barrages, gas and liquid fire. When he got back, his nerves had all gone to pieces. He had no job, but a little capital; this was eaten up by the inflation. He tried everything but without success. Competition was too great. As he sat there in the little room he relived in memory those difficult post-war days. In spite of the great distance both in miles and years his hands still shook and his voice became uncertain. It was the same old banal struggle with hunger and unemployment.

Then one day he broke out and travelled here with his young wife and child. Here he found peace and recovered his health. He was a happy man and devoted to his wife and children, the younger of which was born on the island and was a model of health and strength.  No cases of presents were borne to Wittmer's house and perhaps that is just the reason why his glance is quiet and his wife happy.

He puffed at his pipe while the children played about with a young Alsatian puppy, and his quietness had a beneficial effect on the young postman who had spent the entire day among pirate queens and naked philosophical dentists with rat-like movements and dirty toes. Wittmer was the island's one and only stable point, unknown and thus happy, although he knew nothing of Kant, the cartography of the human brain or Jean-Jacques Rousseau. My thoughts returned to him with quiet pleasure on the long road back to Post Office Bay.

The day had been long and arduous. I had tumbled about among the wings and painted scenery of a fantastic stage and had finally found a real person of flesh and blood. When Ritter and the Baroness have turned to dust and "Paradise" and "Eden" have sunk into a smok-

ing hell, Wittmer will still be sitting in his cosy little house smoking his pipe. The sun will rise and set, and he will forget to count the days.

The name of this man's house was not "Eldorado."

Shortly after the appearance of the Danish edition of this book, I received a letter from which I learned that this prophecy had already been fulfilled.

The Baroness, Baby and Lorenz, Dr. Ritter and his disciple, Miss Dora, had disappeared from the history of the Galapagos and that in a manner which corresponded to the mysterious and tragic atmosphere that lay over the island. The letter was from Captain Alan Hancock who had once again visited the Galapagos in the *Velero*. He had visited the colonists of "Paradise" and "Eden" and this time in tense excitement, for Dr. Ritter had sent him a letter asking him to come as quickly as possible, as things had happened and would happen, which were too terrible to be the subject of a letter.

Hancock came, but the evening before his ship anchored in Post Office Bay the German philosopher died of poisoning. Miss Dora sat in their primitive hut, half out of her mind with fright and grief and the story she told was like the feverish fantasies of an overstrung mind.

One evening Lorenz had knocked at the door, been admitted and had begged to be allowed to stay. The night before this the Wittmer family had been wakened by wild howls and shrieks coming from the Baroness's property, but had not paid much attention to it as quarrels and dramatic jealousies were nothing unusual in the Baroness's household. Every now and again the "Pirate Queen" would simply order her big Baby to hunt the tubercular cook, who was already marked down by death, over the rocks and stones till he finally fell down and unresistingly allowed himself to be beaten, while the Baroness looked on and encouraged her gladiator with wild shrieks. On this evening Lorenz came to the Ritters quaking all over and begged to be allowed to stay till he could get a ship to Ecuador.

According to his story, on the morning after the Wittmers had heard the wild cries, the Baroness and Baby had disappeared completely. A yacht had put in at night, they had taken their belongings and left Lorenz to his fate.

Lorenz stayed quite a short time with the Ritters, then one day Nuggeröd, our pilot from Santa Cruz, ran into Post Office Bay in his little *Dynamit* and took him on board. They never reached Santa Cruz, but for the next three weeks their boat was sighted from several other islands sailing now here, now there, seemingly without aim or purpose, until it disappeared altogether.

Captain Hancock looked up the Wittmers, but they could not tell him anything he had not already learned from Miss Dora. He took her away with him to the mainland and then continued his scientific investigations among the other islands. On one small, deserted, volcanic island he found Nuggeröd and Lorenz. They lay a short distance from the shore, their bodies dried up by the sun, but still not so unrecognizable that they could not easily be identified. Of Nuggeröd's native sailor there was no trace, nor could the remains of the boat be found.

Captain Hancock had to return without clearing the matter up and the Floreana mystery is to-day presumably still open to conjecture. Hancock himself thinks he has built up the right solution.

In other parts of the group nothing had either been

heard or seen of the mysterious yacht that was supposed
to have taken off the Baroness and Baby. Nor had news
been received of these two originals from other parts of
the world, although a search was made for them after
Hancock had got into touch with the nearest mainland.
This brought the Captain to the conclusion that Lorenz
had finally had enough of the thousand and one little
tortures to which he was subjected, that his rage got the
upper hand and he had murdered the pair in their sleep,
burying the bodies and inventing the story of the yacht.

It is, however, possible that there was something more
than jealousy and the desire for revenge at the back of
the murder.

The Galapagos have always been a pirates' nest and the
air is still thick with tales of buried treasure. Was it
not possible that Lorenz overheard a conversation between
the Baroness and Baby and thought that he had found
out where such treasure lay buried? That he then killed
his two competitors in cold blood and came to an agreement with Nuggeröd to go treasure hunting among the
islands?

That would account for the curious voyages of the
Dynamit which were observed by the other settlers
during those three weeks and would also explain why the
three inhabitants of the boat landed on an island which
otherwise had nothing of interest to offer.

Did Nuggeröd and Lorenz then quarrel about the
imagined treasure and kill each other, or were they
wrecked and driven ashore on the island? If so, where
is the boat and the native sailor? It is not impossible
that he stole both boat and secret and abandoned his
employer to die of thirst under the merciless sun! Then
where is he now?

The whole affair is shrouded in a veil of impenetrable mystery. Ritter could perhaps have given us the key to the puzzle, but he died the day before he should have spoken and Miss Dora kept on repeating that she did not know what it was that Ritter wanted to tell Hancock, the news that was so revolting that he could not confide it to paper.

What position did Ritter take in the matter? How much did he know of the murder and the imagined treasure? and why must he die at such a suitable time for him or those who desired silence?

One question piles up on another, the threads grow confused, and the scattered, uncertain material that is at one's disposal only permits of guesses.

Certainty will surely never be had unless the Baroness and Baby turn up one fine day in some other part of the world and clear Lorenz of a suspicion which undeniably rests on him. But whatever he may have done, he has atoned for it on a block of lava under the terrible equatorial sun.

The worst hit was Mrs. Nuggeröd, who is in Santa Cruz with a fatherless infant born just at the time when her husband sailed to Floreana and his fate.

CHAPTER XI

*Which tells two stories about mosquitoes and warships,
the mate feels a shark's tooth, a sea-animal is afraid
of water, and we meet one or two sensible people*

AFTER my return there began a regular pilgrimage to both "Paradise" and "Eden." Everyone wanted to see the giraffes, and they came back with their tails between their legs. Their reception had been even more Spartan than mine, consisting of a cupful of tepid water, while none of the nice gifts which Hancock and the passengers of the *Stella Polaris* had had taken up by donkey were ever produced—and we had seen both Johnny Walker and Veuve Cliquot going ashore.

One evening a sea-lion swam up to the side of the ship, looked curiously at us and sauntered up and down several times, keeping one fin on the planks as though it wished to polish the ship. At the same time a large shark kept swimming round the keel and we expected a mighty battle. But the tiger of the sea appeared to be afraid of the sea-lion, for as often as their ways crossed, the shark made a wide detour while the sea-lion swam on as though nothing had happened.

There is, by the way, no truth in the old belief that a shark has to turn on its back to bite. We saw countless sharks bite downwards, and it is only when the morsel is quite near the surface that the shark turns over. This turn is simply the result of the position of what is to be bitten and it is certain that this widely spread belief can only have been put about by shark fishers. The hook, cast and line prevent the brute from taking the bait from above, and so the white belly must be turned upwards while the sharp steel jaws close round the pork.

We visited an old crater that lay some little distance from the shore called the Devil's Crown, and clambered about the steep rim, while Mr. Möller photographed our mountaineering. Lava is bound to have some complicated chemical composition, but according to my hurried analysis it is composed of green soap, slag, and broken glass. At least that is how it feels when you stumble and slide down it with only a thin piece of khaki between Mother Volcano and the more sensitive parts of your body.

Our scientists collected whole cases of insects, and when they had finished with Floreana we set sail for Santa Cruz, where we cast anchor late one evening, greeted by a multi-voiced choir of mosquitoes. We spread our nets and crept inside. The mosquito nets had a heavenly smell of muslin and we dreamed of carnival and black pierrettes, of taxis arriving up to hotel swing doors and disgorging a crowd of clowns and shepherdesses into the pouring rain—for those were the days of carnival at home.

Do you know the story of the man who was hunted by mosquitoes? He was sleeping in a tent in the virgin forest and his mosquito net reached right down to the ground, but the little dears got down on their knees and crept underneath. Then he climbed up a tree to find peace but each mosquito took a firefly and looked for him by the light of its lantern. Finally, the man crept into an iron tank and closed the lid over him, but the mosquitoes smelt him and stuck their noses through the walls of the tank in their efforts to reach him. Then he took a

hammer and tapped down their noses one after the other
so that they were stuck there. In the end there were so
many mosquitoes fastened to the tank that they were
able to lift it into the air and fly away with the man.

That story will perhaps give you a slight idea of the
lengths to which these tormentors will go and show you
why in the tropics the mosquito is more feared than the
lion or the cobra.

The morning after our arrival Bobby was so nibbled
that his already rather knobbly skin had the appearance
of a lunar landscape. It is a curious thing about these
animals, that the more they eat their victims the fatter
these become.

A mighty Danish standard and a huge Norwegian flag
were waving on the shore in welcome to the *Monsoon*
from the Scandinavian inhabitants of Santa Cruz who
soon came rowing out towards her. They were of a
different stamp from the hermits of Floreana. Worm-
Müller was a Norwegian and had spent most of his life
abroad, in the U.S.A., South Africa and Ecuador. He
had been broker, business man, coal miner, railway
engineer and roadman, was a brother of the well-known
Professor of Oslo University and filled with good spirits
and optimism to the rims of his spectacles. He had come
ashore with one of the wrecked Norwegian expeditions,
and after the crash went to Guayaquil, founded an agency
business and became the Norwegian consul, but left
everything and started afresh when the Norwegian
Captain Brunn founded his own colony and fishing
station on Floreana. The colony flourished and expanded
and there followed happy, busy days on the island till
one day in July, 1931, Captain Brunn was drowned off
the black cliffs of Isabela and everything went west. A

simple cross made from the wreckage of his own boat was planted on his sailor's grave among the cliffs and put finis to the story of his colony.

Worm-Müller stayed on for some time alone in the empty house at Post Office Bay. All their expensive equipment rotted, the dynamo grew rusty and he had only the wild animals of the island to keep him company. During those lonely hours spent in the empty house, he drew up the balance sheet of his restless life and decided to settle down. He wrote to his wife in Ecuador and together they moved into one of the abandoned houses on Santa Cruz, where one of the Norwegian expeditions had for a short time had a canning factory. The elderly couple have lived there ever since and like it immensely. Expensive machinery was falling to bits in the rooms under their house while a most unnecessary tractor looked out from a shed.

Time stood still. One could almost hear its quiet, regular breathing.

In the bay swam swarms of fish, good, fat fish that should have been riding up the rusty rails from the quay to the factory to be cut up or dried whole on the cliffs, packed in tins and cases and sold for high prices during Lent.

A little apart from the Norwegian colony lived the Dane, Raeder. His way also had led from the great world to the Galapagos. In the service of the American navy he had built bridges and harbours and been the consulting engineer in charge of the erection of 150 petroleum tanks in Venezuela. He had seen Chile, Peru, Argentine and Ecuador and lived for sixteen years in Mexico City where he had scored a decided success as an amateur bull fighter. There he had met his present wife, a charming woman from Kalundborg and a gifted water-colour painter.

They finally landed in Chile where he was to carry out the work in connexion with large harbour works, but a day or two later came one of those revolutions which are as common as thunderstorms in South America, and opinion turned against all foreigners and their contracts were annulled. The Chileans had once again grown desirous of showing that they could not get on by themselves. At this point Raeder was fifty-eight. He had saved a modest competence and had grown tired of the quarrels and strife of this bewildered world. A few weeks later he had bought tickets for Santa Cruz.

This island is rich in pigs, tortoises, horses and wild goats, while in the gardens grow otoy, oranges, pineapples, bananas, maize, melons, lemons and a quantity of other good things to eat, and once a month the boat from Chatham comes and brings the few things they have to import from the mainland. One cannot starve to death on Santa Cruz.

The Raeders live in a charming wooden bungalow with lovely furniture and beautiful water-colours on the walls. In the evenings the couple sit on the veranda and enjoy their home-grown coffee, while the evening breeze brings coolness and helps to turn the leaves of some exciting book.

Mr. Möller and Sonny tried to shoot sea-lions on a small island called Jensen Island, and Jack nearly became involved in a fight with a large, angry sea-lion and the breakers behind, but the discussion ended most amicably with the sea-lion as a tame, soft rug under Mr. Möller's desk.

The mate and I became furiously angry with a fifteen-

The Marquesas

foot shark which kept on circling round a particularly tempting bait without daring to take it, and this finally irritated Sören so much that he clambered down into our motor-boat, which was bumping against the stern, and stuck hook and bait into the shark's mouth. It was rather a primitive method of fishing, but successful.

The shark wagged its tail a bit, but, after being given five sleeping tablets from my little Browning, let itself be pulled on board without further protest and its tail fin was nailed to the bow as an awful warning to all its brothers, in accordance with the time-honoured custom.

Our scientists worked from morning till night and brought curious animals back with them; so curious, indeed, that we had to abandon our homely everyday life on board and engross ourselves for a moment in the study of the fauna of the Galapagos—five minutes' interval to take a look at the pens!

The animal life of the Galapagos is unique. Not because of the number of the species, but because of their kind. There are animals there the history of whose development seems to go back to dark prehistoric depths which no one has yet been able to plumb. In the mountains giant tortoises trample broad paths through the cactus bushes. Their shells are mightily rounded, their feet can be as large as horses' hooves, and specimens have been found measuring five feet in length and three feet in height. One of these giants was brought on board and christened "Columbus." It was capable of carrying three grown men on its back and waddled over ropes, chests and other obstacles like an armoured tank. It became Bobby's tormentor, always choosing his sleeping

place as its base of operations and planting its feet without warning on the tip of his tail.

The number of these giant tortoises is rapidly declining. They have been carried off by expeditions, and tourist steamers and the whalers have decimated their numbers for many years. The reason is that the flesh of these giant tortoises is a delicacy and the larder can run about the deck for months without being fed, filled to the rim with lovely fresh meat which is the best medicine for scurvy and other plagues of the long sea voyage.

Now, it is true, the government has forbidden any hunting of rare animals, but Major Aguilera sits in Chatham, his men clean their cartridges, and the Ecuador navy lies in the harbour of Guayaquil. Its engines were taken to pieces by inquisitive engineers and now nobody knows how to put the pieces together again. The last voyage undertaken by the ship was to the Galapagos, but the admiral was not sufficiently conversant with his compass and, turning back home, told the representatives of a wondering world's press that the islands had completely disappeared as the result of a mighty volcanic upheaval.

One of the ubiquitous Norwegians was granted permission to accompany a relief expedition as pilot, and thanks to his help the Galapagos rose once more safe and sound from the bottom of the sea together with their Norwegians, Danes and giant tortoises.

On another occasion the proud vessel was to take a new governor to Chatham. They steamed for days and they steamed for nights, and finally they sighted land. They ran into a harbour and put the governor ashore where he was immediately arrested. The ship had somehow got to Peru, and at this period an unusually violent war was in progress between that country and Ecuador, the fleet had to put up with being taken as a prize until peace broke out again—one of the few, short intervals they allow themselves when it becomes too hot for fighting.

But to return to the animals! Sea-iguanas crawl about in the sea at the foot of the cliffs, and up above live their country cousins, the land-iguanas. In size and appearance they are very much the same, it is only the colour that is different. The land-iguana is a dusty-grey or yellowish tinge, while the sea-iguana varies between reddish-brown and grey-green; the latter is the more amusing and more peaceable. It grows over three feet in length and is an exact copy of its primeval ancestor down to the smallest detail.

The sea-iguanas are distinctly marine animals and find their food among the plants at the bottom of the sea, where they swim like fish, moving their curled-up tail from side to side with a winding motion and letting their legs hang idle by their sides. The amusing thing about these excellent swimmers is that they are afraid of water. They live in colonies in the immediate neighbourhood of the sea, dwell in hiding places among the cliffs and stare inquisitively at the disturber of their peace when he comes along the shore. It is only at the last minute that they decide to escape and waddle with astonishing speed a dozen yards farther off, where they turn round and look back with their coal-black eyes!

If you hunt them in real earnest they take flight inland and not into the sea. This fact has given rise to many speculations. Many people are of the opinion that the sea-iguana was formerly a land animal—a land-iguana which turned sailor. Its complete lack of web between its toes seems to point to this, as does its instinctive reliance on *terra firma* as its safest hiding place.

We chased a large iguana so enthusiastically that in the end its every means of escape to a nearby mango grove was cut off; not till then did it dive head first into the water and, swimming a dozen yards or so along the shore, quickly climbed out again and disappeared with dizzy speed into some bushes.

The animal life of the Galapagos is altogether most amusing in and near the sea. The islands' insect life is also supposed to be very interesting, but what difference does the layman find between an English fly, an Arabian or one from the Galapagos Archipelago?

There is enough life along the shore that does not need to be studied under the microscope. Trusting, clear-eyed sea-lions play with their youngsters in the pools among the lava rocks, and they are so ignorant of man's real character that they will let him play with them if he likes. We caught the young sea-lions and played with them while their parents looked on without too much disquiet, and we photographed them at such close range that the water in which they were playing splashed our cameras.

The albatross and penguin regard the Galapagos as the northern boundary of their domain and the wingless cormorant lives on Isabela. The history of the develop ment of the cormorant is again most interesting.

The cormorant, that stout flier which skims the water beside the shores of so many seas and lakes, has practically no wings here on Isabela. Many think that the slight development of the wings comes from little use. The fish swim in mighty shoals past the cormorant's very nesting place and it only needs to dive from its rock to have a beakful of food. It does not require to fly, and limbs which are not used disappear in the course of generations.

The kindly but grotesque pelican fills his pouch with fish and the flamingo mirrors itself in the waters of the lagoons. All the birds of the tropics and the Southern Antarctic meet at the Galapagos and help to make these puzzling islands more curious still.

Tunny fish, bonitos, dolphins, sword-fish, and rays turn somersaults on the sea's surface. Here is a still undiscovered land of Cocaigne for the knights of rod and line and the little birds in the bushes fly inquisitively round the visitor's ears and perch naïvely on twigs a few feet away from him. It really looks as though the Galapagos possessed something of the peace of Paradise—apart from the places where man has pitched his tent and which he has called "Paradise." Man is not good for the Galapagos.

The *Monsoon* began to grow impatient. She did not like these long periods of inactivity in quiet, sheltered bays, and wanted to be on her way again.

Then our scientists made their last expedition into the hills, accompanied by Mr. Möller who wanted to take a look at Raeder's experimental farm, and the next morning we weighed anchor, the Danish and Norwegian flags on the shore dipped farewell, and we set course for Barrington Island, the last of the Galapagos group that we wished to visit.

Once off Barrington the skipper steered us into a bay that swarmed with turtles. We caught one huge fellow and enjoyed its famous beef-chicken-fish-flesh for dinner.

Beneath a wooden cross on the shore rests the last of

the pirates of these waters. He died and was buried in the year 1920.

Our scientists scraped the bottom of the sea clear of snails and sea-urchins while the rest of us continued our games with the wild, yet tame sea-lions and made excursions into the island. Mr. Möller shot a full-grown sea-lion and a fine young one which he presented to Stubbe, who, however, had not the means of preserving such large animals. Their skins were as soft as silk and their eyes large and brown. On a zoological expedition one cannot be sentimental. Science and such like come before everything; but all the same we were sorry for them. All of us.

The ship was surrounded with swarms of sharks. They ate the bait from the hooks and finally took up permanent residence beside the ship and waited for galley refuse or whatever else was thrown overboard in the course of the day. That became a bit too much for us, so we threw a sea-lion's corpse into the sea and in an instant the whole scene was turned into a splashing confusion of black fins and greedy teeth. Guns and revolvers were fired into the foaming clump and when the cannonade ceased, fourteen lifeless sharks were lying there.

It will be a long time before we forget that bloody scene and how the greedy jaws fastened on the red flesh, tearing it apart, while the sea became dyed with their blood. The sea-lion was as big as a man and a certain association of ideas was unavoidable. It was that, perhaps, which so excited our lust to kill. There were so many outstanding accounts to be settled.

That was our farewell to the Galapagos and the next day we left—after we had held a ship's conference. The skipper and Mr. Möller had discovered that we had too little drinking water in the tanks and we decided to ration it till we could replenish the tanks at the Marquesas. A day or two later we discovered that there had been an error in our calculations to the extent of over a hundred gallons in our favour, whereupon we went with relieved feelings on deck and took an extra shower bath—in fresh water!

We sailed southwards to reach the south-east trades and the weather was the best imaginable. We had a 3000-mile stretch before us, farther than that across the Atlantic and the longest of the whole voyage. Time passed slowly.

Mr. Möller carpentered in the cabin, and all the steel engagement rings that were to have been used for barter and to raise the morals of the South Sea Islanders were employed to turn grey horse blankets into elegant curtains for the provision room.

Bobby's jealousy of Columbus blazed up one day when we fed the turtle with cactus leaves. He hurled himself on the unsuspecting animal and with an angry snarl snatched its breakfast out of its mouth. He never did it again. All the rest of the day he sulked and was busily occupied in removing the cactus prickles from his nose with his long-fingered paws.

The long evenings were spent in earnest debates below deck, failing which we did crossword puzzles or played patience.

The food became more zoological than we were accustomed to. The weevils organized races in the rice and the maggots paddled about with their tails in the sugar and grew large and fat from lack of exercise. We put the best face on it we could and were glad of this unexpected addition of fresh meat.

The wind came and went; it thundered, lightninged, rained and was fine. The engine puffed now and again when the wind could not be botherd filling the sails, and after sailing for a month we saw a dark cloud rise up above the horizon. The cloud remained in the same place, took off its coat and became an island, rugged, steep and wild and with such a cloak of melancholy and inaccessibility as we had not come across since the little Salvage Islands. It was Hiva-Oa, the largest island in the Marquesas Group. We anchored in Taahuku Bay and rolled the name round our tongues. Ta-ahu-ku. It sounded like a whole chapter from Stevenson. Had we really reached the South Seas at last?

CHAPTER XII

*Tells of blood and bibles, brown people that are forced
to become white and whites that would
like to be brown*

THE Marquesas have witnessed one of the darkest and bloodiest chapters in the history of the unjust treatment of primitive peoples by the whites.

The whites conquered the Marquesas, depopulated the island's valleys and ruined the few remaining of the original inhabitants by means of misplaced missionary work and European diseases. The chief rôles in this drama were played by whalers, merchants and ignorant officials. Neither our generation nor the politicians of the future can make good the damage, even if they should feel themselves so in duty bound, for the life-nerve of the Marquesas has been destroyed and only the beautiful shell is left.

Only a few centuries ago the deep valleys of Hiva-Oa still rang with the joyous sound of children's voices and the songs of the women; war-cries echoed among the cliffs and the air shook with the triton's fiery fanfares.

The inhabitants of the Marquesas had come from afar, paddling across the seas in their beautiful, richly carved war canoes. They formed the advance guard of the great Polynesian migration of many centuries ago. They were fine big men, tattooed in many patterns and with a high cultural level. They built large huts, carved pictures and ornaments on their dishes and vessels, clothed themselves in home-woven cloth and slept on straw mats the colours and patterns of which were quite up to the level of the best examples of European peasant art. There was happiness in the valleys of Hiva-Oa in those days when the noise of battle had subsided and they danced to the rhythm of sharkskin drum and bamboo flute.

The old chief and his headmen gathered together under the great breadfruit tree in the centre of the village and decided over the weal and woe of the island.

Then one day in the sixteenth century the wheel of fate turned once more. A Spanish flotilla ran into Taahuku Bay and sent out its boats. The Marquesas had been discovered.

Spain had no joy of the islands. The star of the country which had given birth to so many great voyages of discovery declined and the veil of forgetfulness sank down again over the newly discovered islands, till in 1791 the Frenchman Marchand and Thomas Cook simultaneously discovered the northern and southern parts of the group. But in that year revolution raged through the streets of Paris, and Europe had more serious things to think about.

During the next fifty years the beautiful islands and their inhabitants were ruled and governed by sailors and whalers without any control from responsible quarters and hitherto unknown diseases began to destroy the natives. In 1800 the inhabitants numbered more than a hundred thousand Polynesians and to-day in the same territory there live scarcely three thousand people, diseased and physically degenerate. The old settlements lie in ruins, the hibiscus blooms where once there was a street and the survivors huddle round the church and the trader's shop. Mangos and avocado pears shower an abundance of sweet, juicy fruits on to the paths, but to no purpose, for there are no brown hands to stretch out and take their soft, scented flesh. Nature expands unhindered in the dead valleys.

Many factors have aided this work of destruction. The natives were subdued without any great difficulty. The individual tribes lived isolated from one another by high mountainous ridges and had no idea of the power of cohesion, so it was possible to root them out one after another. The diseases of the whalers and the traders' alcohol helped to the best of their ability. White deserters and marauders mixed with the natives, took their women and desecrated the gods they had worshipped from time immemorial and their traditional taboos, so that the natives also lost their respect for them. Thus their heathen morals were thrown to the winds before the Christian code came to take their place, which all helped to smooth the way for tuberculosis and other infectious diseases.

Traders went ashore to buy copra, the Bible in one hand and a bottle of rum in the other. The few race-conscious chiefs were driven into the mountains, where they waged a desperate guerilla warfare with the conquerors; yet there was only one way in which the war could reach a peaceful end—death.

Missionaries first came to the Marquesas when the islands were taken over by the French. They tried to make good the crimes committed by the pioneers, to help the sick and teach France's glorious history and the ten commandments to the healthy. But the black-clothed padres forgot that a healthy mind belongs to a healthy body—Roman Catholics are seldom good hygienists. Their priests and nuns clothed themselves in the tropics as they do in the north of France, they wear cowls reaching down to their feet on top of much warm underclothing, buttoned-up collars and thick heavy boots over their woollen socks.

They taught the natives of the Marquesas that the naked body was sinful. It took some time before the Polynesians understood this morality, for since the dawn of time they had been accustomed to go naked above the waist and the sun and rain had hardened their beautiful bodies. Finally, however, they saw their sin in all its frightfulness and submitted, and now they are more modest than most whites.

They are poor and seldom possess more than one suit of clothes. These get soaked in the tropical rains, by sweat or when they wade through a stream, after which the sun shines down and dries them on their bodies and they catch cold. As a race they are extraordinarily sensitive to changes of temperature and the majority die of pneumonia. They bathe fully clothed and should one of the mighty white men pass, they dive under until only their heads remain above the water, remaining true to the last to their new moral code.

There is something wrong with a gospel which tries to force stuffy and unhealthy ideas of modesty on primitive peoples and which conceals golden, tanned limbs in cheap cotton printed in loud colours. There is something wrong with a mission which turns the daily bathe into an indecent action and stifles the natives' inherent artistic sense and their faculty to express it in carvings of wood and stone. Their traditional Dance of Beauty has been condemned as the work of the devil, and in its stead they have been given oleographed pictures of the saints in inexcusably bad taste.

One does not like to sit in judgment on those who have consecrated their lives to the propagation of the gospel in uncivilized parts; in most cases they are real idealists who do not for a moment doubt the rightness of their endeavours and the sacredness of their work. Yet could not religious vocation be backed with a general instruction in the history of the fine arts and an elementary knowledge of ethnography and the cultural importance of ancient customs?

Individual denominations have taken a lenient view of their ancient songs and dances. The Church of England has in places even allowed the peoples to keep their old secret societies, the masonic lodges of the South Seas, after deleting some of the most barbaric rituals, and the Seventh Day Adventists take an equally lenient view of the question of clothing, but at the same time forbid smoking and the eating of pig's flesh, and that where tobacco is almost a standard delicacy and the pig a national animal and the only available form of animal food. The natives' scented garlands have given place to dirty straw hats, and their simple love songs have had to yield to hymns whose melodies are as strange to the Polynesian's musical ear as Chinese music is to ours.

The tremendous competition that arises from time to time between the different missionary societies on the same island is the acme of bad taste. The native is tempted, threatened and cajoled from every side, and does not know where to turn. No one tells him that it is the same God that is on each programme. He was sent to the battlefield of Verdun as soon as he had learned that he must not kill, and he experiences jealousy and hatred between the various sects at the same time as he reads that there is but one God and that we should love one another.

The Catholic Mission owns the best of the plantations

on the Marquesas and the Adventists are strongly capitalistic and own huge coffee estates in South America. The natives scarcely earn enough for the necessities of life on the small lots that are left them of their fathers' ground.

Any serious attempt to go into the question brings you to the conclusion that it must be dreadful to be a missionary if you are intelligent and ordinarily human—but you do not meet many missionaries of this kind. The blindly fanatical are in overwhelming majority, while now and again you meet one who has taken it up as a profession and lives a happy-go-lucky existence on a fat island where the natives bring him charitable gifts, while his family and the mission's supporters at home are plaiting him a martyr's crown.

There are not many martyr's crowns to be got in Polynesia. The good, strong, pioneer missionaries have been replaced by others of a different sort, and those who spend their days on the islands say that it is time the foreign missions were put on a different basis. But that is godless blasphemy in the ears of the parishioners at home knitting stockings for the native children in blind belief.

On the side of the government there have also been sins of commission. The Marquesas and most of the other islands are governed by administrators who are relieved every three years. The post is a jumping-off place for promotion, a station in the journey between Cochin-China, the Congo, and a pension, and but few of the officials have any desire to make themselves acquainted with the language and mentality of their subjects. After all they soon have to pack their bags again. The Marquesas are ruled according to the "Code Napoleon," a

code that was written in 1804 by the French for the French and not by an iota has it been altered to meet different circumstances and points of view.

Copra and souls, that is what the white man is out for in the Marquesas, and thus he chokes the native with one hand, while he raises the cross up to heaven in the other.

Hiva-Oa lies far back from the high-road and, apart from a distant echo of psalms and hoots from the steamers heavily laden with sacks of copra, nothing European penetrates to it.

I have tried to give a small picture of the actual conditions, but it is not entirely, nor even more than half complete. You can only get a true picture when you look up the stream that runs through the Atirona Valley. Nowadays it chatters alone. No happy children play by its banks, and no more will its cool waters cling caressingly to brown, naked bodies. The hibiscus blooms in vain and its red flowers fade and fall lifeless on to the stones below.

Their poetry has been throttled by narrowmindedness and corrugated iron, while the old gods sit on the top of Temetius and look down at the realm from which they have been cast.

On the other side of the valley there shines a marble cross rising thirty feet above the Christians' graveyard, where brown women sleep their last sleep by the side of chaste nuns. Here lies the mad, genial painter, Paul Gauguin, not far from the worthy bishop who fought him and damned his heathen influence on the Christian natives. Some well-meaning society has removed from his grave the unhewn stone that one of his nameless friends laid between the faded leaves, and has given him

a tame and delicate placard with letters of gold. One can hold differing views on the desecration of graves.

Above them all, both brown and white, whispers the evening breeze in the ever-murmuring palms and high up in the blue sky two white terns play their game of love. Waterfalls run like pearling tears down the furrowed cheeks of Temetius and ripple through the dead valleys. Atuana is the only town of importance on Hiva-Oa. The administrator and the white trader live there; there are a couple of Chinese shops, and the red tower of a church rises above the palms. The Post Office and wireless station lie on the coast and from there the road runs in a gentle curve past the Police Station and the branch of A. B. Donald's store into the valley, crosses a brook and dwindles away to a small path—a dozen native huts and a school and that is all.

Donald's store is run by an old Scots sailor, Bob MacKetterick, who received us with open arms, and we plundered his shelves and storeroom of sunhelmets, cigarettes and many other nice things that one can with difficulty do without. Bob invited us to tea, Bob stood us beer, and Bob became our good friend and helper during the few weeks we spent on the island. The only thing in which he could not help us was in finding ethnographica. All the time that he had been on the island the entire population had cooked in nothing but enamelled pans and eaten with tin forks—and it was, after all, his business to sell them. Neither could the administrator help us, for a few years before a very fine gentleman had come to Atuana. He spoke a distinguished French, was in possession of recommendations from prominent personages in Paris and was given the post of assistant to the administrator. He used his

The Valley of Death—the Marquesas

A native hut on Takaroa

position to scrape together all the wooden gods, carved bowls, war clubs and other valuable things that were left, without paying for them. One day he disappeared, and it was not till long afterwards that it was discovered that he had opened a curio shop for tourists in another part of Oceania and was supplying all the liners with rare and expensive souvenirs. The man was Swiss and his recommendations forged. He was thrown out, but with a bulging pocket-book. Quite a smart piece of work—but not pleasant hearing for a scientific expedition!

The white population of Atuana leads a happy life. They have reached the state in which the lack of dance halls, football matches and tax assessments has become an advantage, and do not worry about what happens on the other side of the horizon. The wireless operator doesn't need to tune in to the news, even though it only requires a turn of the hand. The devil take Hitler and Mussolini. They are a thousand miles away and not interested in Hiva-Oa, and Hiva-Oa is not interested in them. Their food falls with a loud bump from the trees and the brown women are submissive and domesticated. There are more pigs and hens than they can eat, and what they do not have on the island is brought by the trading schooners which come to fetch copra, and which sail about with a whole store of luxury articles, floating Selfridges suited to Atuanarian circumstances.

We wandered through the valleys treading on overripe mangoes, yellower and more juicy than those which, swaddled like babies in silk and cotton-wool, now and again find their way into the shops of the European capitals and are sold for two or three shillings each. We clambered about the mountains and were given as many oranges as we could carry by smiling boys who rode

their horses barebacked; and Johnny, a Samoan, who had cut the entire crew's hair so that we all looked like circus poodles, gave us lessons in basic-English.

Johnny manufactured wooden idols, straight from the tree, for tourists. He made a strong distinction between Americans and other peoples.

"Me sell goods to American millionaires, when he comes ashore. Me say one—two—three hundred francs and he say only 'Yes' and pay. When yacht go away, me millionaire too.

"My father his father carved gods, him set god on paper; my father carved gods, him set god on paper; me carve gods, me set god on paper; my son carve gods, him set god on paper!"

In these few words Johnny had given an apt explanation of how primitive art had been able to continue practically unaltered for generations, and when he had finished he started to give us a most convincing description of the glories of Tahiti.

He talked like a waterfall, and cut hair like a cowman, but all the same he became one of our best friends during our stay in Taahuku Bay. We adopted his expressions and became good tempered as soon as we saw his brown face grinning so that his eyes became two black brackets round his snub nose.

Johnny had his pride. One day he brought a basketful of vegetables which he wanted to sell us for fifteen francs. Mr. Möller offered ten, but Johnny turned his back on him in dudgeon and presented the basket with all it contained to the mate who was the nearest to him. That was at any rate a gesture!

One warm, sunny morning a little cutter glided quietly up and moored near us. Her sails hung idle and loose, and in the stern stood a white man, as thin as a skeleton, punting her for'ards. It was Alain Gerbault, the world-famous French war-ace, tennis champion, circum-navigator and author.

After his voyage with *Fire Crest* had ended in the red ribbon of the Legion of Honour and a stormy reception in the harbour at Le Havre, he had built himself a new cutter, a shining miracle of teak and mahogany put together with copper nails and equipped with electric light, fans and every conceivable kind of gadget. He had sailed out again in his new boat and had now arrived at the Marquesas in the course of a voyage without plan or goal, hunting the sun and the happiness that his money could not give him at home in Europe.

His only article of clothing was the natives' loin-cloth, the pareo; he was clean shaven and wore no hat. He has sleepy eyes under heavy lids and his lower lip has a tendency to hang down. The whole appearance of the man is that of an over-civilized, refined type, such as one often sees in the more expensive Boulevard cafés of Paris. Sometimes he answered not at all when you spoke to him and when he did he lisped indistinctly. One cannot help wondering that this somewhat feminine, morbidly smiling or childishly peevish eccentric should have been cap-able of the feat of sailing alone in a cutter round the world. However, under his curious exterior there must lie qualities hidden, that have made the improbable possible.

Alain Gerbault has quite "gone native" as the whites in the tropics say of their brethren, who have been beaten, gone to pieces and end up in a straw hut among those whom we regard as being on a lower level. Yet he descended the ladder quite of his own free will, with

plenty of money in his pockets and the best of connexions. He plays football with the young boys and takes them with him in his boat from island to island. He teaches them the crawl and to swim on their backs and gives them lessons in practical seamanship. He is a vegetarian and teetotaller. He is a character and seems to have found his niche in the little islands of the South Seas. Possibly he will settle down on one of them for the rest of his days and become a new Paul Gauguin, no copy of that robust, amazing Bohemian and hermit of pre-war days, but a representative of the bizarre, somewhat anæmic castle-in-Spain architects of the post-war era. He forms the left wing of the white race, while the well-padded Catholic "Pater" is on the extreme right and the materialistic representative of the government forms the centre.

The *Monsoon* was waiting for the mail-boat and letters from home, and Mr. Möller employed the time in heron-shooting and filming waves with an infanticide from Tahiti who had spent fifteen years holidaying with the Marquesas police. Then the motor schooner *Denise* arrived with swollen post bags of which we received a good share.

We had finished with the Marquesas and according to our original plan should have gone on to Samoa, but the local authorities were of the opinion that the *Monsoon* had to go into dock, and as Alain Gerbault warmly recommended the Papeete yard as the best in the Pacific, it was decided to go to Tahiti. So now we would see if Johnny's enthusiastic description was right, if it were really true that there were six whole taxis on the rank at the quay, and that the brown ladies of Papeete kiss one on the mouth whether you like it or not. We were to see the town and the island of which the entire world paints fantastic day-dream pictures, Pierre Loti's island and the home of the Cythera since Alexander the Great, Venizelos or whoever it was had them driven out of Greece. The crew clapped their hands and sang "God bless ye, merry gentlemen," curious behaviour for normal sailors, and the skipper was caught putting pomade on his beard to hide his grey hairs. Midway between Hiva-Oa and Tahiti lies Takaroa, one of the western Tuamotu islands. Tuamotu, Puamotu or "the low and dangerous islands" are a collection of more than a hundred low atolls which form a belt between 130th and 150th degrees west and are a serious obstacle to navigation. We wanted to visit Takaroa and perhaps take a look at the neighbouring island Apataki, and longed for our first encounter with a real coral island and a real cinema night with moonshine on the blue lagoon, seductive guitars, the scent of flowers and the Southern Cross above our heads.

The lagoon-night we were not to experience and the Southern Cross turned out to be a giant leg-pull, an ignoble advertisement for false romance—closely related to Hamlet's grave in Helsingör—but we did encounter the coral island and we also met Jensen, and these two factors will ensure of Takaroa always being given a friendly reception in our memories.

But Jensen deserves a chapter to himself.

CHAPTER XIV

*Concerns Jensen's merits, Stubbe's country practice, the
skipper's hula-hula and attempts the hopeless
task of describing a coral reef*

IT is Jensen's fault that we have passed over chapter XIII.
Like every other sailor, Jensen is extremely superstitious
and it would have been unfair to him to let him appear
in the thirteenth chapter.

Jensen was not his proper name; he was really called
Herotekara Mapuhi, but we could not get our tongues
properly round that, so we rechristened him. He was
standing well forward among the ranks of the curious
as the *Monsoon* berthed alongside the steep side of the
coral reef in the centre of the entrance to the lagoon,
where the current made the water boil and at both high
and low tides tugged at one's moorings with all the
strength of its six knots.

He stood out from the brown uniformity of the crowd
by reason of a linen jacket that was nearly white and a
bright red pareo. His jacket was opened wide at the
neck so that one could see a wonderful full-rigged ship
which was hopelessly caught in the sargasso seaweed of
his chest.

Takaroa was not used to seeing strangers. It was
merely a coral ring which had been cast aside on one
of the busiest days of the creation and had been forgotten
in the subsequent confusion. No one had even remembered to give the island proper vegetation or to provide
the means to grow it. The coconut palm was the only

thing which could keep itself alive there, but it flourishes in a handful of sand and simply loves to dip its roots into salt water. All the other useful plants like yams, bananas and breadfruit trees had to be imported from other islands and were treated like convalescent patients, being planted in imported earth in large holes cut out of the chalk, while large shields of palm leaves protected them from the eternal trades.

Such an island breeds sailors, and Jensen was one of the best. The old town in Marseilles and the Skipperstraat in Antwerp held no secrets for him, and what he did not know about the girls in 'Frisco and fever in Lima was not worth any experienced sailor's while knowing. He was getting on in years now and had retired, being kept by his family and making himself respected by speaking French and because he was the father-in-law of Tommy the Mormon chaplain, who kept things dusted in the temple during the continual absence of the high priest.

I won Jensen's friendship because my French was reminiscent of his, and as soon as the hawsers had been made fast I hopped over the rail and went for a long walk through the town with my new friend. We were fated to be bosom friends and that increases confidence.

Jensen gave me a short résumé of Takaroa's spiritual life. There is both a Mormon temple and a Catholic church on the island, and the natives oscillate between them according to how the priests bore them. It is not unusual to find the same man among the Mormons on Saturday and in the Catholic church on Sunday—there are so few entertainments on Takaroa!

Wherever our morning walk took us we met friendly smiles. The Takaroans still possess much of the untouched Polynesian's trustfulness and charm, and they still like to decorate themselves with a hibiscus flower behind their ear or in their black hair. They are hospitable, open and honourable, without a thought of material benefit or deceit. Living away from the steamer routes has its advantages!

Jensen was a serious man. He was like a four-year-old child that has been spanked without knowing why. Being a Mormon by conviction, he might neither smoke nor drink, but being the chaplain's father-in-law he felt somewhat superior to dogma and allowed himself certain liberties, such as smoking and drinking. He showed me the few sights of the island which Baedeker had not yet discovered. We admired the new lighthouse which the local harbour authorities were building. If the calculations of the native architect are accurate and the loose coral blocks do not fall in first, it will be more than eighteen feet high and you will be able to see it right from the other side of the coral reef.

We passed the football ground where forty men were engaged in massacring a ball. The game was governed by less complicated rules than those in force in Europe and only the right and left wings possessed a pair of boots—which they shared. Jensen gave the players a friendly smile and drew their attention to me as we cut right across the pitch in the middle of a strong attack. His nephew, the goalkeeper, waved to us with both hands, giving his right back an opportunity to shoot a goal, which was disallowed by the referee—who was also one of the outside forwards—as the other goalkeeper was offside. I was friendlily invited to join in, and put Jensen on a fallen tree trunk while I scored two goals, one for either side so as not to hurt anyone's feelings.

We landed in the midst of one of the upper-class families who were just having their lunch in their private palm garden. They welcomed us with hearty smackings of lips and invited us to take our seats in the sand round their groaning soapbox, and with some hesitation I stuck the first three fingers of my right hand into that part of the popoi pot which was the least frequented. Popoi is breadfruit which is kept in a hole in the ground covered with fermenting palm leaves, until one is absolutely certain that the fruit is rotten right to the core and has acquired the right aroma. This seemed to be very well prepared popoi. The dessert consisted of dried fish, to which Jensen treated us, withdrawing it carefully from the pocket of his drill jacket and lovingly blowing the fluff off before he presented it. Fish which has been cut into strips and dried in the sun becomes black and melancholy and tastes like second-class string.

Each country has its own customs and even Takaroa had its lighter side—when it grew dark. Jensen told me that he had persuaded the island's chieftain, nice old Tavanna Pori, to arrange a ball for the crew of the *Monsoon* in the town hall that evening. The town hall was a hut roofed with palm leaves, just opposite the Mormon temple, and there we collected as the sun set, together with all the inhabitants of the village. At eight o'clock we moved off in close column to the ball, each in white trousers and tennis shirt and with a red hibiscus behind one ear. A flower behind the left ear means that one is free and fair game, behind the right ear it acts as a warning signal —already taken, married, or misogynist. However, I shall not tell who wore their flower behind which ear!

The atmosphere on the benches round the trampled clay floor was actually a little depressed. There sat the

swelling beauties in wonderful creations of dainty sail-cloth in many colours and with bare feet.

Here, however, I am afraid I must pause and shatter an illusion. The women of the South Sea Islands are not beautiful. They have figures like that of a whale and legs like those of a billiard table, and they tempt one to leave the words "Lead us not into temptation" out of our bedtime prayer. But they can dance well.

A balloon with a diameter of thirty feet can appear elegant when it glides through the air on a gentle breeze, and equally so can a Takaroan girl appear majestic when, with a delicate Danish sailor in her arms, she foxtrots to the strains of an orchestra playing the hula-hula in six different ways on six different instruments.

It was really a little dull at first, just like at the beginning of a club dance at home. The boys stood shyly outside in the open and peered round the four corner posts into the hall, seemingly preferring to eat three coconuts—with the shell—than to be the first to take the floor. It was left to our skipper to make a start. He dances in a very personal style which reminds you of a hornpipe, all-in-wrestling and "knees-up" all at the same time, but which is always a great success with those who are not on the floor at the same time as he, and it was not long before the party got really going.

In the course of his duties the master of ceremonies showed that he possessed astonishingly muscular arms. He would seize the nearest bachelor and hurl him right into the arms of some wallflower and so it happened that I suddenly found myself making a kind of cradling motion on the bosom of a brown beauty queen of a good twenty-two stones live weight. I had no time to observe whether the holes in the floor had been made by the stamping that evening, but if that were not the case, then Takaroan cement must be the one and only material for building armoured forts.

The music wailed and the dust rose up thick round our ears; we perspired and danced and had a wonderful time. Jensen stood in a corner and looked on with sparkling eyes, while small children lay in every corner and slept while their mothers danced. The fun grew faster and more furious till at ten o'clock it reached its peak, when loud clapping indicated the sensation of the evening—refreshments were now to be served.

Two men appeared with a petrol tin and a cup without a handle, went from person to person through the whole hall and poured them out a free drink of lukewarm water. I must to my shame confess that from this point on I do not remember much. I only have a dim recollection of going to the boat a little while later, leaning on Jensen's arm and softly singing: "Tane, vahini, hula-hula metai!" so that the stars wavered in their course, turned round and smiled.

The next morning Jensen came to the quay to ask if we had a doctor on board. I thought of Stubbe and said no. Then he told me of their many sick, of the doctors who never came and the families stricken by unknown diseases they were powerless to cure. Then I thought of my fellow men and our full medicine chest and said yes.

Stubbe had to spend the whole day visiting his patients. He went from a coughing tuberculosis case to a midwife suffering from kidney disease, looked at inflamed wounds, and squirted collodium into hollow teeth, washed out eyes and distributed medicine right and left. It was touching to see how grateful his patients were. As a return of thanks they sent live chickens on board, came with coconuts and bananas from their valuable imported plants and even the poorest of them brought large, curious shells which they had found on the shore. Nothing was too good for the man who had brought them a little relief.

Jensen showed great interest. He followed in Stubbe's wake and sampled the medicines. He stayed long by the side of a tubercular friend and in high tones praised his cough mixture. He smacked his lips and rolled his eyes so appreciatively that I proposed a slight cough. We went aside and practised, to the great joy of a swarm of small children and a Chinese trader. As we passed the town hall, his cough had already a hollow background and by the time we reached the quay Jensen was one of the best cough imitators in the world. I winked at Stubbe and Stubbe winked at me, and five minutes later Jensen left the *Monsoon* with a gay trill on his lips and a large bottle of the life-giving mixture in the capacious pocket of his jacket.

Every native in the island from sucking infant to doddering centenarian, stood throughout the day in a queue which stretched from quay to the cabin, waiting to sell Mr. Möller shells in exchange for glass beads, earrings and mouth organs. It is interesting to observe how the exchange varies from island to island. On Takaroa glass beads were strong; in several other places interest was all for mouth organs; while on Santo in the New Hebrides it was impossible to talk the natives into taking them. Mr. Möller could sit on tree stump and play them whole concerts; they would listen readily, but were a deal to be struck with these musical instruments they had only a pitying smile for the giver of the concert and his instrument. They wanted tobacco.

The skipper was so jealous that he hopped like a sick hen from one foot to another—shells were his hobby, but Mr. Möller had the same taste, and here was a whole museum passing right under his nose, but yet out of reach.

Jensen asked me to fetch "the little black box which makes pictures," it being his dearest wish one day to have a picture of the entire Herotekara Mapuhi family. I said that I would be only too pleased to grant this modest favour, but the next half-hour proved that Jensen was related with the island's entire population. I took seven large groups before he declared himself satisfied, and in return he procured for me the opportunity of photographing the chieftain, Pori, in full gala dress in front of a hibiscus in his beautiful garden.

He was a nice old man and looked almost regal in his clean white uniform with a tricolour scarf round his waist and a glittering French order at his breast. There was about him nothing of the comical there usually is about natives in European dress. His French official uniform suited him and his age-old culture saved him from absurdity.

He was a grand old man with a fine face and clever eyes, and we stayed all too short a time on his happy island. Too soon had we to leave his friendly subjects, those large women with soft light movements and indolent grace, and athletic men with regal bearing and splendid muscles under their golden skin. But an expedition has a timetable and timetables are not interested in lazy days passed in the shade of palms; their fingers are on the calendar and their eyes on the clock.

As we left Takaroa, old Jensen was standing beside the flagstaff. He pressed into my hand a wonderful shell and a chain of smaller shells to put round my hat. He was a little shy when giving it to me and didn't rightly know where to look. I must admit that I too did not know what to say. Parting is difficult for friends who have eaten from the same popoi dish, and a large bottle of yellow cough mixture does not make it easier —to say nothing of purely spiritual sympathies. It is often difficult to find the right words and at such time one does best to say nothing.

When the skipper cast off at bow and stern the current swept us immediately into the channel, and borne along by the ebbing tide we rapidly drew away from the quay. A crowd of children stood on the shore and, calling out "Ya ora na!" waved to us with their broad-rimmed straw hats. Jensen did not wave. He looked a little tired, the poor old chap. Those had been glorious days for him. He had smoked American cigarettes till he was nearly sick, and had impressed his fellow citizens with his knowledge of languages. He grew smaller and smaller. It looked as though he were shrinking into himself. The children broke up in small groups and wandered off to the football pitch, and in the end Jensen was left standing there alone. Sadly he buttoned his jacket over the wonderful picture of a full-rigged ship, cast a last look over the sea, spat into the water and went slowly away through the palms—the cough mixture gargling melancholily in his pocket. He took a piece of dried fish out, blew the dust away and chewed it thoughtfully. The feast was over.

The *Monsoon* passed Takapoto and we caught a glimpse of Manihi to the west. To the south lay a hundred other small atolls and in the south-west Apataki, our next port of call.

There was nobody at home on the island. The entire population had paddled over to the other side of the lagoon to harvest copra, and we only met a couple of toothless old women who entertained us with breadfruit and gave a small hula-hula performance on deck for our benefit. But we did see a coral reef for the first time.

I shall try to describe this miracle as I first saw it— and besides must ask my readers to keep it always at the back of their minds as being a constant, muted, submarine accompaniment to all the rest of the book, fantastically beautiful, an experience far beyond one's most daring dreams, a wonderful poem in the most beautiful colours and shapes in the world, and at the same time a furtive enemy, a brutal threat to shipping and the merciless murderer of the *Monsoon*. But we never thought of that on Apataki.

We only saw the fairy palace and its swimming butterflies and humming-birds and never grew tired of admiring it all the way from Apataki to Vanikora. It was always alive, always varied and always filled with new colours and shapes. It was an inexhaustible field of study for Stubbe and a vision for the rest of us.

Imagine a submarine wood lit up with green floodlights and seen through a wall of blue glass. White patches of sunlight dance round on the white sandy floor out of which shoot colonies of curiously formed trees and bushes. Some are like huge, yellow sponges, others brown with a thousand twists and turns. There are mallow-coloured colonies, composed of quite small yet perfectly formed members. Each member is an animal but has the same shape as a snowflake under the microscope. There are antipathidæ, cinnabar and raven black, and at their feet bunches of grapes made of green seaweed swing

159

in time with the beat of the waves, as graceful as ballerinas and as green as jade.

Here and there a rock formation rises up vertically to the surface—and in the rocks are vast, deep grottoes with eternal dark-violet shadows, and from the jaws of these grottoes dangle the pock-marked suckers of an octopus.

Little fairy fish hide among the twigs in the wood, black, lemon, and cobalt blue, spotted, striped and plain, with fins that wave high above their backs like long ribbons and shapes that seem to contradict all sober sense and zoology. Large green, blue and red parrot-fish shoot about with white beaks shaped like those of their winged namesakes; and small fish respectfully keep out of the way of the black and rust-red sea-urchins with their prickles standing out in all directions.

Crabs of every shape, size and colour run sideways and backwards across inert, clumsy sea-slugs which let the water pulse in and out of their stomachs; and blue and leather-coloured starfish play at planets above the wood, while a purple jellyfish represents the moon.

Slender spotted misgurns in every shade of brown and grey lurk in holes between the coral, and giant mussels whose shells measure over two feet at their broadest point hide maliciously in the sand, so that only the wavy line of their opening is free. This is a trap of steel which snaps down on its prey like lightning and holds it as in a vice. Many a native has been caught in this way at low water and drowned when the tide came in, and those who have escaped from their clutches have as a rule paid the penalty with a toe or their whole foot.

A coral reef is not without its dangers. Quite apart from the fact that a cut from a piece of coral only heals with difficulty and leaves a large black scar, there are other factors of which one does well to be careful. Stubbe and I were taught our lesson on Apataki.

I was quite alone on the reef and had waded out a mile or more from the shore through the shallow warm water that came up to my thighs. The fish glided through between my legs and I took care not to tread on any malicious mussel. On my way back I saw two pointed fins cleaving the water a hundred yards away— between me and the shore. A pair of sharks were taking a trip in the shallow water of the lagoon where the fish were numerous.

They saw my legs and whispered something to each other, then put the rudder hard over and came up to take a look at my checked sports stockings. I myself had thought them striking but the assistant in Copenhagen had convinced me that they were ideal for the tropics and I had relied on his judgment. Ideal they were not. A pair of sand-coloured ones would have been better. Luckily there was a coral rock near—it rose almost above the surface—and in shorter time than one can think I was standing on top of it enjoying the view.

The sharks were not very large, only about six feet, but their teeth seemed to be in the best of condition and the looks they gave me were more than curious. One of them tried to smell the toes of my shoes, but in doing so grazed its little tummy on the coral and, insulted, swam away with its companion after taking several turns round my refuge.

Between my rock and the safety of the shore was the best part of three hundred yards and I believe that this distance has never yet been covered so quickly by any one up to the knees in water at any sports ground in the world. Just as I reached the shore, I stubbed my toe

L

against a stone and to its very great surprise there was no swearing to be heard, for the simple reason that it was dry, and all its neighbours were dry, and where it is dry the shark stands no chance.

Later the same day Stubbe wanted to go out to the reef for scientific purposes and I gave him a few tips. He chose another route, where the distance was less and the water shallower, but where there were several large rocks. As he was wading out and whistling: "Ah, how beautiful it's here in the woods and no robbers to be seen," an octopus slung its slimy arms round his bare leg. He shrieked, gesticulated mightily, hammered with his toy pail on the octopus's head and kicked so heartily that he sat down plump in the water, giving the octopus such a shock that it let go and made off. Stubbe got palpitations and a nasty coral wound, but he, like I, had learned to take care when he moved in the warm, shallow water between the coral rocks—and we will never forget the lesson we were given.

Afraid? Neither of us! Not for a second! Who is, when they tell the story some time afterwards?

There was nothing more for us to do on Apataki, so on the next day we put out on the ebb tide, set sail before a somewhat feeble breeze and wrote letters far into the night.

We were approaching Tahiti.

CHAPTER XV

*We turn a somersault, land in a Chinese shop and have
garlands put round our necks. Bobby is
arrested while we escape*

THE tourist who comes to Tahiti with Pierre Loti and
Stevenson under his arm and his head full of recollections of coloured picture postcards and the travel bureau's
pamphlets, must be a sufficiently good mental acrobat to
be able to turn a somersault without breaking his neck
and so losing his good humour.

Papeete is a bucket of cold water on all day dreams and
illusions about the South Sea Islands. The town kills
them swiftly and surely with the aid of rattling bicycles,
hooting motor-cars, humming sewing-machines, travel
bureaux and ice-cream bars. Papeete has broad streets,
flat beer, cinemas, dentists and sign posts presented by
Dunlop and Citroën, who have not forgotten to remind
the world of their generosity. Time has not stood still
since the days of Raruha, and the saxophones bleat in the
"Queen's" restaurant—to the astonishment of American
tourists who "do" the Pacific in a hunt for ukulele music
and the idyllic. The women of Tahiti have gold teeth
and are familiar with the word "bartender," and the fox-
trot has crowded the hula-hula off the narrow dance
floors of Papeete.

That sounds dismal in the ear of a romantic and it
would be terrible if they really had succeeded in altering
the Queen of the South Seas' face by means of face-lifting
and paraffin treatment. One may break Madame Tahiti

in, make her waddle round on high French heels and exchange her red pareo for a gown, but one cannot mould her native charm. It still exists under her superficial rouge, only one must stay some time on the island to find it.

By the Quai de Commerce lie a number of yachts that were actually sailing round the world, and only intended to visit Tahiti as they had so many other harbours. They never got away; barnacles and a luxuriant green growth cover the sides of these boats from the waterline to the keel. For them time is an unknown conception, and their clocks lie like antique instruments of torture in the cabin drawer, where they tick away, chopping up time into monotonous and exactly similar sized seconds until they stop unnoticed, with a slight sigh for the frivolity of man and his lack of the sense of duty. The owner of the clock lies on deck and tries to spit on to a red flower floating on the blue water. All the little butterfly fish that swim among the dead coral of the quay dash together in fright when the spittle reaches the water's surface.

Your first day in Tahiti is a disappointment, the second a surprise and on the morning of the third you would do best to pack your bag and see that you get away before the charming girl has caught all your senses in the delicate mesh of her graces.

By day Papeete is very prosaic with wooden houses, bars and photographers with shameless prices, to say nothing of tourist sharks who have forgotten the art of blushing. At every street corner is a Chinese shop with many more between. Here, like elsewhere between Suez and Panama, the Chinese problem is very acute. These little yellow stoics arrive with their bags full of cheap

Chinese manufactured goods, squat down at the first street corner they come to and hold a sale. Then they order more cases from Hong-Kong or Canton, buy themselves a little shop, expand and give credit, expand still more with the help of their mighty "Tong" and give the lazy, carefree planter still more credit—greater credit than he can ever hope to pay.

Thus the plantations of Tahiti and the inheritances of the natives gradually find their way into the hands of the Chinese. The yellow ones increase like rats, and soon these rats have quite quietly and all unnoticed undermined yet another piece of ground in this way. The snowball grows and rolls on. At the present time several small islands belong almost entirely to the Chinese and as they are naturally good French citizens, the local authorities, i.e. the governor, find themselves in an awkward dilemma when they try to stem the yellow tide.

As a general rule, the Chinaman is a French citizen only on paper. The native broadcasts his money over the island like chaff before the wind; the white man drinks it away or puts it in local undertakings or securities, just according to his inclinations; but the yellow man collects his centimes one by one, ties them together with a piece of twine through the hole in the centre, packs them in cheap newspaper and sends them to the great country in the west, and that can give a national economist something to think about.

Hu-Sen-Chang and Wang-Kong-Lee stand in their shop door and gaze thoughtfully out. Their faces are expressionless and as though turned to stone. In the shop the hard wooden balls of the cash register rattle and the change drops like a continual gentle rain into the greasy drawer. White and brown customers meet in the door, and the European storekeeper just across the road has not the Chinaman's ability to hide his inmost feelings behind a poker face. Everybody hates and despises Wang-Kong-Lee but they all buy his goods because they are cheap and only very slightly inferior in quality to those of the white man.

The lights burn long in the Chinese club of nights, and the rattle of counters penetrates far into the nocturnal quiet of the street, while the sickening scent of the opium pipe carries small, black-eyed men with apathetic faces across the sea to where the slimy, yellow water of the Yangstekiang mingles with the blue of the Pacific, to where limitless rice fields fill the valleys and heavy oxen snort under the yoke. It is in the club that they arm themselves against the hatred and disdain of the whites; in their associations with their fellow sufferers and under the colour of the same Tong they find the courage to remain silent and patient during the coming day.

It is not till the evening that Papeete opens its brown eyes, yawns, stretches itself and returns for a few warm hours during the night to the old days, and gives free rein to its insatiable desire for a feverish enjoyment of life.

Loviana is dead. Her world-famous hotel "Tiare" has passed into other hands and the rooms which used to echo the curses and laughter of the pearl traders and South Sea skippers and resound with the clinking of glasses and the songs of dusky maidens, now have melancholy, white-covered tables which call sadly to each other and wait in vain for the proud days and warm nights of the past to come back.

Loviana's garden is as dense as it always was, and the

166

annexe is still there with freshly made beds ready, but
the stream of people has been diverted to the "Queen's"
in the Rue de Rivoli, from whose red swing doors comes
the never-ending sound of roaring laughter, hoarse voices
and hot music.

You drink beer at "Queen's," beer out of large, fat
bottles, ice-cold and in limitless quantity. At "Queen's"
one-third of the huge space is reserved for those playing
at six huge, green billiard tables; a smaller portion of
about eighteen square feet is graciously given over to the
few couples who wish to dance, and the rest of the
restaurant is dedicated to Bacchus—he is worshipped at
small tables separated by Japanese screens—so zealously
that Venus, who is also invited, feels forgotten and superfluous. She sits in a corner and pouts, if she hasn't preferred to take part in the fun till the jovial old gentleman
has disappeared under the table, which happens at eleven
o'clock.

At this quite pointlessly early hour Madame Queens
sets her slaves in motion with a light, tired gesture of her
aristocratic hand, and the slaves go from table to table
and collect more or less enormous sums from the Jewish
pearl buyers, Scandinavian sailors, American millionaires,
German beachcombers, French policemen, English
artists, Spanish adventurers, Greek agitators and native
princes that constitute her clientele.

Tahiti, you must remember, still has a native aristocracy. King Pomare the Great and the Last left a large
family, and although it is only the cunning old Queen
Mauru and her two daughters who receive any advantage
from their titles in the shape of a considerable pension
from Paris, his other offspring still bear their titles of
prince and princess with pride.

Once the beer froth has been wiped from the tables at "Queen's" and the chairs have piled themselves up, those who have neither the money nor the desire to continue the orgy in the hotels by the shore have the choice of two possibilities. They can either go home or not. The former is by far the more difficult and we shall pass over this possibility which actually only exists in theory. Adopting the latter there are again two courses open. One leads to the Chinese restaurants and the other to the quay; but either way both meet at five o'clock in the morning at the market place.

The Chinese route is the more prosaic and hence less to be recommended to the newly arrived greenhorn. It consists of a cup of coffee with a piece of bread and a palaver with a perfect host of arriving and departing people of every colour, religion and financial position. To the Chinaman all are equal and he pours the coffee into your saucer whether you are a coolie from Shanghai or the Archbishop of Canterbury, and his price is always the same, one franc—not inclusive of any politenesses.

Opposite the restaurant lies the market hall where from two till five things become more and more lively. It is Les Halles of Paris reproduced in brighter miniature. The wagons come rattling in from the country, fishermen rise wet with slime from the water and there is much eager gossip. The market is Papeete's only newspaper. Printed competition has often been tried but each time suppressed by the government, which desires to govern without any troublesome and unpleasant commentaries. That they will not be able to do as long as there is a daily market held in Papeete; but the spoken word is blown away by the sea breeze and is infinitely difficult to lay hold of. The *Gazette Officielle* which is published by the government and controlled by the governor is, it is true, more loyal, but not nearly so amusing as the "Gazette de la Rue."

But let us get away quickly from all this political talk and join those who preferred to spend the interval between the shutting of "Queen's" and the opening of the market, on the quay. You soon discover that you are not alone in suffering from this curious insomnia which persists in spite of all the laws of nature and the exertions of the day.

There is a rustling of life in the thick shadows of the trees and from the little park in front of the hotel "Tahiti" comes the sound of conversation and lightly plucked strings. Someone is singing softly on an iron bench at the foot of the Bougainville monument, and the air is heavy with the scent of flowers; almost too heavy, a little too narcotic—or so you find it the first night. But the next day you are already accustomed to it and it would come like a sensible loss, were it to disappear.

Tiare Tahiti.

From the open porthole of one of the boats comes the sound of women's laughter and the music of a harmonica. Each sound seems to be wrapped in cotton-wool. The moon is high up above the lagoon and Murea closes off the space with its jagged profile, while the Queen's little island swims on the water like a sea bird a short distance from the shore.

Two women appear from somewhere with a guitar and a ukulele. They have garlands of scented tiare tahiti round their black hair and the moon is mirrored large and round in their dark, sparkling eyes. The women of Tahiti are world-famous. For many people they are the epitome of all that is beautiful and romantic. It is the

same with them as with their mother island, the first impression is a disappointment, the second an enchantment. They are not actually physically beautiful, that one must say straight away. The models of most of the photographs and drawings that have exalted the women of Tahiti in the European illustrated press, have all been half or three-quarter white, powdered, painted and dressed in theatrical costumes. The real Tahiti girl is plump, too heavy and solid for European taste; her lips are too thick and her nose too flat. But her skin is like café au lait, her eyes like those the poets sing, her movements have rhythm and a queenly grace as she walks the streets in bare feet, the soles of which are trodden hard as leather, so hard that she can tread out lighted cigarettes. They all have one thing in common—they never grow up. And they love music.

One moment they are plunged in the deepest melancholy, to change in an instant to a mood of sparkling, carefree gamin humour. Their speech is a cheerful chatter with short, hoarse syllables and much music, and their confidence in strangers is limitless.

There are not a few sailors of all nationalities who, tempted by the wonderful songs of the sirens, have thrown their sea chests ashore on the Quai de Commerce. Their ships have moved heaven and earth and all the French police in order to recapture these deserters, but Tahiti is large and the country round Papeete offers any number of safe hiding-places. Thus it is not unusual for one to meet a dark-skinned youth with blue eyes and blond hair. His surname may be Schmidt, Jones, Bergström or Hansen, and his father will be somewhere in the mountains, where he eats breadfruit, stretches lazily on the veranda, turns his back on the tourist cars and listens to the wind telling fairy stories to the palms above his greying head.

Night steals unnoticed from the Quai de Commerce. Lovely, quick melodies slip in and out between sad songs, the girls plait garlands, let their bare legs dangle in the water and frighten all the little butterfly fish swimming about there among the variegated coral.

The guitar falls silent, but only to let the ukulele sing, and so the hours are sung imperceptibly away, till a sheaf of golden beams shoots up from behind the mountains and announces that day is advancing—and the market begins.

Then the night birds meet the early worms in the halls; the chop-suey restaurants are once more filled to the last seat, and the events of the night, great and small, are related from table to table.

Across the street nature opens its paint box and sprinkles its brightest colours over a whole acre of ground. Here the glowing fish of the coral reefs meet the glaring fruits of the mountain, the golden-yellow mango, the green water-melon, and the orange-coloured paw-paw. Violet sea-urchins and brown starfish, harlequin-coloured lobsters and bright red crabs with black spots fight for the favour of the innkeeper and housewife, and above them all soars a chatter and a babble which forms a wave, rising and falling to an irregular rhythm.

In the market of Papeete you can find all the rare fruits that grew in Aladdin's cave, and all the fish of which you dreamed as a child, and then there will still remain a number, to dream of which you had not enough imagination. It is the cornucopia of tropical nature, a mass performance that surpasses the Arabian Nights, and for a few centimes you can have your share of these

wonders, eat the soft, yellow flesh of the mango till the scented juice runs down your chin, and become the possessor of a fish whose pattern and colours will not find their equal among the rarest gems in the treasure house of an Indian rajah.

The sun gilds the kaleidoscopic scene: the wagons begin to roll through the streets of Papeete on their way home: the Chinamen take down their shutters: a new day has begun.

The white jasmin garlands lie fading on pavement and street and are trodden under by bare feet and hooves till they end as shapeless, yellow masses in the gutter. But this evening, to-morrow and every day to come new garlands will be plaited afresh and no one will be able to destroy Tahiti's charm till the last has faded and died— not even Cook, Ford, nor Singer.

We stayed five days in Papeete and became Tahiti's humble slaves. Alain Gerbault's recommendation of the shipyard proved to be more than justified, but a large white schooner, *Tiare Taporo,* was lying in the dock and it did not look as though she would be afloat for another two months, so that a telegram would have spared us this little detour.

We were visited by a well-dressed young Dane, who introduced himself as Henrik Levinsen from Aarhus and asked if we would not like to pay him a visit. He kept an exclusive little bungalow hotel by the shore and this former amateur rider and officer seemed to have found his right niche in the wonderful district of the Punaruu pass.

Two wonderful, well-groomed thoroughbreds stamped in his stable; white doves hovered like a cloud over the calm lagoon which sent its gentle waves up under the piles of the veranda where they whispered insinuatingly of canoeing by moonlight. American tourists played at being English lords and English lords played the tourist beneath Levinsen's roof and enjoyed the cheapness of the franc.

The proprietor of all these glories showed us his collection of Tahiti paintings and entertained us to a wonderful dinner of local dishes. There was raw tunny fish, soaked in lemon juice and served with coconut sauce; white pigeons as large as chickens and chickens as large as turkeys, as well as a number of delicious dishes whose ingredients were as tasty as they were mysterious. After dinner the kitchen staff danced the hula for us, and altogether we spent one of those days which shine like fireflies when you look back into the jungle of memory.

When we arrived back we found that Bobby had been arrested. He had spent a wonderful day on shore. He had had garlands put round his neck and had plunged into the first fight of his life, which had ended in "jug." The mate had to bail him out, but in view of his youth he was let off with a warning.

We experienced the arrival of a cruising liner and saw stout-bellied brewers from Chicago wandering about the streets with garlands round their necks and heads, paying exorbitant prices for badly faked clubs and spears, till the steamer gave vent to a couple of impatient moans, whereupon they streamed over the gangway with bursting bellies and sweating brows—and the prices fell again.

We already looked upon ourselves as old-timers, but it was time for us to leave. We could wait no longer. A couple of native divers had been down and stopped the worst of the leaks with oakum, and after they had encouragingly told us that the *Monsoon* would fall to bits like

a matchbox before we were halfway to Samoa, we were ready to go.

We paid a last visit to "Queen's," sang Tahiti songs and chanteys, and the mate danced the hula-hula with a hibiscus flower in his mouth and a French policeman's cap on his head. A prince who was on a visit from Hawaii did a step dance on a rickety table covered with fat beer bottles and was arrested for the fourth time that week. Madame Queens waved her elegant hand for the last time as it struck eleven, and we sauntered arm in arm out on to the quay.

Someone tried to persuade one of the girls to go to where Mr. Möller was sleeping in a camp-bed on deck and kiss him on the brow. She agreed immediately, but was frightened by Bobby, who stuck his criminal's face in the middle of the gang-plank and so Mr. Möller was allowed to sleep on undisturbed in the bright moonlight.

The gentle strains of songs and music came from the quay long after we were in bed, and the scent of the garlands we had laid on the table was so strong that it became mixed with our dreams, while through the open skylight came soft, melodious words accompanied by the sentimental tinkle of a ukulele, Tahiti's song at parting:

"Iti ra vatu, iti atea roa,
E ua mihi au ia oe.
Te moana mi o palitifa,
Tei riro ei otia.
O to taua mi here rii e,
A rohi a faaitoito e vai.
To here i roto iau
E chèri iti e Adieu!"

CHAPTER XVI

Romantic visions and American realities

WE passed Murea, where Tito Wessel, the owner of the *White Shadow,* had made his headquarters in the Pacific, turned off to the north and ran in to Raiatea. There was nothing of interest for the expedition there, but on the other hand we met two cousins, Brodersen by name.

A long time ago the father of the one had settled in Raiatea and grown coconuts and bananas. The father of the other had been a sailor and landed on the same island together with the rest of the crew of a ship-wrecked boat. They believed that they had come to a desert island and in a short space of time some of the sailors had killed each other whilst others had committed suicide in their fear of hunger, savage natives and the future. In those days the South Sea Islands were less hospitable than they are now.

The Dane was the last survivor and, dragging himself over a mountain ridge in an attempt to reach the other side of the island, he walked straight into his brother's plantation. Romance is not the monopoly of books.

The two cousins had coffee with us in the cabin, after which we sailed on and reached Bora-Bora. There was nothing for our scientists to do there either, though for us—or at any rate for me—it was the realization of all my dreams about Polynesia.

While the others are celebrating Easter and indulging in a little trading with the natives, I will sit down in the sand and try to describe a moonlight night on one of those

South Sea islands which still live untouched and in happy ignorance of the great happenings of the outside world.

Bora-Bora is a little jewel of beauty. It consists of a mountain rising up in lonely majesty from the broad white sandy shore at its feet, a thousand palms lie mirrored in the water, and a broad reef and foaming surf encircle the lagoon, beach, palms and mountains. Of course, it has to be beautiful if I am to give my little sketch a flattering background, but the sceptical reader will perhaps be more convinced of the truth of my description if I tell him that this was the island on which the film "Tabu" was made, and that it was these rocks on which Ramon Novarro sang the "Pagan Love Song."

The American producers searched the whole South Seas to find scenery of fabulous beauty. They even turned down Tahiti, the queen of the South Seas, and sailed past hundreds of other larger and smaller laughing islands and finally planted the tripods of their cameras on Bora-Bora.

The inhabitants of the islands have luckily forgotten all that now. The American's money has long since found its way into the shops of the Chinese traders, and Ramon Novarro is only a faded memory of happy days which, in the course of time, will take their modest place in the chain of history that began in the eighteenth century, when white men set foot for the first time on this island which lies off the beaten track, and forgot it again, but left strange thoughts in the men's heads and a curious unrest in the hearts of the women.

Since those days Bora-Bora has not lost much of its original character. There is perhaps a thought more clothing to be seen—by day. The night belongs to the natives, and it is of the night that I will try to tell you;

Tahiti

of a night on the reef and the island of the dead, a night that saw only three people on the island awake—Teura, Tini and me.

Have you any idea what a tropical night with a full moon is like? It is mystical and makes you restless. It has all the silent magic of a fairy tale, but is without sweetness. The light is a dazzling blue, with jet-black shadows under the trees and in the valleys. There are coloured shadows where the tupapaus, the evil, incalculable spirits of byegone ancestors, lie in wait to seize the lonely nocturnal wanderer by the throat. The air is soft and tepid. The palms do not rustle as they do in novels, but stand there motionless, black and threatening, with stiff, ragged leaves. Now and again in the plantation a coconut falls with a thud to the ground. A war club descending heavily on a head must make the same noise. It seems as though the tupapaus have crept a little nearer. Their fingers stretch greedily from the bushes towards the pandanus covered huts, and the native moves a step away from the white path towards the water which soliloquizes quietly in the pale, sharp moonlight.

Teura was a fisherman, of pure Polynesian blood. He was forty years of age, but grinned like a boy of fifteen. Tini was his friend, the brother of his wife who had presented him with five strapping sons and one daughter without the blessing of the church. They lived in the same hut, a little way back from the flat shore of the lagoon and were the joint owners of a pirogue, a small fragile canoe hollowed out from a tree trunk and furnished with a razor-edged stem and an outrigger, so that it did not capsize at the first breath of wind when it blows down from the mountain, wrinkles the lagoon and

forms an incalculable, dangerous eddy when it meets the strong, eternal trades on the other side of the reef.

Teura had invited me for the night to go lobster fishing. Tini was to come too, and we were to leave the narrow landing stage at eight, which would leave us plenty of time to take a look round, as the lobsters could not be caught till nearly midnight when the flood tide was rising over the reef.

The pirogue, or va'a as it is called in Polynesian, shot through the water like an arrow. There wasn't a ripple on the surface which was as smooth and shiny as quicksilver. We only heard a gentle spatter as we lifted our broad-bladed paddles from the water and thrust them quickly forwards to make another cut in the bright, yielding surface and to pull them hard back again. The phosphorescence of the sea shone now and again in our wake, but that night it had lost its power, had been pressed to the wall by the moonbeams, as artificial light is killed by the rising sun.

We paddled silently for a while, till Teura steered the va'a to the shore of a little island between Bora-Bora and the reef, and ran quickly to a straw-roofed hut. We heard a muffled palaver in the shadows and shortly afterwards he returned with a net and a two-pronged spear borrowed from a brother who, half-asleep, had wished him good hunting as he gave them to him. Then we put out again and soon only a very low coral island separated us from the roar of the surf. The silhouettes of palms stood out against the clear, blue sky; the white shore was dazzling bright in contrast to all the black and blue, and there, where sand and lagoon met, the water shone with a phosphorescent gleam, as green as the shadow of an emerald on ivory.

"Fenua Menong," said Teura. The island of the dead.

"It is taboo," he continued after a short pause. "Would you like to see it?"

I nodded. We did not talk much. The exertion of paddling demanded the full capacity of our lungs, and, besides, my Polynesian vocabulary did not carry me very far. The island seemed to swim towards us. The water foamed at our pointed stem and with a practically inaudible sigh we let the va'a run up the white sand. A gentle jerk, a crunching under the outrigger and we had stopped. We jumped out up to our knees into the water and waded ashore. With every step we waded back a century, deep into the pagan days when the tupapaus had not yet been driven back into the blackest of the night's shadows, but were the sovereign lords of a crowd of quaking natives.

It was as still as death on Fenua Menong. The shadow of death lay over the dark bushes and a white strip of sand bored its way like an arrow into the darkness. It was the path that led into the interior of the island. My friends stopped where it began and pointed forwards. They themselves were good Catholics and told their beads night and morning; but the tupapaus walk at the full moon and Fenua Menong is still taboo. Fright throws a longer shadow into men's souls than church towers do, and they preferred to stay by the moonlit shore, although the white man could defy the spirits with impunity and tread the taboo underfoot. The tupapaus fall back before a white skin.

I hesitated for the fraction of a second and then moved forwards up the path. In the centre of the island I came into a broad clearing a good ten yards wide. Blocks of weathered lava lay strewn about and the trunks of the palms closed in like a wall behind them, keeping watch on either side, black and dumb. Behind my back was the narrow white strip of the path, my only connexion between this moment and the twentieth century, with civilization and a sober frame of mind. This connexion was never so near to being broken as on that night.

The cold moonbeams falling on a stone that rose steep above its surroundings in front of me, seemed like a threat. I was standing in front of the singing stone, Bora-Bora's most sacred thing, the centre of the old heathen worship and one of the few things that the white man has forgotten to put with the others to grow dusty in glass cases in close museum rooms whither no one comes.

It was here the sacrificial songs used to rise up like a pillar into the night; here the high priest used to strike the chosen human sacrifice to the ground and hand a still warm and steaming eye to the king who ate it before the watchful eyes of the Aroi, while Hina, the goddess of the moon, smiled her smile that is as cold as death, to devilish Hine-nui-te-po, the god of night. The sacrificial fire flamed high, cries resounded and the high priest's shadow flitted here and there in the light of the flames a thousand times more dreadful in its grotesque enlargement on the wall of palms. Taaroa, the mighty god of the universe, smacked his lips over the death cries of the sacrifices, whose souls flitted across the sea to Pu-lotu, the island of souls, where they rested among beautiful women who sang soft songs in their praise.

It was so quiet that it almost hurt. Somewhere in the wood a coconut fell to the ground with the thud of a descending club. I turned quickly round and my elbow struck the sacrificial stone a sharp blow which sent a mighty resounding note ringing out into the night. It rose and rose, and the thundering echo answered from the palms, which held the note and cast it here and there among their stems, till it finally penetrated me to the marrow.

The singing stone had sung its ancient song. Bloody memories poured out from all the dark corners and the dead eyes of Hina stared down at me from her blue camp above. It must soon be midnight.

As I ran back towards the shore I noticed now the branches of the bushes struck at my bare arms and chest and the creepers strung themselves across the path and set traps for my feet. Behind me stormed all the incensed gods of the past and all the tupapaus of the present, and in front of them all ran Hine-nui-te-po, the ugly god of night. In his right hand he swung an iron-wood club and his left grasped for my hair. However, I reached the white coral sand before the howling horde, which stopped with a jerk at the extreme edge of the shadow thrown by the trees, for the tupapaus and the ancient gods live in the darkness of this enlightened century.

Still the note of the singing stone followed me. It throbbed soft and threatening in my ear the whole night and I can hear it even now, if I listen. Taboo is still taboo, and at least on Fenua Menong, the island of the dead, no white man may break unpunished the commands of the ancient heathen rulers, who, dripping with blood, dispense their magic into the cold moonlight of the warm night.

Teura and Tini were sitting beside their canoe on the shore silently smoking. The white of their smiles shone to greet me and, breaking a white bloom from a branch, they stuck it in greeting behind my ear. We had to be on the reef in half an hour.

My friends never asked me about my experiences in the black bush. I only found out that in the days when Teura was still a boy, two fishermen had moved over on to Fenua Menong so as to be nearer their ground on the reef. They laughed at the old men and disregarded all their warnings, but a month later their newly built huts, they themselves, their families and all their possessions were whipped into the sea by a mad cyclone which cost not a life on the main island.

Teura spoke quietly with Tini in the soft speech of the Polynesians. Lying there on the shore, brown, well-built and naked but for a blood-red loin cloth, they resembled two young sea-gods who had stepped out of the blue water to play with seashells and the love of some young sea-maiden. Teura hummed a verse of a Tahitian song. The short, soft syllables clung gently to the music—Polynesian is itself almost singing and now it merged completely with the music. Tini beat time with his head while a white jasmin flower danced between his lips. When the song was finished they began together to teach it to me. They clapped their hands like children when I pronounced the words correctly; they encouraged me in every conceivable way and were not sparing in their praise.

We were friends. I was clothed as they; plied my paddle and did my share of work on their fishing ground. I could talk in their own language of nature, of the wind, the moon, the stars and the sea—matai, avae, fedia, miti. Here there was no abject crawling before the skin that happened to have been born white; no hypocritical profit-seeking in the background, as there was in so many other places where I met Polynesians. That night the wheel was rolled back, the gulf closed up. They offered me cigarettes, handed me paw-paws whose juice is as refreshing and whose flesh as aromatic as that of the melon; they made me tia-shoes which are fashioned on the spot from coconut fibre as a protection against the sharp coral and treacherous muraenas which might be lurking in the holes between the coral rocks of the reef.

It was midnight and we set out for the strip of white in the north. The rollers flung themselves with a roar against the steep outside wall of the reef; towered up in fury at this unexpected obstacle to their wanderings across the Pacific; arched their backs and broke in thunder and foam over the reef, from which they streamed down in mad eddies, and ran out with spent force and gentle splashing into the shallow lagoon, to die finally with a gentle sigh on the sand of Bora-Bora. The white sandy bottom rose up to meet the keel as we approached the reef. Dark coral columns stood out black against the light of the sand, and like dead forests reached their bare, jagged branches towards us, while the shadows of fish moved noiselessly among their tops.

Tini and I went on in front, Tini carrying the spear and I the net, while Teura paddled the va'a along behind us, ready to relieve the net of its burden when the catch had filled it. The lobsters were swept over the reef with each wave that came. The waves towered up to a height of six feet before they broke and then as though they were in an aquarium we could see the fish and lobsters quite clearly behind the green glass wall in the light of our flaming torches made of palm leaves tied together.

Then the side of the acquarium broke and in the same

instant its contents were emptied at our feet, giant fish and floundering lobsters on a bed of green eels, soft sponges, sea-anemonies and white foam. We were on top of them with a bound before they had time to escape in the undertow and the next breaker came. I seized the lobsters and Tini plunged his spear through the fish which remained fast on the prongs, jerking and reflecting all the colours of the rainbow.

Again and again the net filled and was emptied on the floor of the va'a. Teura beamed with pleasure and Tini sang a hunting song, a few jubilant verses as he chased farther over the reef, plunging and withdrawing his spear, jumping through the surf and stumbling over the treacherous holes.

We were wet from crown to foot but never noticed it. The sport had got into our blood and the water was as warm as a bath. When our last torch went out in a shower of sparks and the force of the breakers had diminished, forty lobsters lay on a layer of wonderful fish on the floor of the va'a. It was two o'clock. We were happy and laughed to each other. The joy of the catch still glowed in our blood as we paddled home, so fast that the phosphorescence of the sea spurted away from our bow.

Teura and Tini sang loudly and triumphantly, and at every stroke of the paddles their muscles rippled like round balls under their skin. I sat in the stern and soaked in the scene with every sense—the moon, the sea, the silence about us, the gentle drip from the paddles, the slight chatter and gurgle of the water under our keel and the two melodious voices. The line of the shore grew rapidly nearer and nearer; the palms on land took on shape; the water became more and more bright, and

the huts detached themselves from the shadows. We drew the va'a on to a large stone, divided the catch into three equal heaps and separated.

A night had passed, one of those nights one never forgets. A few hours in which the centuries disappear, the idea of time is suspended and life is lived in all its primitive, direct force beneath the beams of the moon, which is eternally young and ever old—life as it was in distant, prehistoric days, and as it still is on the small islands far from the highways of the Pacific.

*

Strictly scientific, objective expeditions cannot occupy themselves with sentimental sketches. Up to now the booty of our ethnographic department had been rather poor. What they had got was either too new or spurious, and they had to get a move on. It seemed as though Polynesia was going to be a disappointment and they transferred their hopes to Melanesia where cannibals and malaria still kept the tourist at bay.

I had to leave my sketching and jump on board, for we were off for Samoa, but first were to visit the American island of Tutuila before going to the New Zealand Protectorate whose capital is Apia. The wind was favourable. Bora-Bora disappeared behind the horizon and Tutuila appeared above it.

Pago-Pago, the harbour of Tutuila, is the safest refuge from storms in the Pacific and for that reason is the base of the American fleet, which at that time consisted of an old minesweeper. Two slender wireless masts maintained daily communication between the station and Washington and Key-West, and a short signal could,

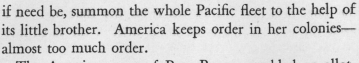

if need be, summon the whole Pacific fleet to the help of its little brother. America keeps order in her colonies—almost too much order.

The American part of Pago-Pago resembled an allotment which was kept with exaggerated, tender care in order to win first prize in some competition. There were beautiful green lawns whose every blade was one and a half inches high, and between them ran asphalt paths, as straight as arrows and without holes, and bordering the path were rows of hibiscus, so symmetrical that one imagined that a troop of marines went round them early every morning and snipped off the flowers till every bush had the same number. There were well-kept tennis courts and a sweet little golf course with nine little holes, and a promenade along the shore which was reserved for the officers of the fleet and their families. For the recreation of the crews there was a cinema which was used as a church on Sundays and a canteen with a glistening new skittle alley and large steel containers from which flowed ice-cream soda and malted milk.

The white inhabitants of Pago-Pago were all in the service of the navy, from the laundryman to the governor of the island. We found them nice, exceptionally helpful people, whether their caps had gold braid or their trousers spots of grease.

The asphalt of the main street ran past the government buildings and four covered guns, continued for a little and then suddenly stopped. From here on it was an ordinary road with loose stones and palms on either side, not nearly such a good motor road but more suited to the island and its surroundings. It led to the native town at the end of the bay.

Uncle Sam leaves the natives to a certain degree to

themselves. He supervises their hygiene and the fight against their diseases but does not interfere with their daily life nor their ancient form of government. Each village has its chieftain who, in his turn, has his under-chieftains and his "talking chief," for the big chieftain is too superior to make a speech in the assembly himself; and each village is under a common district chieftain, who lives in Pago-Pago and whose house is the largest and finest in the village.

The Samoans are famed far and wide for their archi-tecture. Their huts are true works of art, having straw roofs like bee-skeps, supported by a number of artistically carved wooden pillars. In the evening they resemble fairy mounds raised up on glowing stakes. The floors are circular and paved with tiny pieces of coral, over which straw mats are laid; and the spaces between the pillars are furnished with palm-leaf blinds which can be rolled down to keep out the wind and the rain. These blinds are kept rolled up for the most part and so the Samoan huts are clean, bright and well-aired. Round about the hut proper are other smaller ones, of which one serves as sty for their black pigs, another as kitchen, a third as storeroom and torture-chamber, and a fourth as bedroom for the more distant members of the family, young people who as yet have no homes of their own.

The Samoans followed the doctrine of communism long before it was committed to paper. Even nowadays they are governed according to the cell system; each family is a cell, the children are educated collectively and the father is head of the cell. Fishing and hunt-ing are done collectively and new houses are built by the united efforts of the entire village.

No distinction is made between legitimate and illegiti-

mate children. Everybody in Pago-Pago is a good, almost fanatical, Christian, though their Christianity has been somewhat adapted to their old traditions and moral ideas, with seemingly most happy results. Since the earliest times the good-looking, well-built Samoan men have had the reputation of being proud and race-conscious and America has respected this proud past, conformed to it and wisely given the natives as much independence as possible.

The native chieftains are allowed to decide on all internal and local affairs, and only in exceptional circumstances where their decisions run contrary to the welfare of the island as a whole, and may possibly run counter to the interests of America, does the governor impose his solution of the problem—but he does it in an objective and diplomatic way and not as a command. As a result the native population is free and happy, and its number is steadily increasing—a phenomenon for the South Seas.

The ancient inherited traditions are still respected. Men who wish to be regarded as such, must even to-day undergo the long and painful trial of manhood—the tatooing. Every male Samoan wears under his lava-lava a pair of tattooed bathing drawers, a maze of patterns from thigh to knee. In the olden days this was the Samoan's badge of freemasonry, and by it they, who are the best sailors in the Pacific, recognized each other when their canoes met in Tonga, Fiji or Tahiti. The custom still flourishes, although the schools and missions have worked to get this barbarism and unnecessary infliction of pain abolished.

It is a pleasant fact that the brown population of Samoa is as healthy, strong and vital as one could have wished for the whole South Seas, and as it could have been had the white man's thoughts gone a little further than the mere filling of his pocket-book as quickly as possible regardless of the means, like the man who killed the goose that was laying its golden eggs rather too slowly.

There is, however, one danger hovering over Samoa. The tourist microbe is trying to gain entry. Where passenger steamers touch, every native population turns into a horde of calculating, cringing, unreliable individuals. The day that the word dollar and cent are understood by the Samoan in all their significance will see the end of the Pacific's communistic community, the only one to be successful in the history of the world.

CHAPTER XVII

The natives dance, the Governor perspires, we drink soapy
water and I receive a good offer. We learn something
of politics and are terribly spoiled in Apia

A DIVERSITY of things happened during the time the
Monsoon lay in the harbour of Tutuila. By that I do
not mean such trifling events as when the mate's fingers
became caught in the cheese's five holes, so that he flew
down the alley behind it and knocked all nine skittles
down; or that our five tortoises caused such a sensation
that two policemen with rubber truncheons had to keep
the queue on the quay in check, nor that the island's one
photographer spoiled a hundred and seventy of my nega-
tives and demanded ten dollars for his work. No, I mean
real sensations like the arrival of a new governor, the
jubilee of the day when the group was taken over by
America and its resultant national festivities with their
impressive ceremonies and varied forms of merrymaking.

All that happened on 17th April and lasted from early
morning till late into the night. That day the sun
shone with such ardour that one half-expected that it
would grow tired and go to bed an hour before the
meteorological institute allowed.

The evening before large canoes had paddled into the
harbour bringing guests from other parts of the island,
singing, all dressed up and equipped with umbrellas.
On Samoa the umbrella is a sign of respectability and
even in streaming rain is carried rolled up in its cover.
These guests were lodged with friends and relatives, and

when the sun rose on the morning of the holiday the road from the village to the Ma'ala was a huge moving carpet of bright colours and red flowers.

The Ma'ala was the central point of the day's activities. It spread itself out and expanded from a pure feeling of self-importance and in view of the occasion had decorated itself with a million glistening pearls of dew. The white officers of the fleet sat in white clothes on a white veranda and waited, while the natives stood, sat and lay in a semi-circle in front of the veranda and did just the same as the white men.

Then the sound of military music came from up the road. It was the Fita-Fita Guards, the native police force, performing for the new governor. They were big, smart fellows in blue lava-lavas with red stripes, shining white shirts and red fezes, and they all but hid the shining, freshly washed government Packard in which the Governor sat with his wife and sweated. He had come straight from Alaska and murmured unconsidered words about sun and heat and these curious beings who wore skirts and stuck flowers behind their ears, instead of wearing decent furs and frosty beards. But the "Stars and Stripes" drowned all his critical remarks.

He was put in the island's best club-chair among his officers and the ceremonial part of the programme began. Many speeches were made both by white chiefs and brown chieftains and under-chieftains. Guns were fired and a choir of school children sang "The Star-spangled Banner," while the said banner was hoisted in a cloud of gunpowder. The Fita-Fita Guards presented arms, heads were bared and the Governor swore his oath of office on the judge's Bible. The natives listened devoutly and

enjoyed all the ceremonial and the heavy gold of the uniforms.

Fifty bronze statues suddenly came to life and marched into the half-moon that had been kept clear in front of the tribune. The kava ceremony was about to begin. The fifty athletes who were decorated with flowers sat down in a semi-circle with their faces turned towards the governor. Between them and the tribune sat a charming young girl with a bearskin and many ornaments. Near her sat two men of high rank and in front of them stood the focal point of the ceremony, the kava bowl.

All this requires an explanation. Kava is a drink which is distilled from the roots of a pepper plant, piber methysticum. The roots are soaked in water and the fluid is then filtered. The result resembles turbid soapy water and in the opinion of most whites tastes worse. It is not intoxicating, but enjoyed to excess over a long period it has a harmful effect and causes running eyes and weak knees. In earlier times it was the woman's business to chew the roots until they were turned into a sort of papier mâché; but now they are pounded in a mortar, which is no longer quite so primitive, but more in accordance with American ideas of hygiene.

Kava is the centre of every Polynesian festivity. It is drunk at births, marriages, and funerals, and eminent guests are welcomed in the villages with the performance of the kava ceremony. The young girl who prepares the beverage must be of noble birth and a virgin. She is clad in gorgeous tapa material and round her neck hangs a rich chain of whale's teeth; her bearskin is made from human hair and decorated with shells.

When the beverage had been mixed in the huge bowl, it was filtered through a bundle of hibiscus fibres and a smooth, polished, ornamented coconut cup filled to the brim with the greeny-grey liquid, whereupon the head "talking-chief" of the head chieftain clapped his hands three times and shouted, or rather recited, a lengthy oration in Samoan. A master-of-ceremonies seized the cup and, raising it high above his head, walked towards the veranda and presented it with a deep obeisance to the governor.

The governor had been instructed beforehand. He poured a little of the contents out on to the ground as a sacrifice to the gods, drank and handed the cup back. According to the rules he should have sent the cup spinning back over the grass, but there are limits to the digital dexterity of an Alaskan! He hurriedly turned an incipient grimace into a somewhat forced smile and once again wiped his forehead with a large, clean, white handkerchief which was already soaking wet. The desire for a stiff whisky-and-soda without soda shone from his blue sailor's eyes.

Seven other officials had to undergo the same torture. The cup sank deeper and deeper in the hands of the master-of-ceremonies, the lower in rank the victim was; and at the last it was practically sweeping the grass. After that the kava ceremony was over and the governor welcomed as is fitting in Tutuila. He pushed his chair back slightly on the veranda, and the more popular and jovial part of the feast began.

It lasted the whole day. There were sack-races and three-legged races, competitions in splitting coconuts for the men and in weaving baskets for the women, and twenty natives tore over the grass after a pig which had been smeared with grease from its curly tail to snout. The first to catch it could keep it. Each of the men squealed enough for two pigs and five seconds after the starting pistol was fired the prize was buried under a heap of prize-fighters. One had tight hold of the snout, another held it by the tail, two by the ears, and six by the legs, while the others fought to get their arms round the body of the squealing pig. It was just one large, confused mass of kicking legs, and the Fita-Fita Guards had to interfere twice before the ant-heap began to disperse. The one whose skin was the thickest to resist the blows and who still kept hold when the others had loosed their grip, was declared the winner. It was he who had had a grip of the tail. He departed in triumph with one black eye, a loose tooth and a sprained thumb, but his hibiscus flower was still behind his ear. Only the pig forgot to curl its tail.

Then began the swimming races from the quay beside the *Monsoon*. Twenty men dived in at the same instant. One of them shot immediately to the front and when the others saw that, they lost all interest in the business and began to play about in the course like frolicsome sea-lions. Forgotten were the governor and the prizes, and before the rowing regatta could begin the Fita-Fita Guards nearly had to jump, truncheon in hand, into the water to shoo the grown-up children away.

The Samoans have always been known as brilliant boat-builders, and their neat, narrow fifty-foot boats are miracles of light construction. The principal race was between two such boats. There were thirty paddlers in each, a cox, and a drummer with an empty petrol tin in the bow. The two boats darted across the water, their paddles keeping perfect time. The spectators on the quay and in the minelayer shrieked at their favourites and when the first boat passed the finishing line such applause broke out that coconuts fell from the trees and the wireless masts quivered.

The governor ordered a pause at midday and spent the time going over the *Monsoon*. He and the skipper greeted each other with the utmost formality—the skipper with the grandezza of a lady of the Spanish court—but inside five minutes they had put all ceremony aside and were slapping each other in the stomach and back and saying "Goddam" and all the other curious words sailors use when they talk of Cape Horn and "rolling down to Rio."

We others gazed at them in open-mouthed amazement.

Then the mate said something about Nova Scotia and South Georgia and the end of it all was that we almost had to use force to get the governor ashore and back into his empty chair on the veranda.

The afternoon passed with singing and dancing by the natives. The Samoans dance with slight movements of the legs and graceful motions of the arms—just like the Tiller Girls—and they sing so beautifully that even the largest of church organs would tie knots in its pipes with envy. It was a war of song between all the tribes of the island, and when the judge gave one the prize he had to be unjust to the others. It was simply wonderful.

In the evening the orchestra of the Fita-Fita Guards played in a pavilion on the Ma'ala, but by then both whites and browns were so tired with the events of the day that the moon was permitted to illuminate the whole, beautiful scene for its own pleasure. Nobody missed anything by not being there. American foxtrots sound so desolately dull and paltry when they are played by a brass band on a quiet evening in Samoa after the bright spectacle and vivid colours of a feast day. Foxtrots and tangos are all right, not to say O.K., within four walls, where there is a dance floor available and the clatter of knives and forks accompanies the orchestra. Moon, palms and the scent of flowers rob the melodies of their tone and they shrink together like dying-pig balloons.

A cat crept on its way rat hunting and the fish rose in the water, while from the governor's villa, the natives' huts and the skylight of the *Monsoon* a many-voiced snore rose up to the brightness of the stars. The skipper giggled in his sleep and the mate struck him in the stomach to make him be quiet.

Jan began to get busy in his capacity of ethnographist. Mr. Möller and he visited one or two villages to look for treasure which might be buried in lumber-rooms. Before they were allowed to begin their search, they had to go through the whole kava ceremony, sitting with their legs crossed and saying "Yes" and "No" and one or two sentences which they did not understand. That is not so easy when you are sitting right on a layer of sharp, jagged coral such as forms the floor of Samoan huts. For Jan kava is not a drink but a punishment, more exquisite than any known to Europe, not excepting the death penalty. You do not die from kava. On the contrary, it has a stimulating effect on the whole organism, so that you are in the best of form to appreciate the taste of soapy water with every sense, and even when the taste has finally disappeared you still feel a violent burning, like that of Spanish pepper, on the skinless tip of your tongue.

Science, too, has its heroes.

The first chests of drums, kava cups and mats were nailed down, and Jan wrote in childish letters on top "NATIONAL MUSEUM, KOPENHAGEN," while Mr. Möller rubbed his hands, as did the natives. Each party thought the other equally dumb.

We were invited to a party in the house of a chieftain in the American part of the village, where some fat beauties performed light, piquant dances for us. After the performance our kind hostesses came round with a plate and were bitterly disappointed on discovering how little we appreciated their hospitality.

A Fita-Fita guardsman came down to the quay with a bottle of beer under each arm and asked me if I would not consider becoming his brother-in-law. It was much better here than in "Tenmark," an island of which, by the way, he had never heard, and his sister's prowess at fishing was unique. Besides that she owned a nice piece of land and he would see about the house. It was to take about a fortnight before everything would be ready, but if I moved in then I would be able to lie on mats and let myself be fed till the roof fell in over my head. If I insisted on doing something, it was not far to Tahiti where there was a superfluity of alcohol to be obtained cheaply and that would enable me to earn an honourable living by smuggling. The stuff was far too dear in Tutuila and besides that forbidden to the natives.

I made casual mention of my wife at home, but she did not seem to constitute any serious obstacle to our plans for the future. She was sure to find another man soon, who could look after her. To have her come out here was sheer madness. It was not worth the price of the ticket. Could she, perhaps, climb up trees for coconuts or spear fish? Could she weave mats or brew kava? I had to admit that he was right. Eva has still much to learn before we move to Tutuila.

I promised to go carefully into his proposal, and was

still thinking it over when we sailed away. My conscience pricked a little as we sailed out of the bay. It would be a disappointment for the sister, and the man himself would not get his cheap whisky from Tahiti. And I would never lie in a straw hut and be fed with coconuts and chicken.

The wind was feeble, and the little there was was contrary. It thundered and the waves began to rise. In the middle of the night a sudden squall threw our books and tins off the shelves helter-skelter over the floor, but the next morning found us lying in the roads of Apia behind the sheltering circle of the reef.

When the wind veers round into the north, the waves beat in with mighty force through the broad opening and the harbour of Apia is then anything but safe.

In 1889 six men-of-war lay off the island on guard. Three great powers—Britain, America, and Germany—had designs on Samoa, but had not been able to arrive at a peaceful agreement. Then a cyclone came and cleaned the harbour up. The British cruiser escaped to the open sea, but the other ships were flung against the inner reef, torn to pieces so that only their iron skeletons were left and the greater part of their crews cast up on shore. That provided the incentive for a peaceful settlement of the question and Germany was given the islands of Savaii and Upolu, America put Tutuila and the Manua group in its pocket, while Britain had to be content with Fiji which had been in its possession for many years. Germany maintained its predominance till 1914 when a New Zealand cruiser landed troops at Apia and occupied the island without bloodshed. At the conclusion of peace the League of Nations put the islands under the mandate of New Zealand.

Their new master has not proved equal to his task. There have twice been serious disturbances—the last in 1928—and the natives grumble continually against the government. A secret opposition, the Mau movement, has planted its roots all over the island. Its leader, the Swedish-Samoan Nelson, was condemned to five years' deportation in 1928, but returned at the end of this term to be condemned shortly afterwards to ten months' imprisonment and ten years' deportation.

People's sympathy, even that of a large proportion of the white inhabitants, is overwhelmingly on the side of Nelson. He is an idealist who has sacrificed the greater part of his once large fortune on the altar of the Mau movement. His large business is threatened with ruin during his absence, and the Samoans turn more and more against the government and its representatives. The government made the great mistake of letting Samoa be governed by the military, who treat the Samoans, who are tremendously proud and race-conscious, like a flock of intractable and ignorant recruits in the barrack square,  and will not be advised by people who have a knowledge of local conditions and above all of the natives' curious mentality.

This lack of insight and tractability and, what is closely connected with it, the too high-handed and stupid treatment of intelligent native leaders and champions, have made New Zealand's sway most insecure and has contributed to the fact that the natives talk quite openly of the good days under German rule. Those who know anything of the Germans' former colonial policy and discipline will thus be able to get a good picture of New Zealand's methods of government. Twice a week the large German colony assembles in the "Concordia" Club

where they drink beer, sing students' songs and heil Hitler. When Germany was still at the helm, times were good. Copra brought large profits and the harbour of Apia was well frequented. Nowadays economic conditions are simply hopeless. The large trusts have united to force the price of copra below the cost of production and the harbour is as deserted as a graveyard.

The more thoughtful elements of the opposition desire self-government for the natives and in addition direct contact with Britain, as have Fiji and the Solomon Islands. They wish to be governed by "the old man" himself and not by the ship's young, inexperienced third mate, which New Zealand in reality is. Time alone will show what will be the result of all this unrest; but something must happen, for the present situation is as unsatisfactory for the ruler as it is for the subjects.

Upolu is Stevenson's island. He is buried on the peak of the highest mountain, Vaea, which lies behind Apia and from which there is a charming view of the town, the bay and the reef. Wild vanilla flowers round the grave and passion fruit ripens on the sides of its mound, while on the tombstone you may read the following inscription which Stevenson himself composed:

"Here he lies where he longed to be
Home is the sailor, home from the sea,
And the hunter home from the hill."

From here Samoa's consumptive lover looked out over the sea and here it was that he talked with the native chieftains who regarded him as their uncrowned, beloved king. The verse was composed on the island and once one has stood beside his grave and seen the sun set over the reef, one can understand the peace and quiet, the gentle, latent warmth that streams from it:

> "Here in the quiet eve,
> My thankful eyes receive
> The quiet light.
> I see the trees stand fair
> Against the faded air
> And star by star prepare
> The perfect night."

That sounds like an evening prayer, at one with the peace and beauty of sunset on this poor, ill-treated, wonderful island.

The Danes who lived on Samoa received us with wonderful hospitality. They overwhelmed us with gifts; basketfuls of the island's most wonderful fruit were sent aboard and we were their guests almost from morning to night. But all good things come to an end and one fine day we were told that we had been given permission to go to Tonga.

You must understand that normally all communication between Samoa and Tonga is strictly forbidden, as Samoa suffers from a plague of beetles that are unknown on the southern islands; but the *Monsoon* was given permission at any rate to sneak through two paragraphs of this strict law, and we were all looking forward to visiting the one and only independent monarchy in the South Seas, where a six-foot queen rules a highly cultivated and intelligent people.

Unfortunately the trip came to nothing. The leader of our expedition decided to sail direct to Fiji and to his sorrow Jan had to cross a line or two of the museum's requirements from his list. We sailed then for Fiji and

Suva. On the way there we passed a succession of small islands and put in at one—Ngau. We ought not to have done that. Suva is the clearing station for the Fiji group and it is forbidden to visit other harbours before your papers are in order.

We had all sorts of unpleasantness because of this, and the authorities in Suva frowned and were most suspicious, but the letters we had from the Foreign Office and the Danish consul helped us to get away with whole skins. We had to anchor outside in the roads, near the white American yacht *Yankee* which was making a voyage round the world following more or less the same route as we. She had a crew of sixteen young Americans who took the place of sailors and each of whom paid his modest share of the expenses.

We had to throw all our fresh oranges and lemons overboard into the harbour and some of our cabins were sealed up, and all on account of that stupid Apian beetle. Besides that the skipper had to swallow a reprimand from the harbour authorities which did not please him. It was really quite undeserved, for it was not he who wished to land on Ngau. He would have much preferred to have stuck to the course on which we had originally decided and that was bright of him—because you can just as well follow an embroidery pattern or a crossword puzzle as a chart of the South Seas. Most of the charts were made in 1828 or thereabouts, and large black letters right across them inform you that they are guaranteed unreliable.

It put us in no better mood when we were told that the local dock could not take us for at least three weeks. It was the only yard in that part of the Pacific which came into consideration, and the *Monsoon* had to be thoroughly overhauled before the worms had done too much damage to the places where the copper paint had peeled off her bottom. She was already leaking like a sieve.

We had to look round for something to pass the time of waiting. We thought of Tonga, but now the wind was no longer favourable.

CHAPTER XVIII

Concerning a Babylon swarming with beautiful women,
a course in Danish war dances and rheinländers,
to say nothing of a storm that swept mainsail
and storm-jib away and brought us
to Noumea

WE decided to go to Vatulele, a small island a few miles
south of Suva. It had not been visited by whites for a
year and so was presumably a better sphere for both our
zoological and ethnographic work than the main island
of Viti Levu with its motor-cars, cultivated fields and
strong European influence.

We were greatly helped by the Danish consul, Hon.
Henry Marks. Henry Marks is an Australian Jew of
German origin who came to Fiji in its wild days. He
went from house to house with a basket on his arm selling
matches. Later he started his own business, developed
it and ended by signing Fiji's pound notes in his capacity
of Mayor of Suva. He was honoured for his valuable
economic services to the colony, and so to England,
during the war. This matchseller's career is rather like a
Hans Andersen fairy story, which may be the reason he
was made Danish Consul, but that I cannot say. Many
of Suva's other big men have worked their way up with
their hands, and their tales of the days when Suva consisted of nine bars and two hotels are worth listening to.

Suva is the most industrious and most civilized town in
the Pacific. Its main features are stamped with the
elegance and cleanliness of the English, but once you get
a little away from the Victoria Parade, which is the main

street along the shore, then you discover that Suva is a cocktail of nationalities, a mill-race where whites mix with Melanesian, Polynesian, Japanese and Indian elements.

Fiji is the eastern outpost of Melanesia, and although the natives are black and have curly hair and nigger lips, their tall stature and more or less regular features are proof of strong Polynesian influence. Suva is a frontier station, from whose harbour traffic goes to Hong-Kong, Panama, Sydney and San Francisco; and like all frontier stations the town has a bright, international character.

Fiji became British in 1874, and since that day this large, rich colony has been an important jewel in the British Imperial Crown. The Fiji islander is not industrious by nature and his help in working the sugar fields and coconut plantations could not be relied on too much. Foreign labour had to be imported. The government's eye turned to the overpopulated delta of the Ganges and soon large sailing ships were on their way from Calcutta to Suva laden with sea-sick Indians. These coolie-ships were dogged by bad luck. Again and again the ghost of plague showed its white face among the closely crowded passengers and thinned their ranks, but energetic quarantine measures combined with a large measure of luck prevented the disease from being brought to Fiji, where its effect would have been catastrophic. An epidemic of measles once took toll of forty thousand Fiji islanders and the influenza epidemic of 1918-19 recruited an army of dead all over the South Seas.

Nowadays the group of islands has as many Indian citizens as aborigines—80,000 as against 90,000—and the Indians form a state within the state with their own

schools, hospitals and priests; but they do not have the Indian castes, which were not brought aboard the transports. Thus Suva has its untouchables, but a Ghandi would be without work in Fiji. On the other hand it has transpired that the good education the young Indians receive in the schools of Suva has put them in a position to form a real and dangerous opposition in the islands' politics; so that in addition to the already existing Chinese problem there has arisen an Indian problem.

The Indians' headquarters are in Cumming Street. Cumming Street is a Babel and not till you have been in it can you have an adequate conception of the confusion that must have overtaken humanity when the artisans began to speak with tongues during the building of the tower of Babel, when the architect explained his plans in Celtic, the masons spoke to their men in New Greek and they answered in a long-forgotten dialect of North China, while the handyman cursed the apprentice in English. If a schoolboy was placed in the middle of the street with his geography book in his hand he would be unable to discover in what part of the globe he was.

Indian women go past shrouded in long white veils, and with rubies set in gold filigree in their nostrils and ears. A little man with a fez, long beard, his shirt over baggy trousers and a grey unbuttoned coat over his shirt shuffles past a shop with Chinese characters on long pendant sign-boards. A yellow Japanese barber plasters his white lather on a brown Samoan, while a German planter roars in pidgin English at a melancholy taxi-driver.

In numberless little booths sit brown, dried-up Indians bent over an anvil, a hammer and a piece of silver in their hands. They are jewellers at work. Just as the Indians

206

have remained faithful to their native religion and ancient customs, so have they kept their love of precious metals and showy jewellery. Bombay silversmiths followed hard on the heels of the coolies from the Punjab, and their work clinks at the wrists and ankles of even the poorest Indian girl. Sparkling jewellery hangs in shining rows on strings behind the dusty, broken shopwindows.

An old Hindu sits at a street corner selling small pieces from a coil of cordage. This cordage proved to be the local tobacco and was of a strength that would strike a hardened sailor to the ground when it is rolled in thin, fine ricepaper and made into cigarettes. The natives wrap it in a palm-leaf and light the broad end. That does not make the tobacco any milder.

The whites in Samoa forgather between five and six in the bars on the Strand Promenade, where they exchange gossip and business news among poker chips and foaming beer mugs till the round clock above the rows of bottles strikes six, whereupon all these jolly, chattering men turned into silent, stiff Englishmen, and go home to throw on their dinner-jackets and have dinner with their wife on the veranda.

After dinner the head of the family listens to the Test Match on the wireless or goes to one of the town's three cinemas—in dinner-jacket and his wife in rustling silk and with bare back. There are so few amusements in Suva. Sunday is the usual English Sunday, boring to death and quite hopeless for foreigners. The majority of suicides in England and the Colonies must take place on Sunday at four o'clock in the afternoon. The young go to Nukulau for the week-end. Nukulau is the island's old quarantine station and is a tiny coral island between the town and the reef. There, out of earshot, they jazz the quiet hours away and return in an overladen asthmatic motor-boat to the labours of Monday.

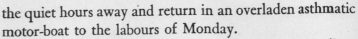

As a result of the large number of immigrant Indians Suva has two police forces, one of natives with white, pointed loin-cloths and blue jackets with a lot of gold, and one of bearded Sikhs with picturesque turbans above a khaki uniform. The former are the more amusing.

They are barefooted and bareheaded, for every self-respecting Fijian wears a curly crown either henna-coloured or bleached with chalk, which precludes the use of hats. You may search long for a more comical sight than that of two such woolly headed policemen strolling along the pavement with bare, spread-out toes and hand in hand as is the natives' custom. In their hair they carry coins and cigarettes, possibly also organic life, and they comb it every few seconds with large wooden combs whose teeth are at least six inches long.

China and Japan have also set their foot in the Fiji Islands. Their dumping prices are very harmful to the large businesses. At first the yellows monopolized the trade with the natives, in which the whites had never been particularly interested; then with the money they had thus earned they enlarged their shops and made their storerooms more comprehensive. Nowadays many people do their shopping in the small shops with cheap prices and the result is very obvious in the main street.

The Asiatic is not loved in Suva, but he makes money and much more than he and his family need. The Tong takes its share of the surplus and it is the Tong that stands behind every little job-bootmaker who sits on the pavement and drives nails into the soles of the poor until one fine day he is able to retire behind a glass window and name plate and acquire white customers.

It will be very exciting to see whether St. Mercury can imitate St. George's trick and kill the fierce, dangerous Chinese dragon. But don't let's get involved in such world problems.

The sun shone and it was gloriously hot and curiously enough it had not rained for several days. The newspapers had written one or two columns about us and we were the lions of the hour. The mate sat in Piers Hotel telling tales of whaling and somewhat later in the evening told ladies' fortunes from their hands or coffee grounds, while the rest of us danced with a selected assortment of the town's beauty queens on the freshly polished floor of the Club Hotel.

We went from one party to another and a dozen sisters Malloy turned the heads of our entire crew in turn. Sonny was in the seventh heaven and related his memories of his previous voyage, so that Emma and Agnes and Joan chose him for their tall, strong Viking, while Margaret, Tilla and all the others fluttered round us and fled to our heroes' breasts till Jan became afraid of the sight of the girls and kicked over the traces, while two of the others fought a duel on account of Agnes' gentle brown eyes.

We went from tea party to cocktail party, and from evening party to garden party, till we finally thought of preparing a kind of dance programme on which all these nice people could reserve the appropriate hour. Now and again our scientists had audiences with a whole series of influential and omniscient authorities who gave them much advice regarding the New Hebrides and the Solomon Islands, which are also under the dominion of Suva.

Mr. Möller was entertained to soup, joint and two veg.

by the consul and was honoured by a governor's hand-shake on the birthday of His Majesty King George V when strong tea and dry cakes were served to all the whites in the town and harbour who could creep or crawl to the reception.

We behaved very well and visited the museum and the stylish English club—once each; we went for picnics with the Malloy girls, and I helped Charley Heren, a good friend of mine, to transport gravel along the roads of Fiji. It gave me exercise and at the same time a good picture of the intensity with which the Indian plantation coolies cultivate the rich soil in the neighbourhood of Suva. Fields of rice stood up to their knees in water; cotton, bananas, sugar canes, pineapples, coffee, cocoa, hemp, vanilla, kava plants and coconut palms competed as to who could produce the most, and yellow lemons tried to out-shout the shrieking colour of the oranges.

Fiji is an industrious colony which is rapidly develop-ing and all romanticism has been carefully eliminated from the vicinity of the capital. Naturally the depression made itself felt here too, particularly the catastrophic fall in the price of copra, but there was everywhere belief in the future and the citizens of Suva have not sacrificed their good humour in the confusion between past and present.

After the days of pleasure a little time for recovery was necessary. Thus it was a real relief to get back to work after ten days of compulsory holidays and set course for Vatulele. On the way we put in for the night into a bay in the island of Mbenga, but the squalls which came howling down from the mountains were so violent that the skipper was not satisfied with our situation and we weighed anchor again and ran for a little, low coral island

to the west. There was a strong wind from the south-
east which caused a considerable swell. Then we
happened to run aground.

We had just run into the lea of the reef round Vatulele
and had manœuvred through a narrow passage into the
rather quieter waters of the lagoon, when we struck a
coral rock and stuck fast. According to the chart we
should have had many fathoms of water under our keel
at the spot where the rock was. The skipper swore like
a Turk and Mr. Möller stood in the stern with a serious
expression, for it was far to the shore and the *Monsoon*
was not insured. Luckily we suffered nothing worse than
a fright.

A couple of kedges, the proficiency of the crew and a
little luck helped us off at high tide and we anchored
some distance away from the treacherous rock in a place
where the sandy bottom smiled up at us inspiring confidence. The wind freshened to a gale and ended in a
storm. It whistled and sang in the shrouds, but we lay
more or less secure in shallow water on good anchor
ground. Land and town were over a mile away and we
were prisoners of the weather.

The next day was Easter and it was still blowing as
hard as ever, and the seas were even heavier. We never
saw the sun, but the *Monsoon* danced most beautifully
between her two anchor cables. We played cards and
waited. It was just the same on Easter Monday and the
day after, and it was not till the Wednesday that the
seas seemed to have quietened down sufficiently for us
to try to reach the village with the engine.

Stubbe and Jan began to work. They discovered a
native schoolmaster who guided them to a cove where
they found wonderful giant prawns which unfortunately

had to end their lives in the formalin jar instead of in Sonny's stockpot. The little animals were sacred and the schoolmaster tried to conjure them with a magic formula, but was not successful. He expressed regret that his sojourn in the mission school had presumably robbed the words of some of their original power and genius; but whatever the reason may have been, the fact remained that the deer little animals had to be hauled out of their hiding places with a net instead of coming out voluntarily and letting themselves be stroked.

The village was fairly large. Its two hundred inhabitants lived in straw huts of the dingy, shut-in Melanesian type which, compared with the clean, friendly houses of the Polynesians, give an excellent picture of the contrast between these two so different races. When the Vatuleleans had got over their shyness of the strange, white men, they were cheerful and hospitable. They invited us to paw-paws and bananas and the schoolmaster asked us to go over the school, where children of from six to fourteen were taught in the same room. The teacher jumped from one peak of learning to the other, Mount A B C, Mount Copperplate and Mount Mental Arithmetic. Every now and again a wet handkerchief rolled up into a ball flew through the air like a cannonball and landed on the head of one of the small ones, who preferred pinching his neighbour to drawing a palm tree or a capital R on his slate.

A monotonous thumping came from all the huts in the village as though a thousand woodpeckers were holding a conference. It was the women preparing tapa, that homespun material which used to constitute Polynesia's clothing, but which is now used partly to decorate their huts and partly to be sold in the shops of the large tourist centres. It is manufactured by beating the bark of the paper-mulberry into thin strips, which are then placed side by side and hammered into a white, papery substance. This is then painted with colours extracted from clay, soot and plants in beautiful primitive colours.

My presence in the village did not pass unnoticed. The tapa beaters laid down their wooden clubs and came into the openings of their doors to have a look. They came a little nearer, and finally a fat, flat-nosed woman plucked up her courage and told me a long story in Vatulelean. I nodded and said "Yes," but should have said "No." You see, it was an invitation to a little dancing under the breadfruit trees.

The spectators clapped their hands and looked expectant and the woman trotted round me like a baby elephant on hot bricks. She seized me and I made an honest but vain endeavour to encircle her waist. Happily the Vatulelean folk dances are not difficult. They consist of a series of good, old black-bottom steps repeated *ad lib.* till the music stops. I used to be a devil at the black-bottom and we got on splendidly because I kept on whistling—mentally—one of the wanton tunes of those days.

This became rather monotonous and I inquired with eyebrows, hands and feet whether she had no other dances in her repertoire. Then two of the women performed a mighty war dance with clubs. They wore vast curtains round their stomachs and jumped about like pedestrians who have got in the way of a cyclist. When it was over and the dancers had lain down puffing and groaning in the shade of the breadfruit trees, the assembled company asked me to show them the Danish war dance.

I looked round for Stubbe and Jan, but as they were

apparently nowhere in the neighbourhood, I plunged into a dance that would have drawn furious protests from all the Officers' Clubs and Peace Societies of Denmark had I danced it there and associated it with our army and navy. It was an improvised mixture of hornpipe, crakoviac, mazurka, charleston and tap dance combined with such steps as come into your head when you trip over a root or your own foot. Any teacher of dancing would have fainted with disgust before the dance was half over, but my spectators clapped their hands madly, which all goes to show that only among primitive peoples can you find a real conception of what true art is and what is bad imitation and false finery. They shouted: "Vinaigre, vinaigre," a word that has nothing to do with vinegar, but which means more or less the same as *da capo*.

Heavens, what a time we had! Our scientists returned from hunting their prawns and beetles and joined the family circle. We ate yams and cooked paw-paws and spent the afternoon looking at the tapa decorations and playing with the young of the village.

It was a variety performance of the first class, and when we left we were all three experts in the Vatulele dance, only Jan was apt to get stuck, because he was ticklish and completely unmusical. Stubbe and I gave a performance of rheinländers and schottisches that was perfect in form and unison, while Jan clapped his hands and tried to put us out of step with a wooden drum. We were fetched away at four o'clock and got aboard dripping wet and with pockets full of dance invitations for the rest of the crew.

That evening Jan developed a genius for character dances. Kalle perspired, and Jack, stamping on the bamboo floor, performed the dance of the Faroes. We plied the ladies with chewing-gum and Sonny tried to find out what "last voyage" was called in Vatulelean; and if the mate had not let go of his girl at twelve o'clock and cast a stern glance at us and his watch, we would certainly still be dancing in the schoolmaster's house on Vatulele.

Between dances ethnographica and insects had been collected. Vatulele was actually the first place where it had been possible to buy old originals for reasonable prices and Mr. Möller took the opportunity to become possessed of the village's large, hollow wooden drum for the sum of four shillings. We bought a sack of meal and took it on board packed in scarves and oilskins, while the mate talked and gesticulated with a native pilot on the question of the way out.

The storm had not lessened appreciably, but it was drawing near the time when the dock was to be free, so that we had to be thinking of getting back to Suva and civilization. We came safely through the passage and tacked against the storm towards Viti Levu. It was hard work. Visibility was poor and the sea ran high. There were coral islands on either side of us and the man in the look-out almost had to stare the eyes out of his head. We kept well out into open water and only reached Suva after a day and a half.

The dock was not yet free, but after a day or two we were hauled up at last and painted from keel to rail with a glistening red patent paint, the mere sight of which sent worms and barnacles scurrying in all directions. The entire crew went on a farewell picnic with their rediscovered girls, while Mr. Möller, Jan and I looked after the freshly painted ship.

That day I received a telegram from my eldest and only daughter informing me that she had arrived in the world on 31st May and regretted my absence. This news lifted a weight from the skipper's heart, for the nice fellows had persuaded him that I had been presented with twins who were to be named after him, and he was still shaking his head and had not quite recovered from the shock when we put out to sea with a cleaned bottom, stopped leaks and freshly painted from stem to stern.

Tears were shed on the quay and the faithless sailors waved to Emma, Margaret, Tilla, Agnes, Joan and all the others, but their handkerchiefs were all too dry. Suva was soon only a little speck with white walls and red roofs astern and the same evening a mighty blue whale came alongside to take a look at the weather and blow.

It was grey and dull with a fine rain and for several days on end it was impossible to take an observation. The wind and the current drove us off our course, and when one day the wind turned into a storm, neither skipper nor mate knew exactly where we were. The horizon was a wall of opaque squalls of rain and the storm howled so that we could hardly hear breakers more than a few ships' lengths away. We had reefed the mainsail and foresail—the first time in the voyage that we had taken a reef in any sail. The mainsail became tattered, was torn from footrope to gaff, and the remnants secured with difficulty.

It was difficult to remain upright on the slippery deck. The *Monsoon* tossed and rolled in the heavy seas and continually shipped water. The rain was heavy and continuous. A wave towered up and bringing down the storm-jib sent it the same road as the mainsail, but at that moment the sun showed its benevolent face again in a tear in the clouds and we could take an observation and were able to determine where we were. We sighted the reef and sailed slowly northwards towards the entrance to Noumea.

We breathed a sigh of relief as the pilot came on board, and then we put on our white things and pretended to be tourists, as Noumea appeared behind L'Ile de Nou, the island of the deported, which has given the name of New Caledonia such a bad reputation in European ears.

CHAPTER XIX

We hold judgment on a Cinderella, see toothless mass-murderers, meet old Julius from Roholte and benefit by his wisdom before we escape after much unpleasantness

"I<small>F</small> that vagabond ship's officer, Pierre Loti, had not fallen in love with one of the lazy girls that hang about the quay at Papeete, New Caledonia would perhaps to-day be the Queen of the South Seas, the harbour at Noumea the goal of the floating tourists' hotels and the whole colony a flourishing paradise. But he did, and now there is only the smoke of the large steamers to be seen on the horizon as they tear in breathless haste to Tahiti with their rich passengers, those Australians, English and French who go there to say 'Isn't it cute' and 'Magnifique' of the mountain lake in which Loti presumably never bathed, to look at the stones on which he sat with the girl Raruha and to wallow in cheap sentiment with a flower behind their ear and a whining ukulele or two in the neighbourhood. Tourist stuff and old women's nonsense!

"New Caledonia, on the other hand—that is a prison, a place where they send their dirty pickpockets and bestial murderers, and that is all. That at least is what the tourist bureaux tell you and even our Petite Larousse only mentions our island as a place for deportation, and the hotelkeepers in Papeete rub their greasy hands while harbour and town are coining money, and all because stupid people believe stories which in either case have lost all connexion with reality and have not the least to do with either the Tahiti or the New Caledonia of to-day. Is that justice? Do you think that we ought to go on being content to be stepchildren? Look for yourself, Monsieur!"

The pilot pointed to the entrance of Noumea, embraced the whole country in a picturesque gesture and interrupted his charming flow of grievances to let Nature herself speak to the foreigner in her gentlest tones.

As an outsider you smiled a little at the man's zeal; but all the same the urgent appeal of his words forced you to take the task of judge thus imposed on you with the greatest seriousness. New Caledonia is France's Cinderella and Tahiti her proud, spoiled sister. New Caledonia has no Prince to take her by the hand and lead her into the ballroom. Loti could have been that Prince, but he was only a dreamer and never saw the gold that glittered beside the hearth.

It was an early morning in the middle of June. Astern lay the blue-black of the Pacific where during the last few days our small boat had been tossed about like a rubber ball. It still stuck its white tongues out at us and thundered against the reef in roaring protest at our having escaped from its rough treatment.

Inside the reef the water was green, clear and quiet like a mirror. We were in the lagoon. In front of us lay Noumea and behind it green hills and steep slopes clad with giant, strange araucaria trees; small islands detached themselves from the compact mass of the main island as we approached and the high mountain chain which forms the island's spine rose up in the background like a distant jagged contour of mist behind a veil of shaded lilac.

The sky was a sparkling blue and it was warm and fresh at the same time, as it is in the north at midsummer. The climate of New Caledonia—there is no better in the tropics—is like that practically the whole year round, and it possesses, besides, such great natural beauty and so rich a variety in the character of its landscapes that you must admit that it surpasses the far smaller island of Tahiti in these two respects.

L'Ile de Nou lies at the entrance to the roads of Noumea like a cork in the neck of a bottle. It is flat and bare; here and there are some old ruined buildings reflecting their melancholy grey walls in the water, lost in deep meditation on the past. This little island is New Caledonia's child of sorrow. It looks so small on the map and compared with the main island disappears altogether, but it has still been able to cast a deep shadow over the name of the colony so that at the mention of New Caledonia a whole world thinks only of the small L'Ile de Nou, its dreary prisons, its murderers and its hungry and inexorable guillotine.

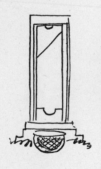

Novel writers know only L'Ile de Nou and in Paris the name of New Caledonia is spoken with a shudder. All that is a terrible handicap for the hard-working pioneers of the colony whose only crime has been that they sought with their bare hands to win gold on the other side of the world for their distant country. The first pioneers of New Caledonia died forgotten by their own countrymen, and are immortalized only by the memorials they themselves erected in the shape of prosperous plantations and productive mines.

Forty years have passed since the bagnios closed their doors behind the last of the deported, and the executioner wiped his bloody hands clean on his trousers before going to plant yams and fight with the maquis, but during the years between, the cold, dark shadow has lain over New Caledonia, throttling it. The colony has still not been cleared of the crimes it never committed.

During the Great War no French peasant dared to give quarters to troops from New Caledonia. They expected a crowd of murderers with conditional pardons, at the best a wild horde of black cannibals, and there arrived a regiment of white Frenchmen, peasants like themselves, only with more calloused hands won in a fierce struggle for a greater France. They had come home to fight for their country and were received by a population that in sheer confusion and ignorance did not know what to say or do.

Such a reception made for bitterness and this bitterness revived again when, after their return from the bloodshed of war, the colonists heard that Tahiti was symbolized as a wondrously beautiful woman on the huge picture map of the French possessions at the Paris exhibition, that Morocco had been given the figure of a proud Arab and that the Congo was represented by a smiling negro with bundles of radiant fruits, while a convict in bagnio dress and with chains on his feet straddled all the seventeen thousand square kilometres of fertile country and all the industrious inhabitants of New Caledonia. After forty years!

Apart from its evil reputation, New Caledonia has only two mementoes of the deportation days. The one is the discharged prisoners who either had not the desire or the means to leave the colony and its wonderful climate, and the few who are not yet pardoned and never will be, the incorrigibles. But their number is dwindling so rapidly that in comparison with the "honest" population it is as good as nil. You meet them now and again in the street, age-old men overgrown with beard and dirt, with sacks on their backs and quite incapable of as much as harming a kitten, however much they could terrify a town or a country with murders and arson in their exciting youth. You give them a cigarette in the same way as you toss a piece of bread to a toothless animal in a menagerie, and their humble thanks has a paradoxical effect when compared with the background of their former raging and brutal dominion in the jungles of the city.

These greybeards are seventy, eighty and ninety years old. Most of them are housed in the hospital's poor-ward and in a few years the last of them will have gone to take his stand before the greatest judgment seat of all.

The other memento which the colony is compelled to preserve is incomparably more active and dangerous. It is the Nessadiou valley. There in the middle of the most hopeless and impenetrable maquis they tried to cultivate the ground with convict labour. They portioned out lots and gave them buildings and implements, but a farm without a woman's hand on the field and in the house is condemned to death in advance, and so those prisoners who were conditionally pardoned were allowed to marry. No free girl wanted to tie herself up with a criminal and the natives shunned them like the plague. What was one to do?

They emptied Saint-Lazare, the worst female prison in Paris, and sent its content of child murderesses, harlots and procuresses to Noumea by steamer and from there farther up country to the colonists in the Nessadiou valley.

The oldest of them are still living there, but are pardoned. They had children, and their children were brought up in the atmosphere which results when Saint-Lazare is given in marriage to L'Ile de Nou with the blessing of the church and of those investigating heredity. Their traditions are continued, their instincts inherited and absorbed; and that is why the Nessadiou valley to-day forms a feverish element in the healthy blood of New Caledonia, filled to bursting with innate evil and devilish in its acquired cunning.

In nine out of ten cases when a crime is brought to the notice of the court in Noumea or the police in a country district, the direct or indirect originator can be tracked to this tainted valley. It is only recently that the French Government has realized that you cannot reap corn where you have sown thistles.

Yet the Nessadiou valley is only an isolated phenomenon, a slum district which is small in comparison to the size of the colony. The voluntary colonization is so infinitely more important. It has its own rude romance, entirely different from the savage, perverse criminal cult which surrounds L'Ile de Nou. It is grey, steep and blunt, stands with both feet deep in the red tropical earth and thus is overlooked by all.

Both the State and private enterprise indulged in a ruthless propaganda to induce people to go there. They were promised gold and green woods, and given impenetrable maquis from which a profit could only be wrung after years of struggle and endless difficulty. Many turned back when they saw the unvarnished truth, but those who stayed gave New Caledonia the best a man has to give—youth, confidence, freedom and the sweat of their brow. They were given stones for bread, and returned thanks with pure gold.

All over the large island lie insignificant little Frenchmen in insignificant little graves. Over their homely coffins lies the island's rich soil and above their last resting place the trades sing their eternal song in the fertile plantations, cattle graze in hundreds of thousands in the wide fields, and from the mines and shafts of the north island busy hands bring chromium, cobalt and, above all, nickel to the light of day. It is a song of work that rises from New Caledonia, a homely simple hymn of the earth; more valuable than the tinkling of Tahiti's guitars, but less regarded. The island offers a future for hands that are accustomed to toil and work, while Tahiti has oblivion and sweet melodies for him who wishes to throw off his grey trammels for a day, an hour, or the rest of his life. It has a future to offer those who are work's veterans and those who have not been able to find the so-highly-prized happiness of work and duty.

Cinderella and her lazy sister have mentalities as different as water and sweet champagne, and that is why it is so difficult to judge between them, which is the first thing you are asked to do when you step on to the quay at Noumea, if, as in our case, the pilot has not already put the question.

There are two things which, from the tourist's point of view, speak strikingly in Tahiti's favour—the town and the natives. New Caledonia's climate, its nature and its white population are capable of a decisive victory in competition with Tahiti; but the town! Papeete is full of swarming life, muted music and an almost intangible charm. The evening in Papeete lasts till the morning. Life is beautiful and not a moment of it is wasted, so long as bougainvillaea and jasmin fill the night air with their narcotic sweetness.

Samoan house

Samoan Islanders waiting for the new Governor

Noumea is poor and miserable. By day it is revoltingly disconsolate and dirty, with low, neglected and
ruined houses, dirty streets and weathered statues of
admirals in magnificent full-dress, and nameless, full-
bosomed women without a dress, in its overgrown parks.
Little, doll-like Japanese servant girls in gaily coloured
batik sarongs glide in and out of the grey houses like
butterflies that have strayed into a ruined factory where
they vainly look for flowers among the dust and cobwebs.
Noumea at eight o'clock in the evening looks like
Pompeii before the excavations. All the windows are
covered with heavy shutters that permit no ray of light
to escape. There are cinemas, but they show no films.
There are street lamps, but they do not burn. The only
mitigating circumstances are a couple of dirty bars where
one can get drunk without any refinements in the shape
of dancing, music or any kind of cheeriness.

Then there is the steamer from Sydney—if it happens
to come. People go to the steamer in Noumea as they
do to the nine-o'clock in a small village station, gape a
bit, stare at the lanterns on the companionway till they
are dazzled and then go home in the belief of having
had an experience.

Once a month there is a ball in the Hôtel de Ville, in
the large room that leads out into the small garden.
The Town Hall's good name does not suffer by these
balls, where the young girls of the town warm the
benches, dance with deference and modesty or refresh
themselves with a lemonade, while their mothers with
moustaches and lynx-eyes scan the room to its farthest
corner—till the band packs up its instruments at a proper
hour, and Jeanne and Angèle would really love to be
taken home by Gaston and Marcel under the nice, round

moon, which curiously enough shines with the same gentle glow on both Papeete and Noumea.

New Caledonia is more provincial than the most out-of-the-way spot in the most out-of-the-way corner in France, for the spirit of modernity penetrates but weakly there. Socially they still live in the conditions of 1900 and gentlemen still dance in high collars and glacé gloves that are slightly too large, at the balls of the rifle club and working men's association. Here, as in France, Paris is the constant topic of conversation and its boulevards are the dream of all the small people. It is there they will meet when the official has his six months' leave after five years and the colonist and bank agent have saved enough money to get through a year's income in a week in one of the numerous "dancings" of Montmartre. Then they will feel that they have had something from their savings and amused themselves royally.

While for them the city of Paris is something incorporeal, the symbol of joy and all that they have left behind, the Colonial Office there is real enough. It is the source of eternal astonishment and the mother of all the little wrinkles and grey hairs which make the small man appear older than he is. If you turn the conversation on to the government when talking with a New Caledonian, you will not need to say much for the next hour or two. He will complain of how a few men in Paris waste his hard-earned money. The influence which the island's own children have in the administration of the colony is practically nil. Mr. Stick-in-the-mud and Mr. Bureaucrat sit side by side in a magnificent office and bite their nails during office hours, and in the meantime everything goes wrong. They built a bridge. The piers were cast with the greatest care in accordance with inaccurate calculations sent in a blue envelope from the engineer in Paris, whence the metal parts were also sent ready made. The iron arch of the bridge proved to be nearly three feet too short.

Six railway engines were ordered for the island's pride, its thirty-mile-long railway, and on arrival were found to be of the wrong gauge. When they were still considering whether to re-lay the thirty miles of rails or whether they should send the useless engines on the long, expensive road back to Marseilles, a high official discovered that his new mistress lived on the other side of a stream, so that he had to go a long way round whenever he wished to visit the beauty in her home. The high official was neither a long-jumper nor a long-distance runner; neither was he gifted with patience or a burning zeal to overcome great difficulties for the sake of his beloved, hence—an elegant, stylish little bridge costing the bagatelle of 200,000 of the taxpayers' francs. With the best will in the world it could not lead you anywhere else than just to the beloved's house, and as the high official would certainly not have appreciated it if it had been used too frequently, one may presume that his memory will be kept alive in people's minds for many years to come yet.

Those are perhaps only trifles in a country's budget, but for people who pay the piper with savings from their stockings, such trifles create discord. The Stavisky affair, whose eddies even reached New Caledonia, enriched the vocabulary of the small French saver with a whole number of new acquisitions and at the same time has given the words of the New Caledonian as he reflects over an aperitif, a hard metallic ring, not unlike the ring of the nickel they tear from the grasp of god cobalt in

the north end of the island in hard struggle with earth and mountain.

No—the town is not laughing and carefree like Papeete, and neither are the natives. Perhaps they are judged too harshly, for one should never let the first impression of a person or a country be decisive; but the Melanesian type of humanity is so gloomy, so dirty and dark-skinned  that you remember with an involuntary sigh the cheerful, clean, thoughtless children of all ages in Polynesia— their smiles, their laughter and their entire freedom from all distrust.

The land of darkness begins in New Caledonia. From here Melanesia stretches out its tentacles into the north, across the fever-ridden hell of the New Hebrides and the Solomon Islands, in whose forests fantastic orgies with human flesh as their centre are still celebrated, up to hot, devilish New Guinea, whose pathless interior hides riddles and horrors which no white man has seen without paying for it with his life.

Now the Kanakas of New Caledonia are civilized enough in comparison to their brethren in the north. They learn French in the schools and mostly belong to one of the creeds through which one may be saved; but one may expect that any day the sheepskin will fall from the wolf's shoulders and then there will be gaps in the ranks of the whites, which will not be closed again so soon, however many punitive massacres the government organizes.

In 1878 two hundred policemen and colonists were killed with their wives and children. Two hundred houses and the fields about them were destroyed, and only nineteen people are reported to have been wounded. These figures give an eloquent picture of the ferocity with which the war was waged; and it is quite safe to presume that no small percentage of those killed finished their existence over the fire of one of the native tribes.

The natives again raised their heads in 1917 when nearly all the whites of military age had departed for the battlefields of Europe, but this time there is absolutely no indication of the losses suffered by the whites. The rebellion is not even mentioned in any of the books on New Caledonia that I have seen, and if the conversation is brought round to it, the white citizens of Noumea begin to talk of something else. It must be hushed up; it has nothing to do with the outside world; but all the same I will tell you as shortly as I can what I managed to find out about it.

It is known with some certainty that the Kanakas lost well over a thousand men. The French authorities in Noumea allied themselves with a large, friendly tribe, set a price of twenty francs on the head of every rebel and promised two thousand five hundred francs to the man who brought to Noumea the head of the chieftain who was the leader of the rebellion. In the course of a short time more than eight hundred black heads were delivered to the Town Hall in sacks dripping with blood. An eyewitness, with whom I spoke, told me of the revolting, sinister scenes that were enacted as the heads were counted and the grinning blacks paid their day's wages. There is, however, no need to go into details; they are more suited to a medical journal than to a decent travel book.

The rebel chieftain's head was also brought to market and its price paid in clinking coin. A pardoned Arab convict who used to go daily to the chieftain's village, where out of pity they gave him food and shelter, stabbed his benefactor in the back one evening and escaped unnoticed from the village with the head he had cut off, in a cloth under his arm.

War is war, and one should not interfere in colonial politics; but am I really the only one who is so sentimental as to feel a slight twinge of conscience at the way in which this primitive man died—a man who fought to drive a foreign race out of territory of which they had seized possession without asking the permission of its rightful owners or making the slightest move to offer them any compensation? From any point of view religion, disease and slavery can hardly be regarded as sufficient compensation for the loss of a country! And then heads cut off and dripping blood——! In a public building occupied by white men and in the twentieth century!

No! Pierre Loti was right. Judgment must be given in Tahiti's favour. In spite of tourist steamers and souvenir shops it is still a land of dreams, while New Caledonia is reality and hard work for one's daily bread, although in a setting that in many respects is superior to much-praised Tahiti.

There were only two Danes in Noumea. One was called Mortensen, came from Bornholm and was formerly the manager of a large plantation. The other was Julius Petersen, "old man Julius" to the whole of Melanesia and one of the few who turned their plantations into cash at the right time before the price of copra fell with the speed and the destructive effect of an avalanche.

Petersen took us for trips in his car and showed us the beautiful island which has become his new country, whilst he gave our scientists many a tip and valuable advice for their coming journey to the wild tribes of the

New Hebrides. We sat in his comfortable dining-room and heard tales of cannibals and black magic, of soil that was as impregnated with tetanus germs as the flies with malaria; and he sat in our cabin and spoke of sealing with Indian hunters, typhoons in the China Seas and of stranding on the Japanese coast where little geishas with cherry-blossoms in their hair taught the cobbler's son from Roholte Japanese.

Petersen helped us to find a diver to stop a leak which the *Monsoon* had sprung during the difficul voyage round the southern point of New Caledonia; and he was tireless when it came to helping Mr. Möller with the chandlers and guiding him through the labyrinth of the French language. The only thing which he was unable to conjure up was a restaurant with lights, dancing and music, where we could take leave of the blessings of civilization before our long voyage into the unknown began.

We were warned against visiting a night club that lay in the mountains some few miles away and which was conducted by the optimistic offspring of a convict. Five minutes after we had been warned, Kalle, Stubbe, Jack and I sat in a swaying car which tore along in the direction of the night club at a speed far in excess of all speed limits. As we rattled up to the house all the guests, both male and female, vanished like rats through side doors and narrow passages. We were alone with the proprietor.

He took a few steps towards us and looked like Lon Chaney in one of his more unbelievable make-ups. He asked us why we had come. His voice smacked of L'Ile de Nou and his words were far from academic. He was told that we neither wished to play with his scrubby

beard nor pull his corkscrew straight; that we merely
wanted a glass of red wine, beer, or lemonade, just something that was long and cheap while enjoying his pleasant
company and the gracious charm of his conversation.

He was, however, not susceptible to empty flattery.
He had nothing of what we had asked for, only served
champagne—some glasses on the rats' tables spoke
eloquently of near beer—and the champagne cost so much
the bottle, cash and paid in advance.

I am afraid that I answered him in slightly impure
French which was not very suited to the expedition's
flag; at any rate I remember one or two of my trimmings
for the designations "shark" and "vampire." Stubbe
nodded in approval of my zoological choice, while Jack
began to roll up his sleeves and Kalle's eyes blinked—
but we were many miles away from law and order and
the rats were beginning to come back. It was pitch
dark on every side and we began to feel that it was time
to be moving.

Our retreat was carried out according to the best stra-
tegical principles—to the accompaniment of a continual
exchange of exploding shells. Then our diplomatic
chauffeur started his engine and a flying bottle rang out
a farewell on our rear mudguard. It was a beer bottle.

We longed for the savages of the New Hebrides.

The newspapers in Noumea were no more reliable than
elsewhere. They called the *Monsoon* a dainty yacht and
the old girl was so pleased that she nearly burst a couple
of planks. The diver had nailed a copper plate over the
leak and it grinned on the waterline like a shining gold
tooth.

We gradually got ready to start. The pilot came aboard

and ran us nicely aground on a mudbank a few yards from the shore. Stubbe swam ashore with a lifeline round his waist and we were hauled from our couch by a lorry and fifty natives. Then we rammed a crane and finally had to anchor in the middle of the entrance to the harbour because the engine had gone on strike.

The mate perspired, hammered and swore, and an hour later we did escape from the narrow entrance and sailed inside the reef southwards to the island of Ouen, where we took a room for the night in a little bay.

The next morning we ran through the Havannah Passage and sailed to the Loyalty Group, the islands Maré, Lifou and Ouvéa—which lie one-two-three in a straight line from north to south.

CHAPTER XX

*We visit lepers, see a pair of unsuccessful Siamese twins
and prepare ourselves to meet the gourmands
of the South Seas*

THE Loyalty Group is a French native reserve and special permission is required from the governor in Noumea before these three small islands may be visited, a fact which has in many respects protected their inhabitants from the unhappy influence of the European.

For the last nine years the Loyalty Islands had been under the control of Dr. Tivollier. This young doctor and his charming wife came to the islands as residents for a period of five years. They fell in love with the place and when their time was up asked to be allowed to return for a further period. As very few French officials experience the desire to play Robinson Crusoe on a remote, isolated island, their request was granted on the spot and Tivollier returned to his subjects and friends on Lifou.

We shall always have pleasant memories of this curious man and his home. He was an idealist, but personally in no way an original or an eccentric. He had an inherent tact and a psychological sense which never failed him, and the natives loved him. They waved to him as he tore over the indescribably bad forest roads in his red Citröen, and he knew them all by name and waved back. He spoke their language and settled their quarrels with each other with the wisdom of a Solomon. He was tireless in his work of trying to improve their hygienic conditions

234

with the miserable means the government put at his disposal.

Lifou is a kind of earthly Paradise where there live tall, stalwart men who are definitely more of Polynesian than Melanesian origin; but there is a snake in the grass among the flowers and its name is leprosy. Elephantiasis, tuberculosis, syphilis and leprosy are the worst plagues of the South Seas Islands, and leprosy is the worst of them for it necessitates lifelong isolation in special colonies and is really incurable. To all intents and purposes nothing is known of the way in which the disease spreads. The bacillus is known, but there is no knowledge of how it forces its way into the body and gradually eats it up alive.

Early one morning, as the sun was rising, Dr. Tivollier took Mr. Möller and myself for a drive through the island. We left Mr. Möller to shoot pigeons and flying-foxes in the forest and I accompanied Tivollier on his round of the leper colony at Chila. I think that I may say that I benefited the most from the expedition.

For three hours we walked from one hut to another along a broad, well-kept road. In front of the huts were little gardens with wonderful flowers, but behind the walls was disease, disfigurement and death. The moment a case of leprosy is confirmed in a village, the unhappy wretch is separated from his family and friends and taken to Chila where his family builds him a house. He is allowed to look for a new wife from among the other patients or to have himself adopted by a leper family if he should be too young for marriage or should there be no unmarried women in the colony at the time. The patients, luckily enough, do not take the internment as seriously as a European would. They quickly make themselves at home and resign themselves to their new surroundings.

Tivollier goes twice a week in his little car to give the patients experimental injections and each time brings small presents with him, giving them flower seeds and awarding prizes out of his own pocket for the most beautiful garden and the best-kept home. The government puts twenty thousand francs at his disposal each year and with this sum he has to buy medicines, pay three warders and give his patients little additions to their daily vegetarian diet, such as sugar and meat. That makes approximately a hundred francs for each of the odd two hundred patients, which is not much in comparison to the millions that are spent in looking after the sick in other countries.

For three hours we went from hut to hut, for three hours Dr. Tivollier showed me the progress of the disease, from the moment that it first breaks out, the slow rotting of the flesh right up to merciful death. During those three hours I saw the ghost of leprosy in the eyes of these broken people and could almost hear its horrible laughter at the impotence of man.

The huts in Chila have no chimneys. The door is the only means of ventilation, and in the one dark, sooty room there burns a log fire the smoke of which makes your eyes burn and smart, until you have grown accustomed to it. The floor is strewn with small pieces of coral on which are stretched one or two straw mats. That constitutes the entire furniture. The lepers lie on the mats, and as most of them are naked no sign of their disease is hidden from the doctor, their family or the occasional visitor.

A woman lifted her head from the mat and bared her

teeth in a white, friendly smile and moved her lips in wordless greeting. Her throat was affected. She had no roof to her mouth and her vocal chords had long since disappeared. She breathed with a rattling noise in her throat and her neck was covered with fresh sores. She was completely dumb. We smiled back and even a grimace so difficult to make can be a smile at such a moment.

A man raised his arm in greeting. All the fingers of his right hand had gone and on his left there was only the thumb left. The entire upper part of his body was a confusion of hard growths.

Death works slowly but surely in Chila. One day it takes a finger and the next a hand, and a month later comes to fetch a foot or an ear—and so the destruction goes on step by step with the patient himself as the passive spectator of the revolting drama. We walked on and on, and everywhere there was the same misery, the same decaying of the living flesh. However, I shall not weary the reader with snapshots of this waiting-room of death.

As we walked back through the village the lepers streamed out from the huts. They had got themselves up as for a feast, with streaks of paint on cheek and brow, and brightly coloured ribbons of pandanus fibre in a ring round their shoulders. They came limping and swaying up to honour the doctor and his unannounced guest who came from the strange lands on the other side of the forest.

Twenty leper children were stationed in front of the school, two big boys blew a fanfare on trumpets, and the leper teacher stepped forward, nervously crushing his old,

torn hat between his two crippled hands and made me a speech. He stuttered out his French, the words tumbling over his inflamed lips, while tears stood in his eyes. He thanked me for bringing a little change into the lepers' monotonous lives, told me that my visits to the huts would never be forgotten and begged me to think kindly of Chila now and then when I had gone.

They wanted to pray for me.

What does one answer such a man? What comfort can words give a leper audience. A few miserable expressions, a few empty sentences can so poorly express one's thoughts and sympathy, and it is difficult to retain the illusion of the superiority of the white races, when you stand face to face with people whose sufferings and resignation have raised them to heights that but few of us would reach without giving up the struggle half-way. Some would have answered with a quotation from the Bible, others with bravado. I could only thank them quietly and calmly; thank them for the feelings of friendship I felt all about me, as one does instinctively with dumb animals; thank them because they had shown me how far patient resignation to an evil fate can take a man.

Then the leper children sang a parting song. Their song was tuneful and rhythmical, with that underground of savagery and tenderness which you find so often in the music of primitive peoples. When you shut your eyes, it sounded like a hymn to life sung by happy children, but when you opened them you saw a crowd of ugly gnomes with distorted features on which the disease had set its stamp.

Behind them lay the school, a small, white building

where the children learned all the things they would never use and where they heard of countries they would never come to see. An enthusiastic scholar had written in white chalk on the dark doorway: "Vive l'Ecole de Chila!" The effect in such a place was naïve and sinister. Long live the school! Long live teaching! Long live everything, but not he who had put that inscription there in his joy at the little life that flickered in his body.

"Ave vita—morituri te salutant!"

The lepers posted themselves at the entrance, while Dr. Tivollier and I washed our hands and then disinfected them. We wiped our shoes on a mat which reeked of carbolic and climbed into the little car. Once more we were driving towards the sun-drenched forest which closed behind us like a protective curtain between death and life. We were still able to hear the lepers singing for a while, then everything grew quiet and we heard only the hum of the engine and the soft chirping of the birds in the bushes.

I spread out my fingers, clenched my fists, looked at my feet and carefully stroked the smooth skin of my cheeks with the palms of my hands. When I moved my toes in my shoes, I could feel them all. They were alive and obeyed my orders. I could see, even when I closed one eye, and I could speak. I functioned like a well-oiled machine. I was healthy.

Chila is a lesson you never forget. It casts a new and brighter light on the sun, the sea and your health; and all the trifles to which you pay no attention in your daily life grow large and stand out from the background in which, till then, they had led a quiet existence. It is not only the melody of life you hear, but also the delicate harmonies of its accompaniment.

✳

The days of our stay on Lifou passed in a flash. Native divers worked for us on the coral reef and brought many sea-slugs and other strange things to light. Our best diver was the chieftain's son and he refused all mention of payment with head thrown proudly back. He was twenty-five years old, his body was like a bright bronze statue and he was as handsome as Apollo. When he worked, he played, and every now and again he would forget to look for what he was supposed to be searching. Mr. Möller's reproaches poured from him like water from a duck's back, partly because he understood no English and partly because he was completely indifferent to all the commanding voices in the world as long as the water was warm and playing nicely on the reef.

It was full moon during those days on Lifou, and we used to sit on Tivollier's veranda and watch the silhouette of the large banyan tree against the night sky, while the moon hung like a huge lantern among the black tangle of its branches. The days were hot and we threw off our clothes and went about in bathing-drawers or handkerchiefs. Native fishermen splashed about near us on the reef, spearing cuttle-fish and biting them to death, burying their white teeth deep in the grey, slimy flesh while the many suckers wound round their necks and shoulders.

We made the most of those sunny days because we knew that it was our last farewell to the brown inhabitants of Polynesia, and because we knew from hearsay of the damp, unhealthy air which we would be breathing between the New Hebrides and the Solomon Islands.   Still, the time to say good-bye came.   Dr. Tivollier went with us as far as Ouve where he had a visit to make and, after we had put him ashore on the low coral island and done a little business with the natives, we sailed on to Vila, the largest and only town in the New Hebrides and the clearing port for the group.

The last that we saw of Dr. Tivollier was a small black speck on the shore of the island whose former white official had shot himself, driven mad by the loneliness—the loneliness that overtakes the white man who does not regard his brown subjects as human beings and feels helplessly deserted in a village which is filled from morning to night with the happy chatter of small children.   This loneliness Tivollier and his young wife had turned into an idyll, set in a frame of busy days in which their chief task was to mitigate the lot of the sick. May there be many like him in the South Seas!

Port Vila, or Fila as it is as often called, is the seat of that confused realm which goes by the name of "the English-French Condominium of the New Hebrides." The fact is that England and France have never been able to agree as to who should have these fertile islands with their unhealthy climate, and this has resulted in a compromise which has neither hand nor foot, costs much too much in comparison to the worth and production of the islands, and satisfies neither party.   The whites have put their stamp on the island of Efate with its town and harbour of Vila, and a dozen or so planters and traders hold the fort.

The relative strength of the two rival nations is most

unequal. France can mobilize 675,000 hectares of plantation land and more than a thousand whites, against Britain's 85,000 hectares and two hundred citizens. There are in addition the thousand coolies France imported from Tonkin and they, both as respects nationality and labour, weigh the scales down in favour of France. The struggle is waged bitterly behind the scenes, and particularly just now are the British furious with their government for giving them absolutely no benefit from subsidies, customs rebates, &c., while the French receive quite a substantial sum as bonus on their copra. The result of this is that the German, Scandinavian and other foreign planters who possess land in the New Hebrides and have till now been British subjects are trying to obtain French nationality and no one can be surprised at Marianne receiving them with open arms.

In Vila there is a customs house with one French and one English official. Post office, wireless station, hospitals and police force have similarly representatives of both nations, and each country has its own courts which judge cases brought before them by their respective subjects. Should a hotheaded Frenchman and a pigheaded Britisher quarrel about a piece of ground, they must haul each other before the Condominium Court. This is a mixed court composed of one English and one French judge, a Belgian plenipotentiary and a grandee from Spain who is supposed to hover above the waters as a kind of neutral, infallible supreme judge. Supposed to—for at the moment his exalted seat happens to be empty, because Bueno Esperanza (such was the promising name of the grandee) felt himself too old and toothless to clothe this responsible post. He went home to listen to the castagnettes and to drink sweet Madeira. The citizens do not miss him, for his large salary can be put to much better use.

The few shops that are in Vila will accept Australian, French and English coins and Bank of Indo-China notes, and as the rate of exchange is different for all four, it is understandable that you have to wait a considerable time before the Chinaman with his slow powers of comprehension has managed to work out on his childish abacus with its coloured marbles the exact price in shillings and centimes of a packet of Maryland cigarettes.  It is equally understandable that the French, who constitute eighty per cent. of the population, should be a little dissatisfied with having to grant the twenty per cent. of English every conceivable consideration; but what is completely incomprehensible is that all the clever diplomats have not been able to discover how to divide the islands in such a way as to satisfy all parties.

It is said that actually it is a matter of complete indifference to England but that the Commonwealth of Australia has got up on its hind legs over the matter, the reason being that Australia is very much afraid of Japan, and Japan has been concentrating on her fortified outposts in the Pacific. Whilst we are gossiping I will tell you, strictly between ourselves, that the Japanese for the last twenty years are said to have been smuggling Schneider rifles and chests of ammunition ashore for the cannibals on the north islands, and have been doing their best to stir up the already sufficiently troubled waters. The responsibility for this statement must rest with my informant; but the fact remains that on Malekula, for example, all the tribes are armed with one rifle a head and they know

how to use them. But I never saw who brought the rifles ashore.

Matters of high politics sometimes take narrow paths in the dark, and the future will show whether these paths have led to their goal.

The Europeans at any rate are very angry because the little yellow people are employing methods of which they, the whites, considered they had the monopoly. However, the government of the Condominium holds sway over the New Hebrides, though I cannot say whether it will continue to lead its luxurious existence for long.

The residents were a pair of quaint types, if one may describe two such solemn personages with so disrespectful an expression. The Englishman was small, had hollow cheeks, a furrowed face and a tiny Hitler moustache. He was neat and well dressed, as dry as a smoked cod, mumbled in his figurative beard and ceaselessly juggled and fiddled with a monocle. His secretary was like a chapter out of Kipling. The Frenchman was a plump little person with a large, extraordinary moustache, round cheeks, curly hair and button-boots with cloth sides. He was a bachelor and adored cats. When he appeared in full uniform with all his braid and orders, he was the living image of an animal tamer of the old school. He was as talkative as the Englishman was silent, and was as gushingly friendly as only a Frenchman can be to someone whom he meets to-day and forgets to-morrow.

The Frenchman lived on the heights behind the town from where he had a wonderful view over the harbour and the island of Iririki where Britain's representative resided in superior English seclusion. Yet the residencies are not the whole of Vila, but rather a sort of

Christmas-tree decoration which has been pasted on to it and which is not really at all suitable to this modest little town which consists of one street alongside the shore, two side streets and a dozen little alleyways, which try to look respectable but soon grow tired and climb on through the rough grass growing between the banyan and araucaria trees, if they do not give up the race and the ghost half-way.

No—Vila is one of the most primitive of the towns of European character that we came across during the voyage. It is still just as in Jack London's time, a Wild-West of the East. Primitive wooden huts line the streets and in front of every other one stands a saddled horse waiting for its master, the planter, who has ridden into town for a drink and to sell his copra. Above the entrance to every second house there hangs a sign on which is written in delicate, elaborate letters of gilt the word "Bar," but this small word with its promise of much merely hides a restaurant, a private dwelling or a laundry. They belong to an epoch when copra cost three thousand francs a ton, when cotton and coffee poured streams of gold over Vila and cacao and mother-of-pearl were better investments than the best Bank of England stock. The signs have not been taken down— but whether from laziness or in the steadfast hope that the golden age would come back again, one cannot say. At the present time there is not much probability of the latter.

Only ten years ago the price of copra was ten pounds a ton; now it has sunk to seven and a half and no longer repays the cost of working the plantation. None of the other products have fared any better. It is only four years since there were lights and feasting in Vila of

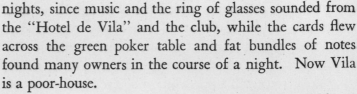

nights, since music and the ring of glasses sounded from the "Hotel de Vila" and the club, while the cards flew across the green poker table and fat bundles of notes found many owners in the course of a night. Now Vila is a poor-house.

Two colonists were sitting mournfully at a table in the club drinking thin Australian beer which they still further diluted with a jug of water. One of them looked like a tramp, but he still possessed some right to call himself the owner of a plantation. Poker and the lawyer had taken the other's plantation and its former owner was now trying to make his way as a combined ship- and produce-broker. That sounds grand, but wasn't.

Their shirts were darned and their trousers had done more than their duty, but their gestures were still grand and comprehensive. The wave of their hands when they offered us a seat at their table was princely and their hospitality that of a king. It was quite out of the question that we should pay for anything. We were their and Vila's guests and one bottle of beer followed another —without the jug of water.

"When we come to Denmark, you can treat us; but here you are our guests! Why the devil have you come so late? Four years ago we would have flooded the whole club in champagne in your honour; the band would have played; we would have let you win at poker and taken you out to our plantations and given you a time you would never have forgotten."

For the local patriot of Vila there is nothing on earth which surpasses it, except perhaps Paris, if you are content to regard that city as a holiday residence and go home before it begins to become boring—an El Dorado which becomes prosaic after a month. There is something touching in this swaggering local patriotism which raises its head so proudly, but is still as grateful as a small child for a kind word about the town—and that is difficult enough to find.

The New Hebrides Club reminded one of a ruined graveyard. *La Vie Parisienne* of 1911 still lay on the table in the excellent company of *L'Illustration* and the *Auckland Weekly,* while the books collected dust and the clock on the wall had stopped. Would it ever start ticking again? The landlord thought so, but he was an incurable optimist. He was a Swiss and a philosopher, and one evening, as we were playing billiards for a glass of beer in the deserted place, we started to talk of Schopenhauer. The landlord lost, but only because he brought Nietzsche into the discussion and got so heated about it that he played too hard.

Vila is not boring, even at the most boring time of day. It is a fire which has burned itself out, but it still smoulders strongly, and it will take much to put out the last of the embers. The year before the town had imported alcohol to the value of eight thousand pounds. As the natives are not allowed to drink anything but water and lemonade, that gives the sum of approximately £6 14s. 10d. a head, allowing old women of eighty as well as infants their full ration. What must the figures have been like when they still drank in Vila? It makes your throat dry to think of it!

At a dance held in the tennis club in connexion with the visit of the New Zealand cruiser *Diomede,* we had an opportunity of observing that the New Zealand fleet's sociability takes the same form as that of other countries' navies, namely, of inviting all the young girls and women in the town on board and leaving the men to sit at home and bite their nails. The officers call this returning hospitality, but the men call it "getting girls." But then sailors are always so vulgar.

The *Monsoon* did not stay long in this hybrid capital. We left as soon as we had all our papers and collector's licences—naturally with a mass of signatures in duplicate.

The mate had taken advantage of the opportunity and the general confusion to acquire a whole series of stamps, on which the value was printed in centimes and pence, for his newly started collection which occupied his thoughts day and night. He had started in a small way in Pago-Pago, was really keen by the time we reached Apia, and in Suva had bought a pair of tweezers and began to count the perforations. After that he was lost, and if you went on deck in the dark during the dog-watches and asked what the course was, you were liable to be given strange answers. In all probability he would reply: "One perforation too few in the right-hand corner," or simply: "A penny-halfpenny Fiji."

One evening scientists and crew drank the pledge of brotherhood in the club and rowed back singing across the silent bay to the ship. The *Diomede* gave a search-light display, and we took our revenge by showing them

just what our own large torch could do in the same line. We scored the greater success with the spectators on shore, and that was perhaps the reason why the *Diomede* began to morse like mad. We did not dare to take down what she was sending out. Our conscience was pricking us rather, for it suddenly occurred to us that we were a solemn Danish expedition with papers from the Foreign Office and respectable intentions; but luckily Mr. Möller had not seen us.

In the morning we weighed anchor and assumed

serious expressions. We were on the road to Cannibalistan; we were going to see the savages of the fairs at home and to find out in the interests of science whether it were true that they were covered all over their bodies with hen's feathers, smelt of isinglass and were fed three times an hour with raw meat and calves' lights. We were very excited.

Sonny sat on the edge of his bunk and tapped the rust off his gun.

CHAPTER XXI

Treats of champagne, God's motor-boat and a great
summer sale in a cannibal village

W<small>E</small> were heading north under full canvas with the trades
singing in the rigging, on past a smoking volcano whose
fiery glow was like the solemn overture to a fairy play,
and up on to the stage for the "Port Sandwich" act.

Port Sandwich lies on the south-east coast of Malekula
and its cheery names make you feel at home at once.
A "Murder River" flows into the bay and an innocent
little brook winds through "Massacre Valley" which is
all most encouraging for a crowd of tourists whom the
well-meaning have told that the place is the worst malaria
hell in the world, and that a scratch on the leg here
means a violent and unpleasant death from tetanus.

All these friendly warnings had one advantage however—they put our fear of the cannibals right into the
background, seeing that we expected to be dead before
we even had time to set foot on land to be killed and
eaten. But don't let us make these green fertile islands
out to be worse than they are, even though our fingers
are itching to tell hair-raising stories of the place, stories
for the truth of which we cannot vouch.

We got many scratches on our legs which we rubbed
nicely with infected earth, we were stung by myriads of
mosquitoes and had many a chat with a friendly cannibal,
but not one of us suffers from tetanus, malaria or a
missing head. The latter to be taken in its purely physical
sense, please!

If you rub a cat the wrong way, it scratches you, and if you tease a cannibal, he bites you. That is in the natural order of things. Speak nicely to a cannibal and do not go ashore armed to the teeth with revolvers, rifles and other weapons, which are terrifying and tempting at the same time, and he will do nothing to you.

It is many years since a white man has figured *innocently* on the menu in this *dangerous* part of the world. The last to do so were a British tax-collector and his assistant, who tried to take not only the Solomon Islanders' money but also their guns—so can you blame them? Haven't you yourself seen red when you opened the door and saw a buff envelope marked "Income Tax —Private" in the outstretched hand of the postman?

We must not judge the cannibals too harshly. They are better than their reputation. Even the Resident in Port Sandwich says so. The Resident is a huge Breton with the exuberant physique of a Henry the Eighth. He made us welcome with a glass of champagne and told us tales of his subjects. I spent the night in his house with its wonderful view of Ambrym and its glowing smoky crater.

Malekula really has a bad reputation, and for this the Big Nambas are responsible. You see, they do not like strangers interfering, and have twice inflicted serious defeats in the forest on a combined British and French punitive expedition. Since then, when anything happened that touched the interests of the whites it has been considered sufficient to dispatch a man-of-war, which fires a shell or two into the beach and goes home again without inflicting further damage, thus upholding their consciousness of the mastery of the whites among the

officials of Vila and enabling the bushmen to enjoy the fireworks from a safe distance.

M. Ballot governs his 6000 natives with the help of six policemen, whom he with difficulty restrains from reverting to the original state of nature from which they were tempted before they donned uniforms. He has not much time left for being murdered. Besides, Ballot is lord of the island's only prison, a pleasant barn whose door stands always open as the guests have no desire to shut it after them. The difficulties encountered by justice are not in keeping the prisoners but in persuading them to leave their quarters when they have served their time. The white man's food and the nice house with real walls are a great attraction, and it sometimes happens that the police have to throw the discharged prisoner out of the prison and propel him with kicks down the hill.

Life in Port Sandwich runs smoothly and M. Ballot has a pleasant time with his Annamite cook and his black garrison. But people are being eaten all over the island. That is a fact no one can dispute. It is only among the "salt-water people" of the small islands along the coast of Malekula that the missionaries have had a slight success. The interior of the main island is a closed book. The inhabitants treat foreign visitors with cold reserve, though they make them welcome and put up with them as long as they are not disturbed. Strangers who come to settle down and try to change their old customs and their beliefs are firmly and summarily thrown out. If they violate old taboos, or young women, they are killed.

The week before we arrived the Big Nambas had murdered six native Adventist missionaries who had tempted a similar number of women from the bush in order to convert them. Of the advance post of Adventism not one stone was left on another, and the entire north end of Malekula was revelling in human flesh. Unfortunately the massacre gave rise to a violent war between the tribes in which two thousand Schneider rifles came into action. When we arrived at Port Sandwich the war was still raging and Ballot grunted angrily at the loss of so many of his subjects.

The bushman has his own strict sense of justice. Six casualties in a tribe demand that vengeance be exacted on six men of the tribe that killed them. The murdered were, it is true, Adventists, but before their conversion they had belonged to the Tinamit tribe whose duty it thus was to avenge them.

Ballot sat over his chicken soup and waited for the firing to stop and peace to settle down again, for he had no desire to make himself and his six policemen a target for both sides. We began to make ourselves comfortable in our chairs. Things were looking promising.

We sailed to the south-west point of the island and, dropping anchor in a quiet, sheltered bay between Tomman and the main island, waited for things to happen.

Nothing happened.

We made a landing and forced our way through the bush up and down the slippery slopes. We sat down in the red mud and visited cannibals in their drawing-rooms.

Still nothing happened.

There were no howling savages, no threatening rifles, no slowly baking "long pig" over the glowing coral bricks of the natives' hearths.

253

It was perhaps all for the best. If we had experienced anything of the kind, it would naturally have made a very interesting story to tell—afterwards; but then we would certainly have had no time to make such good use of our eyes as we did, and that would have been a pity. We were the spectators of "Everyday Life in the North" as it must have been in the Stone Age. The only things to remind us of civilization were the Schneider rifles and the two safety pins which a chieftain wore decorated with alternate red and black Swedish matches in his ear.

The natives of the New Hebrides are on a very low cultural plane. They do not lie, they do not drink, they do not steal and their word can be trusted. One only needs to mention their cannibalism and their weakness for poisoned arrows to round off this horrible picture of an extremely primitive and undeveloped civilization.

They live in scattered villages and each village has its own language, so the white man and bitter necessity have together invented an auxiliary language, "Beche-la-mar" which is a first cousin of pidgin English and a concoction of simple and unadorned sailor's language with a little French and a dash of Melanesian words of which the most frequently recurring is "kai-kai, which means "food" and "to eat."

We gradually made ourselves practically experts in this mode of expression. One or two examples will show you the extremely simple character of the language:

A motor-boat is "lonnis," the English "launch."

A motor-car is "lonnis belong ground."

A typewriter is "lonnis belong 'riting."

An aeroplane, which was depicted in a number of the

Illustrated London News, was dubbed by a sharp, intelligent mission-boy: "lonnis belong Jesus."

A nettle is "small feller tree, he kai-kai man."

A man who is very fat is "close to come down," and —should one be a little sceptical of the culinary delicacy of human flesh, one is routed with the following argument: "Oh, masta!—all getu kai-kai long pig he savvez good—you never tast', you no savvez!"

A sausage is "banana belong cow," and a warship, somewhat disparagingly, "tin-cano."

If you inquire as to a baby's sex, you will be answered "He no bull, he cow"—that, of course, is to say when the child is a girl.

As a language it is easy to learn, requiring a vocabulary of two hundred words and imagination and humour. The skipper had been speaking it since we left Denmark, but that we did not discover till now.

Most fantastic of all is their equivalent for violin: "Some feller something belong white man. Suppose you scratch belly belong him, he cry."

Now and again the missionaries deliver their sermons in this language. Here is a little example, the story of the tragedy of the apple in Paradise:

"Adam and Eve he stop along garden and mango tree he stop. Jesus Christ he come talk along Adam: 'You no kai-kai apple, suppose you kai-kai apple Him Big Feller wild!'

"Eve he come along up behind, he talk along Adam: 'You come kai-kai apple!'

"Adam he too much fright, he talk: 'No, no, no, no!'

"Then Eve he talk more along Adam, and Adam he come kai-kai apple along Eve.

"Jesus Christ he come talk, and he sing out: 'Adam,

Adam, Adam, you kai-kai apple?' and Adam he talk 'Yes' and Jesus Christ he too much wild, he talk along Adam: 'You go . . . well hell along bush, you . . .!' "

You will understand that the missionaries of these parts must be equipped with great powers of self-control in order to preach thus from a pulpit, but "Beche-la-mar" is the one and only method of communication. Ordinary English is double-Dutch to the natives. This curious speech stood us in good stead during our stay on Malekula for it was here that the expedition found its richest field. Curiosities and antiques streamed out of the huts and the *Monsoon* chests were filled to the brim so that the question of space became a burning one.

During the time that we lay in the New Hebrides each day brought new consignments on board. It would be too much to go into details, so I will confine myself to a sample period and describe one of the purchasing expeditions which we undertook into the virgin forest of the mainland of Malekula and on the island of Tomman. The scenario of it would run something like this:

A light, elegant canoe glides noiselessly to the shore and four men jump out. They are in khaki and tropical helmets and have revolvers ready in their hands. They disappear fearlessly into the tangle of creepers.

Next scene: Natives, beating of drums, spears, nose-rings and wild shouts. Shots. Smoke. Victory.

Close-up of the hero with a modest smile between his determined chin, noble nose and hard but gentle blue eyes.

We too would have loved to have looked like that, but as in all probability photographs of our picnic expeditions will be published, I prefer to stick to the truth in negligé.

Robert Louis Stevenson's grave near Apia

Crocodile River, New Hebrides

Right—the whole scene over again:

It is not a light, elegant canoe that glides noiselessly to the white coral strand. It is our dear, broad-beamed, faithful "Moses" who indignantly lets the waves smack his broad bottom and settles down on the sand like a faithful donkey that has finally got tired of his master's stupid tricks. Four men jump out up to their knees in the water and haul the obstinate punt far enough up for the high tide not to be able to reach it. They are most certainly not as well dressed as a film director would require.

Mr. Möller was what a mathematician would call a quadrilateral cube in semicircular style, that is to say something like the quadrature of a circle. He was dressed in leather straps with khaki in odd places where you do not expect to find it. On his head was an elegant, immaculate borsalino, in his mouth a kind of pipe which, owing to its formation, had earned several disrespectful nicknames which you only dared to whisper secretly and which have nothing to do with this story.

Then there was Jan. He was wearing a Boy Scout's shirt, yachting cap, stockings and gym shoes which were so well ventilated as to approach the sandal type.

Stubbe was wearing cloth shoes with red laces which tied in a criss-cross up a pair of legs which he himself considered shapely, a shirt whose colour betrayed that it had been washed at home, a pair of baby trousers and a straw hat which will never be stolen. Even the most primitive aborigines have some sort of taste.

My own contribution to this mannequin parade was sea-boots, bathing drawers, bare legs and several days' growth of beard. In my hand I carried my camera, a Brownie which was tied together with my pyjama cord

R

and of a nice red colour wherever the rust had eaten into it.

Our Colt revolvers hung against the bulkheads in the boat to which they gave a decorative effect. The landing party's entire armament consisted of a butterfly-net, three jack-knives and a small baby revolver in Mr. Möller's hip-pocket. It was never fired and its owner is in considered doubt as to the correct procedure in loading it, for the sports department of the stores forgot to enclose the directions. Possibly they would have been superfluous, for our armament expert, Sonny Boy, tried in an idle hour to take the thing to pieces and put it together again.

We started along the path. It was the one used by the bushmen when, tired of their daily boarding-house fare of yams, pig and little children, they feel like a piece of fish or shellfish by way of a change.

The creepers hung dangling over our heads like fat snakes, and now and again fat snakes hung down like creepers from the boughs of trees. You get tired of being afraid of creepers and clutching hold of snakes, so in the end we pretended that we didn't see either. They only interested Stubbe.

He was always turning up with all sorts of animals. One day he brought home a half-choked giant snake nearly six feet long, which came to life again in the specimen box on the way back, frightened two bird-lice and a spider to death and was most lively and talkative when turned out on to the deck. Stubbe had a morbid passion for every kind of disgusting crawling creature, and as the rest of us were only interested in animals which either looked pretty or were eatable, he imagined himself a kind of unrecognized genius—like a pearl that has rolled into pigpail. That is why we got rid of him before we reached our destination.

We had hardly started when he entered a handicap steeplechase with a green lizard and disappeared like a hippopotamus on fairy wings into the thick of the virgin forest. The last that we heard of him was a plaintive howl of pain. He had either been bitten through his cloth shoes by the lizard or burned himself on those charming little trees whose effect is a happy combination of nettle, boiling water and bee-sting, and does not wear off for at least three days.

We left him to his curses—in Latin—and went on our way.

In front went the first, after him the second and then the third. Now and again we changed the order, but one was always the first and the two others regarded him as the bravest, because, to flee, he had to do so over the other two. The path was as narrow as that. It wound along as though it wanted to write the word "minimum" in the soil of the forest.

We walked on and on, stumbled, recovered, and walked on again until finally we approached a village.

Three black pigs and seventeen black cannibal women in charming negligé—coco-matting and a handful of grass—fled confusedly into the bush in all directions and stood on their heads. The cannibals' entire capital is composed of pigs and women. With the former he can buy the latter, and the latter can live on what the former provide. The husbands are very jealous, hence the hasty flight at the sight of three white Adonises. The contraction of marriage is a very simple ceremony, which usually takes the form of the bridgegroom knocking out a couple of the bride's front teeth, in contrast to our

Western civilization where such ceremony usually precedes a divorce. The scientists had better fight it out as to which is the more civilized.

The women of Malekula ought to be photographed with a press camera, one of those that can take horses jumping and bombs dropping. They rush into the huts like rats and keep mousy still as long as strangers are present. As you see, they are remarkably different from the feminine European.

It was as though the village was deserted, and we would have betted that it was, had we not heard voices just before and seen the women in full flight. It was as quiet as the grave. The silence was uncanny. The kind of silence there is in a bedroom when you wake up with a start convinced that there is a dangerous criminal under your bed and a homicidal maniac hidden under the dressing-table.

Smoke was rising through the roofs of several of the huts.

The bushman is a nervous person. He lives in eternal conflict with his neighbour. There are so many murders and accounts that have not been settled—or he has reason to believe that one of the more distant tribes is out on a foraging expedition in connexion with some planned banquet. On Malekula one never knows whether an invitation to dinner means that one's presence is required as the guest of honour or as the main course.

That we were white did not particularly pacify the bushmen. They have too often seen trim schooners putting in to shore and abducting twenty of their strongest and youngest men, taking them over seas to the sugar plantations of Queensland or neighbouring islands— week-end trips from which you only return after five or ten years, if then. It was no wonder that father sat tight under his thatched roof and took the bamboo cases off his poisoned arrows.

The leader of the expedition waved his hand and called out: "Hallo, boys!"

His voice was so friendly that two white turtle doves came fluttering down from a banana tree and very nearly settled on his shoulder.

A dark countenance appeared in a crack. Our ethnographer lifted his yachting cap and bowed nicely to the distrustful owner, who crept carefully out of the hut's one window and chimney—the door.

Others followed his example from the other huts, and finally all the men of the village were standing in an expectant circle round us. They had bows and arrows in their hands, but it looked as though the ice would thaw. Two bars of unsmokable tobacco worked wonders. They charmed a smile from the chief—a greedy smile that sent cold shivers up and down your spine. The old warrior put out his hand for his present.

He was worse than naked, for a broad belt of bark round his body emphasized his nudity beyond expression. His whole body was covered with sweet little corkscrew curls of wool and his skin was so filthy that you could have grown radishes on it with ease, provided, of course, that you confined yourself to the round variety.

The bushmen are hydrophobes and so soap is the worst article of trade you can take with you on a shopping expedition to these villages. They either do not know what it is, when they try to eat it and then are insulted to death, or they do know it and nearly burst with merriment at the sight of a cake of the finest brown windsor. Tobacco is their all in all. There are people who say that

261

tobacco has a soporific effect. They have never seen the effect the mere sight of it has on cannibals. They turn into nice, good, little boys at the merest whiff of the most inferior tobacco that has been manufactured since Sir Walter Raleigh spat the first tobacco juice on to Queen Elizabeth's freshly polished parquet. It was nothing less than a miracle.

We fell into conversation, we became friends, we clapped each other on the shoulder and slapped each other on the back so that we became covered with patches of brown and blue. We had such a time! Every business man knows that this is the necessary atmosphere if you wish to do business, and that was just what we wished to do. We wanted to fill ethnographical museums, schools and private houses with curiosities from virgin forests and coral islands, and Mr. Möller had decided that that day should see a Great Summer Bargain Sale in Cannibalistan. Tobacco was to go and ethnographica to come.

It was not difficult to find goods on the racks. We were fanciers of everything that was to be had, from kitchen utensils to private wardrobes and jewellery, and our customers were quite enchanted with the store of flowered woollens, tobacco, glass beads and pocket-knives which Mr. Möller poured out from one of those attaché cases which were so fashionable for women ten years ago.

The chief difficulty lay in estimating the equivalent worth of the goods to be bartered. These cannibals have hook noses, thick lips and black curly hair. They look exactly like sunburned Jews. Their facial characteristics are Papuan-semitic, but they are not Jews in the metaphorical sense of the word. They will never make financial magnates. They cannot stand paper money at any price, and their language possesses no words with which to convince them that the "Bank of England promise to pay the Bearer on Demand the sum of——." They would ten times rather have a worn shilling than a brand new pound note. I cannot say whether that comes from their growing anxiety about the movements of gold in the international market or because they are afraid of the long journey to Threadneedle Street and Mr. Montagu Norman; I merely state the fact.

In other spheres too their ideas of value are somewhat curious. For example, for most of what they have to sell they cheerfully ask ten pounds in silver, but will smilingly accept an old, worn-out pipe as an equivalent for that sum. They will hesitate to sell a bamboo comb for a dollar, yet will joyfully exchange their grandfather for a box of safety matches—and that is saying something, for if the old boy has not been eaten, he enjoys considerable respect in the village.

Business was excellent.

One cannot describe all that was found under the straw roofs of the huts. It all piled up outside—arrows, bows, clubs, wooden dishes and mugs. The wives wrung their hands at the thought of how they were to cook without utensils in the days to come, and the children howled because father brutally took away their most treasured toy, the stone doll that had been in the family since great-grandmother was a little girl, and exchanged it for a mouth-organ half of whose notes were out of tune and the rest missing.

When the huts were empty, the strip-tease scene began. The men took off their bracelets, the tortoise-shell rings from their ears and the string from round their waists, in exchange for which they were given glittering ear-rings from Nürnberg, flowered calico from Lyons and precious stones from Gablonz. They shone and sparkled in the sun like glorious phœnixes. And then somebody happened to mention the assembly hut.

An embarrassed silence fell over the assembled company. The chief took a chew at his betel-nut and scratched his head carefully, so as not to hurt his newly acquired Homburg. The elders cast sidelong glances at him and the young men stood there in some embarrassment.

You see, the assembly hut is the most sacred thing in the village and tribe. It is the house of mysteries, the gentlemen's club, which no woman has ever dared to enter. There the members of the secret lodge, Sukwe, hold their Monday meetings. There the sacred swine are slaughtered, and there they howl down bamboo tubes and beat drums till the women creep in terror into the darkest corners of the huts and cover their ears, believing that the devil is having a frolic with their brave warriors, while in reality these gentlemen of nature are having a good time, smoking bad tobacco and telling risqué stories till the taboo poles before the hut blush more than is good for them.

Those rash words made the assembly uneasy. The club house is their pride. Many generations have made their contribution to its equipment, each doing its bit, and to-day its interior is a well-filled ethnographical museum of the very first class.

"Yes, but it is just these old things that interest these whites, and there are still many bars of tobacco in the beautiful case and we have nothing more to sell in our huts or on our bodies. Perhaps it can be managed."

The chief closed one eye and squinted over at the old men with the other. They nodded ever so slightly, but not more than what could be explained away as a chance movement should the others not agree. But the others did agree and soon the entire circle looked like an exhibition of nodding Chinese gods on an old seaman's chest.

The motion, being now passed by Commons and Lords alike, was written in the statute book and whites and blacks moved off in close formation towards the large hut beyond the sacrificial trees and devil-drums. The great sensation, the last most important lot in the great Summer Bargain Sale was about to be disposed of.

We crept on all fours through the space between the floor and roof and found ourselves before a waist-high barrier of bamboo poles. Behind that was the holy of holies. It was pitch dark in the hut. Some embers were smouldering on a hearth. This was the sacred fire that no stranger may touch without exposing his insurance company to unwarrantable risk, the sacred fire that is lighted every New Year's Eve and must burn the whole year through without going out.

The chieftain lit a bamboo torch from the embers. It flamed smokily up and in its flickering light our wondering eyes saw a scene that any writer of children's tales would joyfully include in a new edition of "The Children's Book of Horrors." The inside was hardly a home from home. You missed the deep club chairs and the rows of newspapers, but most of all it was a woman's hand that was lacking. Over everything lay the dust of the last six centuries.

Roses should grow in such a place, but there were only skulls, big white and yellow ones. They were mounted on bits of wood and set up in the corners and under the beams of the roof where we would hang up Japanese fans, paper flowers or a "What is Home without Father." The defunct's social standing is indicated by the length of shaft, like the amount of gilded railing round one of our tombs. In South Malekula they have the nice custom that instead of keeping yellow photographs of your dear departed, you keep their heads. The head is cut off a fortnight after burial, dried over a slow fire, so that the skin and hair are preserved, and the face is then smeared with clay and painted with brilliant colours and striking patterns. It is then mounted on a wooden shaft whose length is decided by the local assessor and finally set up under the club-house roof.

It is all a question of getting used to it.

Persons of the highest rank, that is to say county councillors, war ministers and mayors appointed by royal warrant, are treated with even greater care and respect. To add to their heads, the local Epstein is commissioned to make a life-size body, which he does with clay and straw built over a wooden skeleton. It is an exact copy of the deceased down to the smallest detail, reproducing his jewellery and lack of clothes. The figure is then painted by an artist of real genius in ultramarine, white and blood-red. To judge from the looks of most of them, the most frequent causes of death in this part of the world are measles, spotted typhus and chicken-pox.

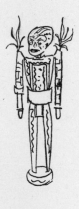

These figures are ranged against the wall beside the altar, on each shoulder a bunch of feathers and the deceased's dried head sticking up between. In course of time the bunches of feathers are replaced by the heads of the sons, and not till then can the family mausoleum be regarded as complete and *comme il faut*.

Apart from these more personal and intimate souvenirs, the club house contained a plethora of things that would make the mouth of any ethnographer water.

Jan stood in amazement before a broken pot and gave vent to low inarticulate sounds. The room was filled with weapons, dance masks, musical instruments and strange things, which from the look of them could have been anything or even worse. Pigs' skulls strung on a cord framed the altar which is dedicated to the worship of their ancestors.

Ancestor worship is the most important element in the religion of the New Hebrides and the pig is its sacred animal. A pig can have a trading value of more than a hundred pounds sterling; but please note, it must be a boar with crooked front teeth. The more crooked the tooth the more sacred is the pig and so the greater its value.

Nature is given some assistance by extracting both the upper eye-teeth when the pig is a couple of months old. Then the two lower fangs have plenty of room to grow up and about. They do not get worn down and one often finds teeth that have formed one or two circles. Such swine are most carefully looked after. When the teeth become very big the pig's owner usually has to feed it. These are the pigs that are sacrificed before the altar to the accompaniment of mystic ceremonies and masked dancers at the full moon when the yams are harvested. The women are not allowed to see these dances, nor may they taste of the boar's flesh.

A man who wants to get on and rise to higher rank in the lodge has to sacrifice a large number of pigs at the altar, and should he desire a wife he can buy one for from four to twenty pigs, depending on fatness and labour productivity—of the wife.

In the marriage trade the hire-purchase system is as well known as in our furniture business and the accounts are kept by a system of knots in a piece of string in father-in-law's hut—one knot for every pig paid. Of course, the rate varies, but it certainly only happened once that a single pig was worth more than a first-class wife. On that occasion panic raged on 'change and all the women of the village hid their faces in shame.

Once having decided to sell their treasure, the savages were wild to get to business. There was nothing which they were not willing to sell. One brought a thigh-bone which looked remarkably as though it had once belonged to the genus *homo sapiens,* but now did duty as a dessert-spoon; another brought his great-grandfather's tombstone from the altar, but at the last moment was overcome by moral scruples and changed the head for one with a shorter shaft, thereby saving his honour and the eight bars of tobacco, and allowing the most important part of great-grandfather to remain in the family.

We chattered and haggled, and loud smacking of lips and watering mouths accompanied the division of the European fancy goods, while Jan's eyes caressed the Melanesian equivalent. The greatest and most complete satisfaction reigned on either side, and the club soon resembled a plundered Christmas tree.

The hour of departure drew near. The heaps of objects we had acquired were divided among the male population of the village, the tabu objects being wrapped in large banana leaves so that the women should not be able to see them and the swindle of the Monday evening meetings thus be discovered. The procession then got

268

slowly under way, out of the hut, down the main street, through the square and back through the jungle.

Mr. Möller went in front. His attaché case was empty but he was beaming all over his face like a freshly minted shilling. Behind him came Jan and I, and at our heels marched twenty native porters with feathers in their hair. They were carrying as many ethnographic curiosities as would fill all the *Monsoon's* cabins and the crew had to share their bunks with four skulls and take their meals on upturned devil-drums swarming with ants. But what will one not do for the sake of science!

A little way down the path we nearly fell over Stubbe. He was standing with his back to us and weeping with joy. Ants in their hundreds were crawling over his face, hands and bare legs. They bit like bulldogs and were larger than rabbits, but that didn't matter. Let the beasts amuse themselves, they were of a new species, a zoological curiosity and would perhaps one day figure in his thesis as "Myrus Stubbeniensis."

What will one not do for the sake of science!

Stubbe followed us, drunk with joy. We others were somewhat sceptical.

The ship swarmed with animals, which had escaped in the general bewilderment. The mess was turned into a menagerie where cockroaches, bird-spiders, geckos and parrot-lice lived in a state of freedom and multiplied. That could be put up with, but we decided to form an Intervention Committee when we got to Java and Sumatra, where Stubbe intended to extend the scope of his activities to tigers, cobras and rhinos. After all, there are limits to what one will do for science.

"Moses" was still lying on the shore, heavy, broad-beamed and dependable. When all our goods were finally stowed aboard, the water was up to the gunwale and the twenty porters had to employ their remaining strength to shove him far enough out for him to float! They stood on shore grinning at us in triumph at our absolutely unbelievable stupidity, while we sat in "Mosses" and laughed at their lack of cunning.

Thus ended the greatest Bargain Sale in the history of Malekula with a touching feeling of satisfaction on both sides. Everything had been sold; both parties believed they had done wonderful business and had to take in fresh supplies. The expedition did this in the nearest store, but for the villagers it occasioned hard work and an impatient time of waiting until the old men hit upon the idea of providing the club with a fresh supply of dried heads for the next expedition that came.

However, this trading in heads must only be entered into for strictly scientific purposes, for as a matter of fact it has been observed that the natives have not the patience to wait for the old men to die, but are apt to assist nature with a little poison in their food, a bang on the head, or they simply enter upon a feud with a neighbouring tribe in order to obtain the necessary raw material.

The three Trader Horns made holiday after a well-spent day and went below to give their hands a really good wash.

"Damned lot of dirt there is in those villages!" said ethnographer Jan blowing into the halo of soap-suds which extended to his ears.

"Yes—and dashed few beautiful white goddesses they keep captive in their temples," said I; and, with a thought to my book: "This will never make a chapter. Readers expect excitement, bloodshed and sensations from a cannibal village and not some nonsense about Bargain Sales."

Thereupon we lit up pipes and cigarettes and went off to Sonny's lucullian dinner.

CHAPTER XXII

In which a murderer discourses on spleen, cannibals dance round a fire on the shore, we are invited to confirmation and visit little girls who stab with large knives

BEFORE we left the bay at Tomman, we met a prince from Tahiti who had fled from his native island many years ago after murdering his wife in a fit of irritation—he just pulled her to bits with his bare hands.

The French had adopted a most unreasonable attitude to this outbreak of temperament, but it did not make much of an impression on us. We were hardened to that sort of thing; infanticide and human sacrifice were becoming practically daily topics of conversation, and we were almost surprised to find that the man had not done away with a whole harim. One's mental perspective becomes a little distorted in daily association with cannibals.

 Our friend from Tahiti was a trader, and he took advantage of 14th July to show his sympathy for un-understanding France and to clean up a little of the shop's stock of three-star brandy and whisky. He gave Mr. Möller a most instructive lecture and explained to him that in these hot countries you have no "savvy" without spirits. He himself must have had plenty of "savvy."

We met him often and his help was most valuable to the expedition, for he was accustomed to bargain with the natives who both respected and liked him. We

272

searched the huts and houses of Tomman and Malekula and collected many bundles of arrows which were infected with tetanus bacilli or poisoned with ptomaine, along with numerous other curiosities.

While this was going on Bobby helped Stubbe to look for animals on the reef, in the course of which a crab caught him by the nose; and the mate made Mr. Möller's old, striped bathing tent into a hood for the motor-boat. This made it look like a pram and was a deserved success wherever we went.

That man of the world, our friend from Tahiti, gave Mr. Möller a good tip the day before we had to sail. If you are in a bad mood, all you have to do is to sit in an armchair with your legs up on the table and a bottle of whisky in your hands. Then you order your dusky minions to put a gramophone at either end of the table and have them play two lively but different tunes at the same time—that puts a little life into the place. When the bottle is empty, you will be drunk and your minions should then put you to bed and you will be in the best possible mood the next morning.

Mr. Möller never tried this method, partly because he had no dusky minions and also because there was not more than one gramophone on the *Monsoon*. But it is supposed to be a good method—on Malekula.

For the last few days of our stay in the little bay we were surrounded by canoes and business was brisk. Soon there was no more to be done; the district was cleared of ethnographica and it was time for us to go.

On the way back from Tomman we paid a flying visit to Port Sandwich to hand over two policemen whom Ballot had sent with us for our protection. We had looked after them carefully and nothing had happened to them.   From Port Sandwich we went to Pentecost Island which faces Malekula.

It was already dark when we arrived off the island, and we did not know where we were. We were making for Point Truchy, but there were no signboards on the shore, only two fires which had been lit in a line on the sand, and after a short discussion with the skipper who said that they were cannibals' preparations for a "white" dinner, we decided to follow the fires.

On approaching the shore we saw naked, black figures dancing confusedly round the fires; but luckily a couple of white people were standing nearby, and as they were not bound to a martyr's stake, the skipper was able to breathe freely once more. They were a Swiss, Dr. de la Rue, and his pretty French wife, who had been sent out to these parts by the Museum of Natural History in the Jardin de Plantes at Paris to collect ethnographica and geological curiosities. They received us with open arms, but did not give us great hope of finding very much on Pentecost.

The natives had almost died out and those that were left had been missionized and ate with knives and forks. Ambrym, which lay farther south, was said to be good and so we decided to depart from our itinerary and sail there. But still we spent an enjoyable day or two on Pentecost before we left.

Only three planters lived on this long island, one of whom was a Norwegian and was called Newman. He was a slender, white-haired gentleman, already a little elderly, and his recollections of Denmark and Norway went back to the time of Ibsen. Since those days he had been in Africa, South America, Saigon, Australia, the Solomon Islands and other similar places, and now he had settled down on Pentecost, and, owing to the bad times in the planting business, was unable to get away again. Three times hurricanes had destroyed everything which he had built up, but after each knock-out blow he had again started afresh.

His Australian wife was an angel, if nothing more. The few surviving natives worshipped her. She looked after them and gave them medicine for which she paid out of her own very limited means. She was a mother to her native servants, and poor bushmen used to lay their infants on her veranda when their mothers died. Yet she has found time to bring up a son and two charming grown-up daughters, as well as her black adopted children. When she grows tired of her work, she sits in her private summer house and plays Chopin and Mozart on a large cabinet gramophone till she forgets all her cares and sorrows.

The pioneers of these desolate, unhealthy islands are strong and unflinching, but their wives are heroines.

Mrs. Newman cherished her flower garden and everything throve under her hands. She had succeeded in inducing violets to flower between the hibiscus bushes, and her roses were covered with large buds just about to break into flower.

Newman went with us to a waterfall which "belonged" to an old Frenchman who lived in constant fear that it might be stolen and taken off to Vila. The old man accompanied us to the fall and sat on a wet stone nearby, from where he could keep an eye on it, while we took the most brutal shower bath of our lives under a douche that poured down from a height of eighty-two feet.

Tourist days are short and our luxury ship had to go on to Ambrym. We said good-bye to our hosts and the

de la Rue family, and puffed across the narrow sound which separates the two islands. Ambrym's smoking crater was hidden in clouds—so now we would see what it was like to live on a volcano.

It was excellent in every way. Mr. Möller bought many curious things very cheaply; Jan poked about in a permanent state of rapture; and Stubbe gloated over some new kinds of soldier-beetle and larva. We laymen all had a good time too. We were well received by the local planter, an Englishman called Mitchell, who gave our scientists native guides to take them to the villages, and while they were away entertained us others in the best possible fashion.

We made trips into the neighbourhood along roads compared with which Coney Island's switchback tracks seemed like broad, even roads. At one moment the path would take us up three hundred and twenty feet, and the next deep down into the valley. Often we had to balance on the trunk of a palm spanning an abyss, and at one place my boy turned round and with a broad grin told me that we had now reached the spot where a few days ago a man had tumbled down to a better life. Ambrym is no country for cyclists.

One night a neighbouring planter, Mr. Morrison, took us on an excursion which it will be long before we forget. A circumcision feast was to be held in a village and this kind of confirmation ceremony was ushered in by a dance which started at sunset and went on the whole night. Native friends assured us that it would be a "very good feller dannis"—and it was!

We stumbled through the dark forest, mad to encounter a great adventure. The country was as described above, only the paths seemed to have been smeared with green soap in honour of the occasion—at any rate everywhere where they were not strung across with creepers and roots. They were tastefully and painfully trimmed with the unbelievably large and effective nettles of the New Hebrides. Kalle cursed the local highway and lighting authorities. He had no love for the exertions of hiking, and we had only induced him to come with us that evening by swearing that we would see to it that he was eaten by neither tigers nor Big Nambas. Nobody had said anything about the nettles.

The caravan was led by a native woman carrying a storm lantern and a six-months-old child on her arm. The lantern dazzled all who followed her and the baby howled. We strayed in the forest and asked our way in a village whose old men were so polite that they answered yes to every question. We wanted to send our native "boy" home to fetch a guide, but she declined the task. Like Kalle, she too had respect for the "Man belong Bush."

Once or twice again we lost our way and went back on our tracks, but at last we received our reward for all our efforts. We heard tom-toms and loud howls in front of us, and shortly afterwards having clambered over four fallen trees on the edge of a precipice we arrived at the dancing ground.

The feast was worth the walk. It was streaming with rain and the moon was not to be seen, but its reflection from behind the grey clouds shed a grey, mystic twilight over the scene. Two hundred cannibals were standing in a solid clump round a stake on whose top were tied a pig's bladder and a pair of boar's skulls with crumpled eye-teeth. Naked backs shone with sweat, white tufts of cock's feathers waved in curly hair, and faces were painted with chalk and cinnabar. They had bark belts round their bodies from which green plants hung, forming a kind of tail which bobbed up and down in time with the dance.

They sang. To our ears there seemed absolutely no difference between the tunes, and the text told of things that had happened on the island in former years, of the eruption of the volcano, of a murder or two and the visit of a man-of-war. The dancers were in a state of ecstasy. Their steps were as monotonous as their songs and their bare feet smacked down on the red mud between the palms in monotonous, enervating rhythm.

Round the first clump, which smelt strongly of sweat, stood a double circle of women. Their hair was close cut and the skin on their heads painted with circles of chalk. Apart from a short apron of pandanus strips, they had nothing on, and they clapped their hands in time with the songs. There was a broad gangway between the men and women and in this a dozen chieftains danced with staring eyes and tripping steps. They had pig's teeth round their arms and necks and held a branch of the sacred croton bush in their hands.

The ecstasy grew, the howls became more piercing and the sinister atmosphere spread. Painted men from distant villages came creeping noiselessly from the bushes and joined the dancers, for the drums had been beating the whole day sending news of the feast from village to village. The drum is the telegraph and telephone of the New Hebrides, and its code system is so involved that it is not only possible to know that a feast is taking place, but also who the host is and how many pigs are going to be sacrificed in front of the sukwen house!

It looked as though this feast might develop into a

fight. Some natives from the village of Ranon had arrived too late, and as they were supposed to have sung the first song, they were insulted when they found that the others had started without them. The Ranon people, however, were too few in number to be able to fight all the others, among whom were some of the most savage and warlike tribes of Ambrym, so they sulkily withdrew and went home brooding vengeance.

We left when a violent downpour set in, but the dancers paid no attention to the rain and continued the monotonous feast till it grew light. As the sun rose, they had a big kai-kai at which they devoured many pigs that had been roasted whole and heaps of yams. After that they all went home.

The ceremony of circumcision took place on the following morning and the young men who thus received initiation and right of entry to the sukwen and the ranks of the men, were shut up in a dark hut for ten days till their wounds had healed. Nobody was allowed to see them or speak with them, and if they had to leave the hut, they had to do so at night when the others were asleep. When the ten days were past another "big feller dannis" was held and not till that was ended was the ceremony complete and the boys men.

I spoke with the chieftain of one of the tribes which had taken part the day afterwards. He was sitting on a tree stump in front of his hut and groaned as he carefully felt the misused muscles of his legs. Yes, it certainly had been a good dance!

We were given a live, wriggling pig for our larder, a parting gift from Mr. Mitchell, and sailed to Atchin and Vao, the two little islands which lie a mile off the coast of North Malekula. Vao was a complete disappointment from the scientific point of view. The population wore clothes, spoke English and had an excellent knowledge of the value of their few old heirlooms which were clumsily faked and given a patina in the smoke of a fire. Atchin was more interesting. Its people did not, it is true, differ very much from those on Vao, but in the island itself there were several large dance places and idols from olden days.

My extremely enlightened guide, a native teacher from the Adventist school, pulled his tie straight and showed me the sights with the rather tired expression of a custodian of a museum, and when we parted his hand was discreetly outstretched—with the palm upwards. But he was worth his shilling. It was like going on a conducted tour through Stonehenge or Bath. I took my revenge by pressing a brochure entitled "Visit Denmark" into my guide's hand when he left.

He rowed ashore in his outrigger canoe and we sailed with the *Monsoon* in the opposite direction to Esperitu-Santo, the largest and most northerly island of the New Hebrides.

After a short stop in Segond channel where bad-tempered and indignant French officials, thoroughbred bureaucrats, tried to make life unpleasant for us, we sailed on to the small island of Cressi, paid our respects to a Swiss planter there and got half a cow from him. We then went on our way with it hanging like a pennant from the yard, sailed past old Julius' former plantation at Turtle Bay and anchored towards dusk in Port Olry, a well-protected bay where the only representatives of civilization were a drunken Father and a half-caste planter.

We visited the priest first. He received us in a room

where a red Dubonnet poster, a black cat and a green bottle completely spoiled the effect of a faded oleograph of the Virgin Mary on the wall. His manner was churlish and refractory and we could get nothing out of him. The planter, however, gave us some good tips and a box of fruit and vegetables. Mr. Möller, Jan and I made a day's excursion over the mountain's ridge into the plain round Big Bay on the other side of the island. Ethnographically the results were poor, but otherwise the expedition was an experience. Nature and the forest were grand and luxurious and the people were the most primitive we had met during the whole voyage.

The first we saw was a young man who was felling a tree. His back was turned to the path and when he heard us, he let out a yell, jumped six feet to one side and seized a Schneider rifle which was leaning against a banyan tree. However, he soon saw that our intentions were not evil and his face softened into what was presumably meant to represent a friendly grin. His teeth were black and shone like varnish and the inside of his mouth was rose-coloured with chewing betel.

Our young friend led us to his village where the grown-up men were just decorating the ground in front of the chieftain's hut for a dance. It was for this that the trees were needed which our friend had been felling with such zeal that he had not heard us coming. This zeal might well have cost him his life, and presumably we had to thank the fact that we were we and not an enemy tribe for his friendliness. There are many ways of saving life.

There were about twenty braves there. They were tall, well built and stark naked except for the stalk of a flower round their bodies and a bunch of hibiscus fore mentality of primitive peoples or did not worry about them.

The cannibals' confidence in the white man's infallibility and justness is almost immeasurable, and it is to our own disadvantage when a white outsider betrays this trust. The cannibals of the New Hebrides have good memories and their tradition demands that an injustice be wiped out with blood. They do not kill for the love of it, but either from religious motives or in revenge, and it is only in times of starvation that they kill to satisfy their hunger. They do not lie in wait in the forest for a "nice steak," like when we go shopping to get something for lunch, which is a very common superstition. Their laws are simple and primitive as they themselves are, and though to us Westerners they may appear unnecessarily grim and brutal, they are always founded on a strict sense of justice.

Our next objective was the Solomon Islands. On the way we wanted to take a look at the Banks Islands, the Torres and Santa Cruz groups. We had no great hopes of finding ethnographica on these islands, but we had to go to Vanikoro in the Santa Cruz group to clear ship and so could take the Banks and Torres in on the way. They turned out to be nearly uninhabited and the inhabitants were either too sick, too stupid or too missionized to carry on any kind of domestic industry.

We found one or two fairly old stone buildings on Gaua in the Banks group which were ethnographically interesting, as evidence of a culture which was presumably older than the existing Melanesian one; on Vanua Lava we met a pleasant English planter, and at Oreparapara we lay at anchor in the fallen-in crater of an extinct volcano, while our scientists investigated a dying village whose six inhabitants were stricken by a skin disease, elephantiasis, and sores on their legs. Their houses swarmed with fleas, which we had to brush off after each visit. It was a terrible picture of decay and misery we saw here between the walls of the crater which were covered with luxuriant vegetation and the bright colours of many flowers.

The Torres Islands were almost as extinct, and apart from some pretty wooden knives we got no booty from this group either. Just as dead and uninteresting was Togategua and Hui, but their coral reefs were the most wonderful we saw and the motley fish which swam about under our keel were larger and more numerous than elsewhere.

We had now "done" the New Hebrides and in spite of all prophecies had come out of it alive. We had not expected much from these islands, but Mr. Möller's expectations had been exceeded many times over and the *Monsoon* was swelling with the stuff we had collected.

One evening a sea-cow started to splash loudly and we began to weave tales of crocodiles, tigers and rhinoceroses, our menu for the months to come. Fate, however, did not allow the fulfilment of these dreams. On the eighth of August at two o'clock in the afternoon the *Monsoon* sailed in through the coral reef into the last fatal harbour, Peon in Vanikoro, the first of the islands in the Santa Cruz group and the last in the *Monsoon's* eventful existence.

On the way there a mighty submarine earthquake had shaken the whole ship, so that we all stared at each other in confusion during the half-minute that it lasted. It was as if the elements had been tuning their instruments for the finale of the last act.

violent than the first. Then events came tumbling over each other like strips of flickering film put together without rhyme or reason and wound off in mad haste.

No one who was on board will forget the minutes that followed as long as he lives. We were then in the middle of the channel with course set a little to windward, and the hurricane-like blasts of wind exerted a tremendous pressure on the whole port side of the *Monsoon*. Foam spurted up over the deck, and sky and sea were one with the mist of rain. We could no longer see the shore. The whole world was blotted out in a grey mist in which were only the *Monsoon,* the sea, the storm and the coral reef shining hungrily through the light green of the water to starboard.

Nearer and nearer came the reef, like in a nightmare when the most terrible dangers come slowly closer without one being able to move hand or foot. Through the foam we could clearly distinguish the shape and colour of the individual rocks and where the reef plunged steeply into the depths turning a sharp, jagged edge towards us. The motor hammered at full speed. We accelerated as much as we could, but the thirty-five horse power was not able to do much against the storm. We were helpless, slowly but surely being forced sideways to destruction. For every inch that we went forwards, we were driven ten to the side. We could do nothing. We were the helpless, bewitched spectators of a play which we knew must end in tragedy unless a miracle happened.

The skipper had long since ordered the wheel to be put hard over to port. The man at the wheel had obeyed almost before the order had been spoken—but the *Monsoon* refused to answer. No power on earth could have forced the stem to windward against the pressure of the mad gusts which howled in the shrouds and rigging. The rudder was a useless piece of firewood. Nearer and near came the reef—twenty yards—fifteen—ten—seven! We were in the channel. There was no turning back. Even if the ship had obeyed the helm, there was not room to turn.

"Hoist the mainsail and ease the helm!" roared the skipper from his lookout, and in the same instant every man on board hurled himself at the braces, the helmsman eased the wheel to starboard, and the mainsail slid up with a speed unknown in the old ship's glorious history. Fourteen hands held and tugged with all their might, sailors, owner, scientist and cook, they all held on for their lives and for the sake of the old boat; but there was nothing to be done.

Before the sail was half up, before there had even been the slightest possibility of easing off and trying this last remedy, the *Monsoon* went aground for the first time with a bump which cut us to the quick, and before the sail was furled the breakers had thrown us on to the reef.

We lay in one and a half fathoms. It was high tide, change of the moon, the height of the spring tide and the wind blew continually with its full force. It was clear to us all that this was the beginning of the end, the sad conclusion of an exciting and eventful voyage, and a curious heavy lump came into our throats.

There was no panic. In fact, apart from a quivering feeling of tension and seriousness, we felt nothing. Orders followed one another in rapid succession and were obeyed without an instant's delay. The breakers thundered against the port side; the keel kept bumping against the sharp hard coral; and yet the motor-boat was into the water like lightning and the mate went with Jack and Kalle to try to drop both anchors in the deep water of the passage, one fore and one aft, which was the only way left of keeping the ship on the edge of the reef and near deep water, the last vague chance of getting her off again when the storm had subsided and the seas slackened. They succeeded in putting out both anchors, but on their way back the motor-boat was slung against the ship's overhanging stern and it was only pure chance that Jack was not crushed against the planks.

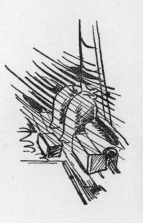

Everybody was in the cabins in all haste packing their valuables and those of the ship. It was only a question of time before she sprang a leak and the water would rise inside. To be sure, the *Monsoon* was a miracle of oak planks and strength, but a coral reef is hard and more merciless than anything else in the world. The squall was over, but the wind still blew as hard as ever. The seas crashed thundering against the ship's side and poured continually over the deck, the lagoon was in a state of commotion, the foam flying from the tops of the waves like the manes of whitehorses, and the whole vessel lay on its port side so that we had to hold on to the rigging and booms if we wanted to cross the deck without falling.

The motor-boat bumped against the planks and Jack sat in her working at the engine, wet to the skin. There had been no time to put on oilskins; but in such a situation you do not notice that you are wet. Sacks of clothes, chests of nautical instruments and bundles of papers were thrown into the boat; then Stubbe and Jan jumped in, the painter was cast off and the motor began its struggle against the foaming seas.

petrol lamps on the quay had been lit: over there warm clothes, hot tea and safety awaited us. Then the motorboat came. Jack's and Kalle's faces shone out in the darkness, glistening with moisture and red from the salt water. The last of the sacks were lowered and then, as a breaker lifted the boat up to the rail, the mate and I jumped in. The skipper was the last to climb over the rail, loosen his grasp and let himself fall. Then the boat glided towards the shore on its last journey. The white stern of the *Monsoon* dissolved like a grey spot in the darkness and disappeared. The mate sat in the bows. We could only distinguish his light-coloured, broad-rimmed Tahiti hat, round which a faded garland was still wound. The showers of salt spray soaked it and the flowers fell overboard. The lights on shore came slowly nearer. The waves no longer broke over us with such force, and finally Jack was able to lay his baler aside. There was no more need to bale, for we were in the lee of the land.

We were given temporary quarters, some in Mr. Dawe's house and others in Mr. Crawford's, the residency. The two sailors slept on the shore in the barrack where the things we had saved had been put. They were to go out next morning at sunrise and, if possible, salvage some more things. During the night the storm and squalls howled over the roofs, and again and again the poles which bore the houses were shaken by earthquakes. That was the death of the *Monsoon*.

Next morning, when the seas had gone down a little, the salvage crew found both the anchor cables parted, the hawse-pipes torn out, planks stove in on either side and the water breast-high in the cabins. It was a disconsolate sight. Everything was swimming in water, laboriously stuffed birds with wonderful bright plumage, idols from the New Hebrides and rare rugs from Samoa. A boot floated about among books and kitchen utensils, Hermann Bank's "A Wonderful Day" bobbed about near the ladder, its wet title page grinning at us like a hideous joke. The water was thick and muddy with coffee, beans and flour. The preserved birds were beginning to rot. Mementoes, lampshades, bedclothes and writing paper, were all mixed up in confusion.

All that is not pleasant to see when the ship has come to be your home. It was like standing powerless beside somebody's deathbed. However, we had no time to indulge in melancholy contemplation of the past. We had to save what could still be saved, and in the course of the day the motor-boat made many trips between the wreck and the shore, and with each trip the ship's contents shrunk a little. As the weather luckily improved in the weeks that followed, we succeeded in salvaging everything, even the tackle, blocks, sails, rigging, and the heavy engine being brought ashore undamaged. Most of it was wet, but it dried quickly on shore in the strong sun.

The *Monsoon* lay plucked and naked on its *lit de parade*. An evil fate had thrown us on to the reef just as the adventurous part of the voyage was about to begin, but a kindly chance brought us all safely ashore, saved the greater part of the cargo and staged the last act on an inhabited island where friendly people competed to help us as far as the means at their disposal allowed.

up for it by purchasing Bobby in person. It would have been impossible for Mr. Möller to have taken him home to Denmark, for going by way of Australia and England the poor brute would have had to have spent a year and a half in quarantine, and so he passed out of our existence and was duly installed as government dog on Vanikoro and elevated to the rank of commander of all "white" and "native" dogs.

Kalle took a tremendous interest in the auction. He sat dangling his legs on a rail above the water and followed events with such great excitement, that he did not notice that the rotten wood was breaking under him until he found himself lying in the water with a cut forehead and a broken arm. Both were patched together again and then, just to show that he was really serious, he went and contracted malaria as soon as his forehead and arm were almost better. That cost him a good many pounds, but luckily only of flesh and fat. He looked like a living skeleton and we were a little anxious about him, it must be admitted. There was not much nourishment in the tinned beef and rancid preserved butter on which Sonny had to exercise his imagination in the kitchen and we began to feel the lack of vitamins. We blossomed out in boils and became studded with pimples which threatened to destroy our school girl complexions; but then there was only one woman on the island for whom to make ourselves beautiful, and she was happily married to Mr. Crawford.

Jan, too, had to pay tribute to malaria, but he got over it all right and was soon playing billiards with the mate and Sonny, an expert, on the company's table, while Kalle, whose arm was still in a sling, told them how to play a game about which he understood absolutely nothing.

Sonny exercised sovereign rights over a pair of ebony slaves who were about forty years old and did not understand much of what he said—but then neither did he. He had learned a lot of Beche-la-mar, but could never make out what the sentences really meant. The scientists and I lived up on the hill as the guests of Mr. and Mrs. Crawford and were greatly envied by the others when they discovered that we were given beer with our dinner nearly every other Sunday. One must remember that on the island beer was as rare as gold in the Thames, and stocks were getting low in this respect too. The sugar barrel was empty. The different households borrowed from one another and we learned that if no ship came by the 15th October we would have to live from fishing and hunting.

We apportioned out the various hunting grounds. Stubbe was to hunt wild pig with the butterfly-net; Jan, because of his height, was allotted the feathered game in the treetops; and I was to put my Bora-Bora experiences to good use and scour reef and lagoon with spear and bow and arrow. None of that, however, was necessary.

Mr. Möller had tried everything to get away. He had not yet given up the idea of somehow or other carrying through the expedition, and had telegraphed to old Julius Petersen at Noumea asking him to investigate the possibility of buying a boat. One or two were offered, but their prices were too high. Then Mr. Möller telegraphed to the Danish Consul, Marks, in Suva and asked whether the government ship *Pioneer* would by any chance happen to be passing Vanikoro in the near future. She would not. Then Consul Hœst in Sydney took the stage.

The authorities at Tulagi had informed him of the wreck, he had discussed the matter by telegraph with Sir Ashley, the governor of the Solomon Islands, and they had agreed that it would be best to offer us assistance and rescue us from our Robinson Crusoe existence. The telegraph office at Vanikoro is not open every day, and as a week had passed before Sydney heard from us, Consul-General Hœst on his own initiative chartered the small schooner *Dawaun* in Tulagi, to bring us back to civilization, dead or alive. In Sydney they cannot have had any idea of our games of billiards and of our plans for fishing and hunting in the years to come.

This arrangement rather thwarted Mr. Möller's plans, for he had still not given up his idea of carrying on the expedition in one form or another, but as the *Dawaun* had already left Tulagi when the telegram was received on Vanikoro, there was nothing to do but to bow to this decision.

We decided to employ the time till the *Dawaun* came in taking a look at the island. It was well worth while! It would have been difficult to find a more beautiful spot on which to be stranded, more difficult still to find kindlier people to impose on and most difficult of all to find a worse climate. It poured with rain every day. Not rain, such as we know it, but the kind of rain we believed did not exist when our geography teacher told us that it was like ropes or manilla hawsers. It was a rare thing for the rain to last long and that was the devilish part of it. You set out in the morning in your beautiful, freshly ironed shorts, your pockets full of cigarettes, and, with a gun in your hand, to shoot red-headed moorhens with blue wings for soup at dinner. Then just as you were standing taking aim and considering

whether you should shoot one or two at the same time, the rain would begin to stream down without the slightest warning. A couple of black clouds would creep up quietly under cover of the treetops and suddenly empty a couple of tons of water on every square yard of forest in the course of a few minutes.

After that the sun would come out again and leer at the wretch standing up to his ankles in red mud with a remarkably foolish expression on his face and pockets full of wet cigarettes. However, we got used to the rain. We learned that it meant an immediate and very necessary cooling of the almost red-hot air and this accounted for the tremendous humidity of the atmosphere. The result of this humidity was that paper and everything else was damp and no metal would keep free of rust. With no little anxiety I saw my little Brownie camera growing redder and redder and the shutter rusting up; however, a slap or two, a little scratching with an equally rusty nail-file and one or two drops of sewing-machine oil made it work again. On that day I took my topee off to Mr. Kodak.

This eternal humidity made all the thousands of brightly coloured flowers, so characteristic of the tropics, grow most luxuriantly. The Vanikoro jungle was a fairy tale, and we listened to this fairy tale every day for two months, without ever growing tired of it. Hibiscus, jasmin, orchids and frangipania beamed at us on every side. In the evening the air was filled with a scent of narcotic sweetness and in the bright moonlight nights the green, hilly countryside was simply indescribable. Apart from the clearings round the quarters of the whites and the timber depot, the island is an impenetrable jungle untrodden by the foot of man.

The name of Vanikoro has only once found a place in history, and that was on the occasion when the French scholar and explorer, La Perouse, and his two ships *Astrolable* and *Boussole* were wrecked on the reef one stormy night in February, 1789.

The Spaniards had discovered the Solomon and Santa Cruz groups many years before, and to get colonization going had spread the rumour that it was on these islands that Solomon had had his famous and mysterious mines. However, nothing ever came of it, for people were a little tired of the gross exaggerations and superlatives of Messrs. Columbus, da Gama, Balboa, Mendano and their colleagues. Thus the only sign of Spain's influence on these groups is their name, yet the fact remains that the caravels *had* brought rich mineral samples back from their voyage and that was what induced France to send out a scientific expedition under the geologist, La Perouse.

An impenetrable mystery surrounds this shipwreck and the years that followed. When a quarter of a century later, an Englishman, Dillon, went to look for the shipwreck in the *Research* he said that he had been able to discover that one of the ships had run upon the reef and the whole crew with the exception of four men been eaten by sharks while attempting to reach the shore. The other ship had managed to get through the passage and had been beached on the spot where the timber company's offices now stand and where we landed after our shipwreck. There they are said to have lived for four months in peace with the natives and to have built a two-masted boat in which the crew sailed away to fetch help, while La Perouse and his secretary stayed on the island. La Perouse died there many years later and as

302

help still had not come and a warlike neighbouring tribe was beginning to make itself unpleasant, his secretary set off in a canoe across the sea. Nothing was ever heard of what happened to the crew, nor is the secretary's fate known. Yet among the natives of Malaita, a larger island more than three hundred miles from Vanikoro, there still exists a legend of a white-skinned man with a long, white beard who came riding across the sea on a plank and who was honoured and respected by the savage tribes until his death.

Much of all that is pure surmise, but it is true that up to a short time ago relics of La Perouse's days were still to be found in the ground round about the timber company's buildings, and that a chieftain on the little island of Tucopia, which lies alone in the ocean a hundred miles from Vanikoro, wore the silver hilt of La Perouse's dagger slung round his neck. He had picked it up on a journey to Vanikoro.

Since those days the name of Vanikoro has been forgotten.

Pigeons which compete with parrots in the splendour of their plumage, coo in the bushes; large, diabolical flying-foxes slowly circle close above the treetops at sunset and snakes glide noiselessly through the grass and along the branches. In the streams alligators lie in wait among the tangles of mango roots; shining insects and large butterflies flutter about in the patches of sunlight, and at evening man's tormentors, the white-winged ants, come to where the light burns on the veranda and commit suicide in its flame or in the whisky glasses, or having cast their gossamer wings cover tables and floor in a crawling mass. Such are their habits. Bats flit about in the light of the lamp and reap a rich harvest, eating

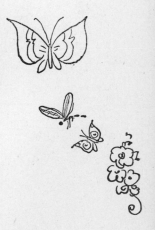

geckos and lizards till they nearly burst, and large, black and yellow spiders dash about in their nets. Nature's traffic police are kept hard at work.

This plague does not visit the bungalows every night, else were life on Vanikoro unbearable. The mosquitoes on the other hand, the dear little anopheles, appear every night as soon as the evening breeze has died away with almost imperturbable certainty, and with them comes fever. Everybody on Vanikoro has malaria, attack succeeding attack at unpleasantly short intervals. Yet man's adaptability is great. Malaria is regarded as a necessary, inevitable event, just as we reckon with having colds in March and November.

Earthquakes are another evil to which the whites on the island must get accustomed. Shortly before we came, a mighty shock had devastated the island. The long quay which runs out into the lagoon was shaken to the core; one or two houses on the hill were standing on four of their original fifty nine-foot piles and trembled at every breath of wind. Mr. and Mrs. Crawford were living in a temporary hut built of branches and their Danish guests slept in the hut's living-room. One of the rooms in their shaking wooden house was given me to work in with the strict injunction to jump out of the window at the slightest quake. As it was nine feet to the ground and the window was covered with a thick mosquito net of solid copper wire, I did not take this course but instead ran like a hare out of the door at the first shock—at the third I half got out of my chair and when the sixth came I remained where I was and went on writing.

Your feelings gradually become blunted and you grow accustomed to what for a plain-dweller are the most unusual occurrences. Now and again we had several

On Vanikoro

Tulagi

shocks in a day and became experts in judging their intensity and the time they lasted, but we never got rid of that tickly feeling in the stomach and that weakness at the knees which you feel as soon as it begins to rumble in the earth below and everything which you are accustomed to regard as fixed and unalterable in this world begins to quiver and quake like a piece of jelly. It is not till you have experienced a severe shock of the kind that knocks your legs from under you, that you properly understand the dreadful panic which is supposed to and must seize those who are shut in narrow cement houses and streets, when an earthquake comes and levels cities to the ground.

In the lumber camp six white men were wrestling with the heavy kauri trunks. When the trees are felled, they are rolled by their own momentum down through the forest on prepared tracks. Their trunks weigh from five to ten tons apiece and the force with which they come down was nearly fatal to Mr. Möller who one day stood right in the middle of the slide to photograph them as they arrived. However, fate was kind to him on that occasion and he also received a lesson in Australian lumberman's language which was quite as flowery as the surrounding jungle.

O SOLE MIO

They were grand fellows these lumbermen, a little uncouth possibly, many of them, but men. There were wild doings in the barracks when they came to "town." They played poker fit to lift the roof and wrestled so fiercely that the company's joiner had to work overtime for the next few days in sorting out the remains of the furniture. One of the men, an Irishman, had a voice which many an opera singer would have envied; another was writing a book and talked in a quite cultivated voice

U 305

of literature and international politics. A third capsized in a canoe out by the reef and together with four natives managed to reach the shore after swimming for five hours. There was never anything in the papers about that achievement.

They came from widely different classes of society and had many different views on life. Here, however, as in the Foreign Legion, no one was asked about his former life or personal affairs. A man was forgiven for being a student, if only he was a man; nor did a spell in jail make a man more popular, if he was not a good fellow at the same time. Many a good tussle was fought out, as will always happen when six men are together night and day for two years without the slightest break. Yet as soon as the battle was over there was always a hand outstretched.

The old truths prove themselves again and again. When man lives in primitive conditions, he is not an evil animal. In such circumstances the bad element is thrust out at once and there is no possibility of its attaining leading positions, as so often happens in more civilized and complicated societies.

On the island they were having difficulties with the native workers, and it looked seriously like strike, blockade and a general flight from the scene of work. It wasn't any question of the number of hours, though it were quite conceivable that eighteen shillings a month plus a little rice and a couple of bars of tobacco might give rise to conflicts; no, it was purely and simply a result of black magic. As you will see, working conditions on Vanikoro are slightly different from those in Europe.

All over Melanesia people die of witchcraft. That is a

fact, and there is no reason why this cause should not be entered on their death certificates, if there were such things in the jungle. On certain of the island groups it is called Devil-Devil, on others Pori-Pori, and here and there the witchcraft is practised by a weila-man with the help of a bundle of bamboo sticks—weila. Suppose a man has a grudge against another; he puts Devil-Devil in his food or looks at him with an evil eye and tells him that he will die on such and such a day at such and such an hour. The man gets terrible pains in his stomach, begins to breathe with difficulty—and dies. That is dying to order, a mighty power of auto-suggestion working on a primitive, extremely sensitive mind which has neither strength nor knowledge enough to fight against the curse.

In the lumber camp six people had died in six weeks and everyone knew what the cause was. The natives fled along the shore, out of their minds with fear, to the company's headquarters, where they wandered about and refused to resume work. Now it is not easy to prosecute workmen and condemn them for refusing to remain in a place where death comes regularly according to a definite timetable. English law knows no paragraph concerning the practice of Devil-Devil, quite apart from the fact that an English official who has been to Eton can hardly be expected to take such a matter very seriously. One man was suspected, and a kind fate arranged that he should attack the Irish songster and get the worst of it in a remarkably short space of time. The excellent result of this little episode was six months' imprisonment for the man and peace in their camp for the others.

The guilty party was called Timmy. He was put to work at once and had to weed garden paths and mend roads under the supervision of a murderer who was fully conscious of his responsibilities. The murderer had been in government care for the last six years and so felt himself superior to the other, both by reason of his seniority as by the nature of his crime. Devil-Devil is an art that anybody can practice; but he had committed his dual murder in accordance with the religious ritual of his tribe and forefathers.

The heathen never understands the nature of his crime as seen from the white man's point of view, but on the other hand he takes his punishment amazingly lightly. For him it is merely a pleasant open-air life in peace and quiet, with a roof over his head at night and plentiful food. The only thing he misses is his tobacco. Money has no real value for him. As soon as a native is paid his wages he hurries off to spend it in the company's shop and so the money returns into the employer's pocket, while the coolie goes back home richly laden with flowered cottons, tobacco, tin whistles and pocket knives which are shared out among all the inhabitants of the village. He himself as a general rule gets nothing, but the next time that a workman is dismissed and returns to the little community, he receives his share of the booty.

During the long weeks of waiting I tried to publish a local typewritten newspaper, but the items of news that could be sifted out of the atmospherics that came from the wireless were so spartan and so hacked about that the "Vanikoro Times" had to cease publication after its second number, and just when I had begun to publish it in English and Danish in deference to its international circulation.

Time began to hang very heavily on our hands. It was

now a fortnight since we had received the telegram informing us that the *Dawaun* had left Tulagi, and although its course lay right in the teeth of the trades, they were not blowing so strongly that a ship with anything of a motor could not easily have covered the four hundred miles in shorter time than that. Another week passed. Then two masts came into view. The natives yelled "sailo" and we tore down to the shore, only to have our hopes dashed on finding a Japanese pearler at anchor in the lagoon. It was a good thing the little yellow skipper did not understand Danish.

Three weeks after the *Dawaun* had left Tulagi, Mr. Crawford telegraphed to the government office and Sir Ashley suggesting that a search expedition should be sent out. But before Tulagi had had time to react to the telegram, the *Dawaun* crawled through the passage with an engine that had broken down and a cursing Scots captain, who was called M'Arthur and was a lieutenant in the New Zealand Naval Reserve.

He had got off his course and had spent eleven days at sea without sighting land. The crew had eaten practically all the provisions and there was no hope of replenishing Vanikoro's meagre supplies and empty larders. However, we had no choice. The *Dawaun* was the only plank on which we could balance our way across the sea to more civilized parts, so we packed our things together, said good-bye to our kind hosts and hopped on board—on the fifth of October at three o'clock in the afternoon.

Three hours later Vanikoro was only a hazy dot on the horizon, it was raining cats and dogs over the hills and the wreck of the *Monsoon* had disappeared for ever out of our sight. Our voyage was really over. The expedition was disbanded and we were on our way home from the warmth, colour, sun and flowers of the South Seas to the cold, the rain and the puddles of a Danish winter. We thought of the North Sea in January and shuddered.

CHAPTER XXIV

*In which in spite of everything we reach Tulagi
and which closes the book with some moral
observations by a man without morals*

THE *Dawaun's* rather exhausted engine had been
repaired by the company's engineer who, however, most
definitely refused all responsibility for its functioning in
the future. He rather disparagingly described his work
as the clumsy attempt of a blockhead to paint a corpse
in natural colours, but to make up for it would take
nothing for doing the repairs.

Such generosity so enraptured the ship's captain, its
passenger, Mr. Gorringe—who had thought he was
making a week's trip from Tulagi to Vanikoro and back
—and some of the departing members of the expedition,
that they decided it had to be celebrated. And celebrated
it was. Unfortunately the engineer was the only person
on the island who had any whisky, the *Dawaun* having
brought a case for him from Tulagi, and so he had to
provide the wherewithal for the celebration. That was
why, standing on an empty, upturned whisky case, he
waved us a sad and rather relieved farewell, whereupon
the motor sobbed despondently once or twice and fell
silent for evermore.

George, the perspiring black mechanic, performed
wonders in his attempts to get the engine on to its feet
again. He tried everything, from spanners and kicks to
artificial respiration but all to no purpose. Thereupon
M'Arthur shrugged his shoulders and set sail. George

had been tinkering with the motor for fourteen years and none knew it better than he, so we tactfully withdrew from its deathbed.

Privacy was difficult of accomplishment on the *Dawaun*. She was no proper passenger boat with smoking-room and "Gentlemen," and room had been made for us in the hold where the *Monsoon's* old sails had been spread out over a hundred or two sacks of copra. Cement sacks or a pile of broken glass would have been better and more comfortable, for a pile of broken glass can be smoothed and levelled, but copra must stay in its sacks and your back has to contend with the individual shape of the sacks as well as with the small, sharp pieces of their contents which can be more than suspected under the canvas. Apart from this, broken glass has not the same sharp, unpleasant, penetrating smell nor has it the same attraction for beetles, ants and rats. However, as we had been members of a scientific expedition, we were not particularly moved by these zoological phenomena.

Jan had the worst of it. A copra-beetle got into his ear—and after all there are limits to what a young scientist can stuff into his head without it hurting him. The mate and I said a decided "No, thank you" to the hold—as we had done throughout the voyage—and took up quarters in one of the punts which lay on deck where they played at being lifeboats. The floor was hard, it is true, but as the floor boards were covered with an inch of water we did not notice it so much. It was not till the next morning that we discovered that the boat had a bung which could be removed. We took it out and the level of the water fell and from that moment we were envied our sanctuary by the entire crew and Mr. Möller, who

had preferred to sleep on deck in a camp bed. This
became lively and entertaining when squalls raged every
ten minutes throughout the night. These squalls gave us
an opportunity of observing the phenomenon that it is
not only possible to walk in one's sleep but also to run—
and that with a pillow under one arm and a pair of
blankets under the other.

The skipper was lodged astern with the passenger from
Tulagi, the planter Gorringe. There, as the result of a
most regrettable mistake he trampled the ship's tame rat
to death. She was soft, round and plump and answered
to the name of "Betty," but of course the skipper did
not know that. You see, there were so many others.

A squall came, which threw the *Dawaun* on to its side
so that the lee-rail dipped under; it boomed and rattled
below deck; all the drawers flew open and the mate
rolled like a road roller on top of me. I peered out to
have a look for the skipper. He was lying on the
threshold and had received the ship's entire supply of
charts, a sextant and M'Arthur's boot-jack on his head.
He sat up, stretched and blinked, but did not wake up.
Vanikoro had made him so accustomed to earthquakes.

We ate our meals on the main-hatch. The two recurring items on the menu were tea and native biscuits,
which are a kind of dog-biscuit from which the meat
has been picked out so that the natives do not fall victims
to gluttony. Their main ingredient seemed to be *papier
mâché,* but they tasted quite good when you had neither
bread, nor horse skin, nor bricks to chew. The *Dawaun*
larder had been plundered on the way to Vanikoro as
has already been mentioned, for two white men and
nineteen betel-chewing black sailors with rosy gullets
could not live for three weeks on part-songs and fresh air

alone. However, we did not mind. We were moving, moving forwards and we would joyfully have fallen on the copra, if that would have speeded up the voyage.

Then we sprang a leak. The technical explanation of the matter was that three rivets which were supposed to hold the stern tube had long since rusted through and the fourth no longer felt inclined to do the other's work by itself, so it snapped off. The practical and immediate result was that the water began to rise in the hold and the copra sacks there became wet and started to smell even more strongly, with the result that the copra-dwellers became still more envious of the innocent punt-dwellers.

After the mate and I had removed the bung and with united artistic sense made ourselves cosier with pocket mirror, cushions and awnings, our bunks were extremely comfortable and dry—as long as it kept fine. Unfortunately it never did.

The water soon rose above the floorplates in the engine room and though this was not being used for the time being, M'Arthur felt that something had to be done all the same. The pump was brought into action. They pumped day and night. Nineteen black sailors is a comparatively large crew for a vessel that can nominally be sailed by two white hands, but we saw that the number was not too large.

A native sailor pumps energetically and effectively for five minutes, working the pump handle as if it were a matter of life and death; but after that he loses interest, chews betel-nut and would rather prepare himself for death than pump another stroke. Then the next one starts. Thus the size of the crew enables each man to pump for five minutes and rest for ninety, and in this way the whites are able to keep the water under.

Then the pump went out of action. Each man had his own pump technique and there are limits to a ship's pump's power of adapting itself to nineteen different temperaments. The nineteen began to bale with jugs and whatever happened to be at hand, and amongst other things we saw our teapot, a petrol tin, in full action.

"It's all right as long as they sing and shout," said M'Arthur. "They will keep the water under, but if they fall silent, then you had best begin to practise your strokes and lower your bedroom into the water. Don't forget to put the bung back first!"

The mate and I went to bed and for safety's sake took with us a couple of dog-biscuits without dog. Then we said good-night to the poor devils who had to sleep in the hold, and told them that it would be impossible for them to get up on deck if anything happened, and that they would drown along with the other rats. But our consoling words met with nothing but coldness and lack of understanding. We shrugged our shoulders and cast the punt off at either end before we turned in.

Next morning we stuck our heads out to take the height of the sun and saw that we were still on deck. Land was to be seen straight ahead and between us and the coast was a small, white schooner which passed over a hawser and towed us into the calm, blue lagoon of Santa Anna, the southernmost of the Solomon Islands. There we were able to lie, lick our wounds, repair the pump and stop the leak with what material we had at hand.

Our tug was none other than the government schooner *Tulagi,* and its only passenger was the island's resident

commissioner, Sir F. M. Ashley, in person. He had been sitting in a deck chair wondering how he could best arrange the search expedition when we appeared on the horizon. He now gave vent to a sigh of relief, bade us welcome and invited Mr. Möller, the skipper, and I on to the afterdeck for a whisky and a chat. Then he puffed out into the lagoon again and we soon followed in his wake, pumped dry, with the leak partially stopped and the pump more or less repaired. In case it is of interest, I might mention that during the stay in the lagoon our anchor had dragged and that it was only by the skin of our teeth that we were kept from drifting on to the reef.

We had become fairly hardened to this sort of thing during the last two months.

The strong trades, alternating with sudden violent squalls from the north-east, hunted us through the straits of Malaita and Guadalcanar, and after sunset the next evening we were rushing on between the small islands and rocks into Tulagi, our harbour of refuge.

M'Arthur crowned his work of rescue by letting the *Dawaun* with all sail set run during a howling squall against a fragile quay.

He kept close in to the shore and his native crew jumped about like fleas and shrieked like four-wheel brakes. Sails flapped, came to life and died, and then clattered down on deck. A light appeared from the depths of the darkness and a pair of hands coiled a hawser round a stake—at last we had reached a harbour where steamers sailed in every direction, to Rabaul, Sydney, America, yes, even to Europe, right up to that little growth on the map which is called Denmark.

M'Arthur treated us to a glass of beer to make up for

the dog-biscuits and give splendour to the end of the
voyage; an English official who happened to be there
shouted "Hurrah" in Irish, English and Scots; M'Arthur
answered with the Maori's war cry; and for the
umpteenth time during the voyage we had to smile appreciatively at "min skol, din skol, alle vackra flickors skol!"
and give the assurance that it was wonderfully correct
Danish. Then we went to bed in the hotel, five in one
room, two in another and two in the much-frequented
corridor.

The next morning we were wakened by a black waiter
who was called Peter, and who brought us nice hot tea
in bed. The bread was spread with butter, real butter
which came straight from a cow and not a tin. We
pinched ourselves and thought that we must have gone
down with the *Dawaun* and wakened up in the seventh
heaven. Through the window we could see the main
street of Tulagi's Chinatown stretching away in front of
us in the burning morning sun.

To the passenger from a tourist liner Tulagi is a ridiculously small town, but to him who arrives with the
Dawaun from Vanikoro it is a metropolis. It has a golf
club, hospital and two restaurants. There is no church,
but then there are more than a hundred convicts who
can be seen in the streets nearly all day on their way
to and from work. Among them are twelve self-
confessed murderers who walk along shouldering mighty
axes, under the supervision of two tiny policemen armed
with short, thin batons—which shows what a wonderful
understanding exists between the administrators of
authority and their best customers.

Only once have these excellent relations been
threatened. That was on the day that the police arranged

a tug-of-war with their prisoners, and the convicts won. The police were so furious that they smashed all the windows in Chinatown, while the peaceful little Chinese withdrew into their back rooms and played mah-jong.

The town lies on a small island, Florida, and the mighty Lever concern and Burns Philp Company have their head offices for the entire group on two nearby islands, Gavuter and Makambo. The name of Burns Philp is known wherever coconut palms grow and Lever's name speaks for itself. It is Unilever which controls most of the world's margarine factories; it is its capital and plantations that are behind Colgate, Palmolive, Lux and all the other international names in the world of soap, while its interests reach even as far as the whaling industry in the Antarctic.

In addition to all these sensations one may mention that now and again a tourist liner puts in to the harbour, and that one may sometimes be lucky enough to discover a Sydney paper which is no more than a week old. What more is needed to prove Tulagi's dominating position in the intellectual and material life of the Solomon Islands!

The harbour was full of small schooners which brought the sovereign copra to the warehouses of the large firms, and the life-hungry planters from their solitude to the life-giving bars, where flows every drinkable liquid, from angostura and gin to the sweet red cheery brandy which brings melancholy pearls of dew into the eyes of the patriotic Dane. In the bars of Tulagi one drinks morosely and methodically. We met a grey-haired planter whom local tradition supposed to be an extremely cultivated and distinguished gentleman when he was sober. We had no opportunity of substantiating the truth of this statement during the short fortnight we spent in the town, but we were able to comfort ourselves with the knowledge that we were not the only ones who had been unable to confirm the truth of the legend. The only person in Tulagi who had ever seen him entirely sober was the old blackbirder, Jock Cromer, but he was so old and childish that we had no real confidence in what he said.

We found recreation in every corner and hole of this extraordinary hair-raising town which yet has such great charm, and we never grew tired of admiring the beauty of its surroundings. The Resident, Sir Ashley, was kind enough to offer me his office as a workroom, which led to many long talks on every conceivable problem, from the reaction of the natives to European influence and the effect of London's traffic on the nerves, but which was not particularly conducive, with shame be it admitted, to much in the way of achievement.

Unfortunately my workroom had windows in front of which the whole archipelago lay spread out. From Government Hill you look over so variegated a sea and so wonderfully beautiful a landscape that I can with good conscience say that I never saw a finer view during the whole of our voyage round the world. The sun sparkled on the water, the colour of the sea changed from deep blue to delicate green and here and there a shimmer from. the submarine coral reefs penetrated to the surface, studding it with a sheen of rose.

Deep below at the foot of the hill lay Chinatown with its painted roofs of corrugated iron, the waves played with a wreck on the shore, and round about on the low hills stood the chalk-white bungalows of the Europeans,

while the green, well-kept turf of the nine round greens
of the golf course beside the shore blinked up to the tops
of the palms.

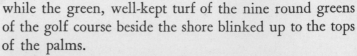

Tulagi has lately been getting itself talked about. A
long time ago gold was found father north in the mighty
unknown interior of New Guinea, and now a horde of
adventurers and capitalists have collected to exploit its
unsuspected possibilities. After an immense amount of
work the crushers and washers have been set going deep
in the virgin forest among swamps filled with fever and
unclimbable mountain chains soaring up to the skies. No
road leads to the gold mines. Every single piece of
machinery, every plank for building the houses, was
taken from the coast to the scene of work by aeroplane.
Nowadays a large mining town lies in the old domain of
the headhunters. They have even started races. The
horses were, of course, taken by air to the saddling
enclosure.

It is many years ago since the attack first began. Now
big business has started, and the real gold-diggers of the
old school, men with check shirts, plaids over their
shoulders, bent and with long, swinging arms, and
washing-pans tied on their backs, no longer feel at home.
They are looking for fresh pastures, new unexplored
rivers in an even more inaccessible country. It is above
all the sport and the adventure they seek, and the alert,
adventuresome capitalist follows readily in their wake and
is only too willing to finance their search.

The morning after our pompous arrival a gold-digger
of this kind came staggering into the hotel and was taken
at once to the hospital. He came from Guadalcanar and
presumably had malaria and pneumonia. He made a
fearful scene in the ward because he was not allowed to

smoke. His partner, the representative of capital, had had to drag him up and down the sides of mountains for the last fourteen days, and he had been carried through the dense jungle on a stretcher made of sacking. They had reached Tulagi in a schooner and it was not a moment too soon for the old man, who was seventy-one years old.

His friend did everything possible to make him comfortable and was genuinely sorry that inexorable Dr. Chricklow did not approve of smoking for his pneumonia patients. In the afternoons he sat beside the old man's bed and suppressed his curses out of consideration for the nurse; in the evenings he played poker with an Englishman, a Japanese and a Chinaman in Chong-Kai's discreet little back room. When the jack-pot was large and his own cards poor, he bluffed sky high, confident in his knowledge of the worth and importance of the quinine bottle which peeped out of his trouser's pocket and shone with heavy grains of alluvial gold which had been washed out of the bed of a river that was to be found now in Guadalcanar, now in Malaita, and now in San Christoval. The other three's eyes nearly popped out of their heads and their ears nearly fell off from the tremendous exertion of trying to get behind the secret. They had no luck. In the course of the night they were bled of a few pounds and the man took his secret with him to Sydney, where his partners already had both hands buried in notes they were willing to pay for more accurate information.

In a few months wheels will be turning and the crusher breaking the raw material into small pieces somewhere on the overgrown bank of a river in Malaita, San Christoval or Guadalcanar. If the gold comes thick from

the washing-pan, the place will be stormed and claim after claim staked out beside that of the two pioneers. It is for this Tulagi waits, looking forward to it just as a young family looks forward to the visit of a noisy, unpleasant uncle whose heirs they are. The government rubs its hands, for the protectorate is economically dependent on itself, like most British colonies, and in these days of depression copra is unable to fill its coffers. For the present, however, the town remains a quite small but strange spot, a few degrees south of the equator.

The planters curse the government, and the government curses the planters because they demand what is impossible but what the government would like to be able to do. And the third great power of the South Seas, the missions, cannot bear them cursing and complain about both—if they are not too much occupied with quarrelling among themselves as to which god is the most suited to the natives—the Adventist, the Protestant, the Catholic or the Methodist. It is all one and the same to the natives. They have gradually acquired so much European cunning, that they are prepared to worship the planter, government official or god who secures them the greatest economic profit for the least expenditure of labour. And they cannot really be blamed for that.

The days passed and then one evening we learned that the X Line's new motor vessel was expected in a few days. It was supposed to ply along the route Sydney-Tulagi - Rabaul - Kavieng - Batavia - Teneriffe - Hamburg - London, and our omnipresent consul had already booked berths for us all on her. She was a large ship, 9000 tons, had coal on the foredeck and was dirty from stem to stern and from the galley to the berths. Her engines made a fearful row, her electric capstans rattled, and the electric light shone white and evil in the cabins. It was roasting in the salons, yet all the same you swathed yourself in tie and jacket in the good old English tradition from the moment you drank boiling tea with your morning bacon till you finished with four hot courses in the evening. We had not lived quite so stylishly on the *Monsoon*.

We often thought of the old ship now fighting out its last battle with the breakers on the reef of Vanikoro. Gone were the poetry of the voyage and billowing sail; we were once more in the midst of unrest, speed and everyday life and when we put in to some harbour it was not for adventure but for oil, and so this book really ought to end here while our boat sets her twin-screws turning and churns up red mud and empty tins from the bottom of the harbour of Tulagi in the Solomon Islands.

The voyage home in this ship was very exciting and varied, for she was a boat of character and temperamental, and as it is rare for a motor-vessel to have personality I feel that I should give a short sketch of the events of the voyage. It began most promisingly by our having to anchor in Tulagi Bay when we had scarcely finished waving good-bye. We had been sailing for twelve minutes. Then the ship refused to go any farther, its super-charger suffering from asthma and the consequent lack of air. There was nothing extraordinary about that, for she was an elderly lady of seventeen who, before undertaking this trip, had been laid up and left to her own devices on the cold, misty Tyne at Newcastle. The X Line had purchased her for a few shillings less than she was worth, which was not much. There was no time to submit her to the thorough medical examination on which the insurance companies usually

insist, and she was sent on her way with all her internal injuries, her palpitations and chronic cold.

The voyage out was the worst she had ever known, and the homeward trip was to be a great deal worse. We succeeded in being a month late on a voyage which the shipping company reckoned would last two months—and that takes some doing. However, we managed to leave Tulagi, after the chief engineer had spent two horrible hours on the engine, and got as far as Rabaul, the capital of the Australian part of New Guinea. We spent fourteen days in this district and got an excellent impression of the feverish life that has broken out in the towns of New Guinea as a result of gold being found on the Morobe peninsula.

Beer streamed across the bars, gold-diggers and South Sea shippers told unbelievable stories, and the old pioneers tried to over-trump these greenhorns with tales of the olden days, when everything was much worse. You believed them politely and in silence, till they told you that even the nights in '95 were darker than they are to-day. Then you had to get up and pay your bill if you did not wish to be rude to grey hairs.

It was a wonderful time. M'Arthur from the *Dawaun* had come with us, and his friend, Skipper Tom Procter, was a real find. He was a grand chap with Cyrano de Bergerac nose and a sparkling, rather low sense of humour which kept his head above water in the storms of life and sea. Mac and Tom were the last representatives of the world we were leaving—after them came ties and good manners; so I will never forget them and the last farewell glass with which we began in the Pacific Hotel on Tuesday and whose bitter dregs we tasted on Sunday morning in the New Guinea Club. They were skippers—no doubt of that! But above all they were two big gambolling boys of the kind who run about the world under the name of men.

In Rabaul several alterations were made in our passenger list. Mr. Möller had long been contemplating jumping ashore and continuing his collecting by himself and possibly later with the help of someone who knew the country. It would have been too expensive to extend our travels with the whole expedition. Ships were very costly in these parts of the world and naturally there could be no question of paying for passages and board for nine persons. On the other hand it was annoying to have to sail past the islands from which the expedition had expected the best results, without setting foot ashore and investigating their possibilities.

It is not every day that one's way takes one past New Guinea, and so Mr. Möller decided to stay on in Rabaul and go from there in a small steamer to Madang, make up a trip up country, buy things for the museums and then return to Denmark with the next boat which would come to New Guinea in a month or two. He negotiated successfully with a magnificent giant of a prospector, Mr. M'Gregor, and then we took farewell of our leader, thanked him for the past months and wished him a good trip.

This wish was more than fulfilled. In the months he spent there Mr. Möller collected so many magnificent ethnographical prizes that the entire National Museum wept with joy when he unpacked them, and so the trip, apart from the mighty cases which were safely stowed under the liner's deck, resulted in a surplus which amply repaid Mr. Möller's large outlay of capital, work and initiative. The *Monsoon's* last voyage had enriched our

National Museum and considerably increased its store of treasures, and that was a slight consolation for the losses and disappointments our leader had suffered.

A small steamer lay in Rabaul harbour waiting to sail for Vanikoro, where she was to load the timber the bushmen had hauled down to the shore, and take it, stowed on deck, the long road to Melbourne. A full crew had been sent out from Sydney, but when the men one day began to chip the rust off the iron deck, they inadvertently knocked eight holes in it with their hammers. The good Australian sailors grew nervous and went ashore. No trip to Melbourne for them in that ship! Quite out of the question!

Then M'Arthur and our own mate, Sören, met over a glass of beer in a bar, and by the time it was empty they had shaken hands on their decision to sail this sardine tin to where she was supposed to go, even if they had to tie her together with string and row her across the coral seas. Thus the mate left us with a clean shirt under one arm and his stamp collection under the other. In February we received a postcard from him—"All well! Sören." The postmark was Melbourne, so the two of them must have paddled the wreck into the harbour somehow or other. Their reunion with the people of Vanikoro will certainly not have been boring!

One of our cooks fell ill and Sonny Boy hopped straight into his job and wages, and stayed there till we arrived home, which pleased Sonny. In place of Mr. Möller and the mate we got two very pleasant Australians on board, the Finance Minister of New Guinea, H. D. Townsend, and his wife. They were not the least bit stiff, but just school children on holiday and we spent a grand, if exciting time with them.

The excitement began when we were still off the north-west coast of New Guinea. Both engines stopped at the same time and all the lights in the ship went out when we were five miles off a coast bristling with coral reefs and dear little cannibals. That was among the Schouten Islands. The wind was blowing towards the coast and we drifted with it; luckily it was not particularly strong. There was nothing to do but shrug our shoulders and exclaim "What, again!" The prospect of being wrecked cannot impress you every time; you can even grow accustomed to that.

Mrs. Townsend was a real good sort. When the breakers over the reef became visible, she told us the stories of all the novels she had ever read in which women are stranded on a cannibal island with two or three men and all the consequent developments. When the ship heard that and thought of her crew of forty-three men and the eight male passengers she did not dare to assume responsibility for the consequences and began to gather way with one heavily groaning engine.

We reached Batavia in Java without much further excitement, and stayed three days there to fill up with oil and have the engines overhauled, which latter was, however, a hopeless undertaking and was only done to seduce the poor Dutch and Malay mechanics into outbreaks which they later regretted. We, however, enjoyed our stay there.

The next stage from beautiful Java was a long one. It took forty-five days to sail round South Africa to Santa Cruz on Teneriffe, and they passed in a deadly boredom that was only relieved by an occasional cyclone which came like shots from a gun, so that we had to turn the ship's head on to the wind towards the centre in order

to escape from the maze of mighty, tangled waves which broke over the deck from all sides.

One day we saw our first albatross—we had again got far south. We played deck-golf and read; played bridge and slept; and then early one sunny morning we saw Table Mountain and Cape Town like a blue silhouette in the mist. We would have liked to have put in, but had nothing to take us there. One or other of us murmured something about getting fresh supplies, for our menu had been rather monotonous for the last fortnight. At breakfast, lunch and dinner we gnawed dry, tough beef, only varied by a turkey on Christmas day; but morale was good, for we were going home and could stuff ourselves full in Consul Olsen's hotel at Teneriffe.

One day after we had left Teneriffe the wireless operator told us that we had had a message to go to Aarhus instead of Hamburg, the cargo having been sold afloat to the oilmills there. We cursed him, and told him not to joke with us; then he showed us the telegram. If he had not had such a large beard, we would have kissed him. Instead we gave him a number of telegrams to our families and the wireless news.

We never noticed the fog in the Channel, paid no attention to the cool reception we were given in the North Sea, and even the roaring squall during which we lay hove to in the Bay, was forgotten. We only stared out into the darkness towards the Hanstholm Light. We breathed a sigh of relief on seeing Aarhus, the lights along the quay and the illuminated clock in the cathedral tower, and thought of the poor people who had been waiting on the beastly cold quay for the last five hours. Then the cargo caught fire.

Copra and petroleum burn almost equally well, and as

the fire had broken out forward, we had to turn in order to have the wind astern, as otherwise there was a very good chance of the ship ending its days in Aarhus bay marked with a buoy. Apart from that the water looked damnably cold and there was a sea running which would not have looked very picturesque when seen from a lifeboat. Luckily the fire was put out inside an hour, and by that time we really had had enough of the old tub. It seemed a bit too thick that, having happily escaped the fate of being grilled by the cannibals on the New Hebrides, we should be roasted just when we could see what the time in Aarhus was.

Finally we found the shelter of the harbour mole. The landing bridge stuck and took half an hour to get out, but then we were home. It took a little time to believe it. Fifteen months and five days had passed since we had last seen Aarhus harbour. That is a long time. Our free and easy adventurous life among carefree primitive peoples and wonderful islands was ended. Here at home there awaited us noisy streets, howling rotary presses and the newspapers' eternal shouting of death, attentats, and political attacks on all and everything—dissatisfaction, commercial jealousy, gossip and scandal.

We who have seen something of both sides of the world may well consider a little which side is the happier. The answer is no longer to be found so close at hand as it was when we set out. Then our heads were stuffed with the doctrine of the rude, barbaric cannibal living a life of sin in pagan darkness and ignorant of our blessed culture and enlightenment. However, it is dangerous to think about such questions. Stevenson and Gauguin died of it. Besides it was by no means my intention to burden this book with large and heavy problems; it should only

attempt to portray some of the pleasure and admiration which nine people felt when they found that the world was round yet not the same on both sides.

It tells of a headmaster of a country school who wanted to try his hand at leading an expedition and who carried through his plan in his own way, confounding the sour thoughts of the doubters; and of the eight men he gathered about him and to whom he gave an experience they will never forget. It is written by a commercial artist who has contracted to make his debut as an author.

None of us was a particularly "great" man, none of us was well known and none of us stood out above the others by virtue of any impressive attributes. That is, perhaps, the reason why we got on so well together. It was this comradeship which formed the quiet background to the whole voyage—and for it thanks are due to you.

All of you!

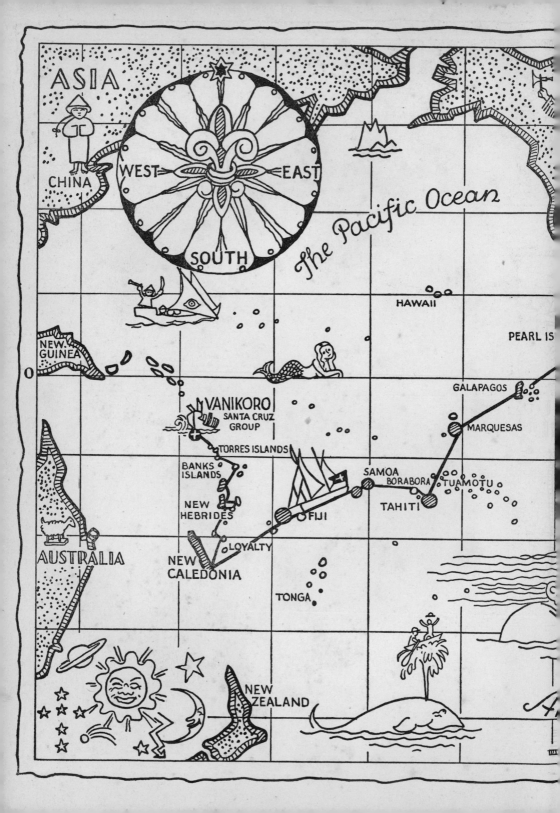